Nomadic Education: Variations on a Theme by Deleuze and Guattari

Inna Semetsky
The University of Newcastle, Australia

SENSE PUBLISHERS
ROTTERDAM / TAIPEI

A C.I.P. record for this book is available from the Library of Congress.

ISBN: 978-90-8790-411-1 (paperback)
ISBN: 978-90-8790-412-8 (hardback)
ISBN: 978-90-8790-413-5 (e-book)

Published by: Sense Publishers,
P.O. Box 21858, 3001 AW
Rotterdam, The Netherlands

Printed on acid-free paper

TABLE OF CONTENTS

CONTENTS

INNA SEMETSKY

(PRE)FACING DELEUZE

This collection brings innovative educational theory into constructive dialogue with the intellectual work of French poststructuralist philosopher Gilles Deleuze whose conceptualizations strongly resonate with contemporary discourse in education. His collaboration with social psychologist Felix Guattari connects philosophy with sociocultural practices. Considering the impact of Deleuze's thinking in social philosophy or cultural theory, a thorough investigation of his legacy for education is imperative (cf. Semetsky, 2006) and conducive to further interdisciplinary studies. Deleuze and Guattari referred to their philosophical method in terms of *Geophilosophy* as beginning with the Greeks. Geophilosophy creates a map or cartography of historical events. Stressing the value of the *present-becoming,* Deleuze and Guattari privileged geography, in spatial terms, over merely a temporal history and positioned their philosophical method against the conservatism, apoliticism and ahistoricism of analytic philosophy. The chapters comprising this volume address issues of primary significance for education ranging from research methodologies to popular culture, to art and creativity, to knowledge structures and learning, to pedagogy, to ethics and moral education, to the problematic of identity and subjectivity.

It is the Deleuzian philosophy of life shared by all contributors that crosses the boundaries between diverse content areas in educational research. The given collection constitutes an exercise in educational (geo)philosophy as an instance of *becoming* of this particular disciplinary field. This *present-becoming* of the philosophy of education is represented by thirteen essays written by scholars across the globe, each chapter being an experiment in nomadic thinking[1]. The metaphor of nomad, used often by Deleuze, is potent as indicating a dynamic and evolving character of philosophical concepts versus their having forever-fixed and eternal meanings independent of context, time, place, subject, or culture. Nomads are excluded from history, yet they break through into history by virtue of their very geography, that is, a movement that cannot be controlled. For Deleuze, all "becomings belong to geography, they are orientations, directions, entries and exits" (Deleuze, 1987, p. 2). In a range of works, Deleuze and Guattari have established a new critical and creative language for analysing thinking as flows or movements across space. The constructive process of production of new concepts, meanings and values embodies an important nomadic *affect* immanent to this very process: it is desire, a creative and erotic element that (in)forms the multiple flows of thoughts and effects. As such, constructivism in philosophy, for Deleuze, is always complemented by expressionism, by "a becoming of thought [that] cries out" (Deleuze, 1995, p. 148) thus disrupting concepts that Deleuze compares, invoking musical tropes, with songs. The nomadic – *smooth* – space is an open territory, providing emancipatory potential to those who are situated in this space in contrast to *striated*, or gridded, space, both musical terms coined by composer Pierre Boulez and subsequently employed by Deleuze.

Nomadic education will have paid attention to places and spaces, to retrospective as well as untimely memories, and to dynamic forces that are capable of affecting and effecting changes thus contesting the very identity of the philosophy of education. For Deleuze, philosophy cannot be reduced to contemplation, reflection, or communication as aiming solely at consensus. It is uniquely a practice of concept creation, and the pedagogy of the concept "would have to analyze the conditions of creation as factors of always singular moments" (Deleuze & Guattari, 1994, p. 12; cf. Peters, 2002; 2004). Deleuze's own philosophical work and his collaborative partnership with Guattari have created novel concepts for philosophy, namely rhizome, nomadic thought, fold, event, Body Without Organs, etc. Positing philosophy as a method of concept creation, the creative – both constructive and expressive – element being a necessary condition for the very *pedagogy* of the concept, Deleuze and Guattari understand such a method in terms of the geography of reason based on a new image of thought that expresses itself in nomadic mode. For Deleuze, a concept is always full of critical and political power that brings forth values and meanings.

The relevance for education is paramount: as Deleuze and Guattari (1994) said, "If the three ages of the concept are the encyclopedia, pedagogy, and commercial professional training, only the second can safeguard us from falling from the heights of the first into the disaster of the third" (Deleuze & Guattari, 1994, p. 12). It is pedagogy – in art, science, and philosophy alike – that must educate us, respectively, in becoming able to feel, to know, and to conceive: that is, *create concepts*. A critical and self-reflective approach to philosophy of education demands establishing a dynamic – nomadic – connection between geophilosophy and the pedagogy of the concept *per se*. Deleuze and Guattari conceptualize concepts as fragmentary wholes existing in relations to other concepts on the plane. They are "only created as a function of problems which are thought to be badly understood or badly posed (pedagogy of the concept)" (Deleuze & Guattari, 1994, p. 16), yet they are not just discursive (they do not link propositions); they are in/corporeal and always express an event, not an essence. Philosophy as a kind of constructivism has two complementary aspects: the creation of concepts and the laying out of a plane (of immanence) with its imaginary, forever vanishing, line reaching towards the horizon of events. Deleuze and Guattari are not interested in concepts in order to determine what something is, that is, its essence, or being. Rather they are interested in the concept as a vehicle for expressing an event, or becoming. Event is a singularity expressed by means of plotting a concept on a plane: concept as an event "secures... linkages with ever increasing connections" (Deleuze & Guattari, 1994, p. 37). The unpredictable connections presuppose not the transmission of the same but the creation of the different: the process that has important implications for education as a developing practice of the generation of new knowledge, new meanings.

Transcoding is one Deleuzian neologism used to underline an element of creativity, of invention. Pedagogy of the concept would defy the habitual transmission of facts from a teacher to a student; instead education becomes "a transcoded passage from one milieu to another... whenever there is transcoding ...there is... a constitution of a new plane, as of a surplus value. A melodic or rhythmic plane, surplus value of passage or bridging. ... [T]he components as melodies in counterpoint, each of which serves as a motif for another..." (Deleuze & Guattari, 1987, pp. 313-314). Thus, education grounded in philosophy defined as the process of concepts-creation becomes possible only providing a teacher and a student serve as a motif for each other. Musical metaphors enable Deleuze to articulate the dynamics of the process, and a surplus value implies growth in meanings and an increase in power: *what the body can do!* Yet, in the present state of society in our information age, its principal technology of confinement may restrict *what the body can do,* both explicitly and implicitly. Deleuze contrasts Foucault's disciplinary societies with the control societies operating through continual control and instant communication, so that it is control (as in William Burroughs) that becomes a new form of power. New open spatial forms – open systems rather than closed systems – are those interconnected, flexible and networked *architectures* that are supplanting the older enclosures. In practice, these new open institutional forms of punishment, education and health are often being introduced without a reflective and critical understanding of what is taking place.

Deleuze provides the following poignant vision anticipating the spread of the institutions of perpetual training and lifelong learning: "One can envisage education becoming less and less a closed site differentiated from the workplace as another closed site, but both disappearing and giving way to frightful continual training, to continual monitoring of worker-schoolkids or bureaucrat-students. They try to present it as a reform of the school system, but it's really its dismantling" (Deleuze, 1995, p. 175). In the same way that corporations have replaced factories, schools are being replaced by the abstract concept of continuing education. By turning exams into continuous assessment, education itself is "turning... into a business" (Deleuze, 1995, p. 179). In this manner, new forms of schooling become the means to provide a continuous stream of human capital for the knowledge economy. If and when human capital replaces *humans*, then, as Deleuze argues, individuals become *dividuals,* a market statistic, part of a sample, an item in a data bank. Yet, it is desire that, in its movement along the transversal line of flight (another of Deleuze's neologisms), can disrupt the prevailing order of things by producing effects in terms of the Deleuzian present-becoming which is always already collective and social.

Deleuze used to say that we ourselves are made up of lines; lines move us, and the strangest line is the one that carries us across many thresholds towards a destination, which is not foreseeable and unpredictable. There is always a space for further explication, for forming yet another transversal line. Chapter 1 in this collection represents one such line of flight towards the new and unpredictable as taken by Ronald Bogue in his powerful essay "Search, Swim and See: Deleuze's Apprenticeship in Signs and Pedagogy of Images". It is images, and not linguistic propositions, that are part and parcel of the very creation of concepts. Bogue employs Deleuze's work on Proust to suggest a model of learning based on explication of non-linguistic signs, such as involuntary memories, images, or immaterial artistic signs. Noticing that Deleuze does not address the topic of education explicitly, Bogue introduces several of his original texts where the indications of a Deleuzian approach to analyzing certain aspects of the process of learning and teaching are nevertheless present.

An educational model suggested by Deleuze/Bogue is based on apprehending signs understood as hieroglyphs that point beyond themselves and require a creative unfolding of the elements enfolded within them if they are to be deciphered. Learning is a means of unfolding signs in practice, and an apprenticeship consists of a progressive exploration of signs and their signification. Deleuze discusses Proust's *A la recherche du temps perdu* as the story of the narrator's "apprenticeship in signs", tracing the stages whereby young Marcel learns that signs are to be apprehended in terms of neither objective nor subjective criteria, but solely in terms of their immanent problematic instances. Deleuze suggests that genuine education proceeds through a deregulation of the senses and a shock that compels thought against its will to go beyond its ordinary operations. In *Cinema 2: The Time-Image* – another source being discussed by Bogue – Deleuze adds to our sense of what an apprenticeship entails when he speaks of Godard's cinema in terms of "pedagogy of images". The medium of film embodying concrete instances of the general pedagogical process typical of Godard's cinema teaches us to see otherwise. This cinematic unlinking of conventional sequences of images and texts and the subsequent re-assemblage of the disparate components in productively disruptive juxtapositions is a mechanism both for inventing signs that foster creativity and for generating problems that make possible fresh questions and solutions. In this sense, Godard's pedagogy of images is a continuation of the Proustian apprenticeship in signs but also an educational encounter with problems that Deleuze addressed in his work *Difference and Repetition* and that Bogue analyzes in detail in his chapter.

Bogue takes us to Deleuze's analysis of Leibniz's logic as the unfolding of internal difference that continuously differentiates itself thereby constituting an infinite learning, *apprendre* in French, hence apprenticeship. The philosophical problem, for Deleuze, is more than a mere question with a single corresponding solution; instead, it is a condition of possibility within which specific questions may be framed. The problem is immanent within questions, and it is not exhausted as the questions are answered. Pointing out that for Deleuze to teach means to learn, Bogue tells us that learning is a process of immersing oneself in a problem and then seeking out the various questions and solutions that the problem makes available to thought. Bogue also brings into the conversation Deleuze's unorthodox philosophy of mind that includes subliminal micro-perceptions and "reading" visual images as genuine pedagogy inseparable from a critique of conventional codes.

For Deleuze, nomads always appear in the lines of flight of social fields. Nomadic existence is always in the process of becoming-other, and David Cole addresses "Deleuze and the narrative forms of educational otherness" in his contribution to this volume. In Chapter 2, Cole tackles the major Deleuzian theme of otherness and applies it to the narrative forms in education. Cole suggests that that the educational narratives can be broken down into the following: legitimization, language-games, the language of desire, nomadism, singular otherness, relative and consumer otherness, and curriculum otherness. Education can produce otherness through the processes of legitimization that Cole relates to the means used by students as a mode of reaction to the ways in which scientific discourses overlay and over-code their realities. Otherness becomes a fact of life in terms of the language-games that teachers and students employ when dealing with power relations and naming what is happening in those relationships. Deleuzian desire has a role to play: otherness is present in education through the ways in which language is produced and as related to desire. There is educational otherness in the nomadic elements of contemporary society, for example, the global movements of people and technological innovations such as mobile phones that have by necessity transformed our relationships with means of communication. Cole says that singular otherness may come about in education through what Deleuze and Guattari term as the qualitative unconscious or the plane of immanence. Finally, there is otherness in our construction of the curriculum in that it may provoke a disconnection with actual teaching and learning, as knowledge has been bounded and separated from the actual action. It is at this point that we may discern the solution to otherness embedded in Deleuze and Guattari's philosophical thought: Cole's essay explores otherness by means of constructing the Deleuzian plane of immanence so that the forces of otherness serve as a means to escape entrapment in rigid boundary conditions in the space of education.

Clair Colebrook's essay "Leading Out, Leading On: The Soul of Education" leads us out (pun intended) from habitual ways of thinking about education and towards a new territory, towards a new truth posited not as a solution but a genuine problem in the Deleuzian spirit. As she indicates in Chapter 3, leading thought away from a current opinion is not the imposition of a higher truth but the provocation to problematize, and to think first of all the truth of problems rather than of solutions. Her essay is exemplary in its provocation to indeed problematize education according to Deleuze and also in connection to the philosophy of Heidegger and Foucault. Deleuze's concept of desire is related by Colebrook to Socratic Eros and thus to pedagogy understood as a process of leading thought away from the already defined opinions and appearances to a desire embedded in the very questions we pose and that will have transformed the very being of a particular question/problem. She notices that Deleuze overturns Platonism by means of deconstructing the opposition between truth and sophistry[2]. Importantly, Colebrook is also leading us to the political problematics which one encounters when facing the very soul of education with its Socratic intensification of Eros: the politics of critique, enlightenment, and the problem of avoiding us ourselves becoming a higher authority on a presupposed truth. Colebrook's analysis of Deleuze's ontology and his positing the relations as external to their terms ensure that *learning* is a task that thought must actively perform in order to intuit the powers that compose relations.

Literary texts, for example, have a certain power to provoke new relations. To learn is equivalent to being led out from oneself; thus one must intuit the desire as that singular striving from which any text emerges. Deleuze's philosophy posits thinking as a mode of desire; this, for Colebrook, leads to two consequences. Thought not only becomes different according to the problems it approaches; significantly, true thinking always moves beyond established relations and constituted terms to the *other* desire in a given encounter. Noticing the difference between Deleuze and Guattari's schizoanalysis and "old-fashioned" Heideggerian hermeneutics, Colebrook emphasizes that the problem's sense consists not in disclosing its being, but in its very assault on method and being. Colebrook suggests that, in the educational context, we should be on the lookout for the force of a text, for the problems of history, for the genesis of new concepts rather than just staying in the constituted discursive field.

Jacques Daignault's essay entitled "Pedagogy and Deleuze's Concept of the Virtual: An illustration of a 'machine à détonner' in the analysis of free software" (translated from the original French by Brett Buchanan) explores the activity of pedagogy as an immanently creative exercise contributing to the common good. Taking Deleuze's philosophy as an inspiration and the Internet as a focal point, in Chapter 4 Daignault draws a parallel between the open source movement that advocates accessibility to free software and information, and the pedagogical liberation entailed in the free and open exchange of ideas. Deleuze's concept of the virtual is extended to the ontological dimension of the Internet where, far from being a copy or representation of the world, the Internet and cyberspace are held to be just as real as the world itself. Daignault suggests that the conception of the virtual addressed by Deleuze in his many works promptly invites questioning of the phenomenon of the Internet. And not only in terms of a controlled society, but in the declension of the concept of virtuality as a *machine à détonner*, where the emphasis on pedagogy would constitute an example *par excellence*. If the Internet can be called virtual, it is because it is a real stratum, and not merely a simulacrum, of the world.

Daignault's analysis of the virtual further emphasizes the creativity of problems and questions that is at work within all that is actual. Rather than considering pedagogy as leading toward solutions and answers, as hoped for by established curricula, pedagogy is akin to the virtual in that it demonstrates, in its creative function, the art of problems/questions opened within what Daignault calls "the pedagogical parenthesis." Pedagogical parentheses suspend the formal laws, norms, and obligations of teaching (as set out, for example, by the contract of the syllabus), only in order to paradoxically realize the aims of the contract through its very suspension. In a sense, we fulfil the pedagogical contract by allowing for the opening of a little slice of chaos, a bit of the unpredictable and unknowable. As a cooperative engagement, teaching and learning – just like the arguments on behalf of free software and open source licensing – can ensure future becoming through the sharing of free knowledge as it leads towards common good and mutual enrichment. Daignault concludes that by bringing Deleuze's philosophy into education we become able to sustain pedagogy as a free creation and offers his personal insight into the activity of teaching. Just as the creation of concepts is the task of the philosophical method for Deleuze, the creation of pedagogical parentheses is held by Daignault to be the object of educational practice. As a performative activity, his brief account of free software itself performs a creative parenthesis within the body of his essay. In a Deleuzian manner, Daignault's essay unfolds into a pedagogical act within a creative *milieu* of the nomadic distribution of ideas.

Gary Genosko's essay "Felix Guattari and popular pedagogy" delivers a long-overdue homage to Guattari among the chapters in this volume. Guattari is mostly known to us for his collaborations with Deleuze, Negri, Alliez, and other post-'68 figures in French thought. In Chapter 5, however, Genosko explores Guattari's unique path as connected to pedagogy and, especially, the youth hostel movement that started when Felix was a teen. Genosko draws a picture of Guattari derived from his involvement in working with marginalized, delinquent, pre-delinquent, and emotionally challenged children. Exploring the relationship between hostelling, far-left militancy, and popular pedagogy, Genosko presents a detailed analysis of how all three influenced Guattari's experiments with transdisciplinary groups in psychotherapy later in life and have led to his practising schizoanalysis. Guattari was learning the very texture of the lessons about organization in extra-curricular youth activities in the hostels movement and from "Institutional Pedagogy". Presenting in depth both history and geography of "Institutional Pedagogy" in France, Genosko examines a critical perspective on institutional psychotherapy in the pedagogical context. Felix Guattari had an ongoing interest in the Group for Therapeutic Education, singling out the role played by the importance given to singularization, that is, a self-organizing process involving the constitution of an assemblage of components, relations with other assemblages, and the analysis of their effects on the constitution of subjectivity. It is a group that is a (collective) subject, and Genosko describes Guattari's sense of a subject-group that formulates its own projects, speaks and is heard, and puts itself at risk in pursuing its own ends and taking responsibility for them. We may conclude that the fact that popular pedagogy and democratic education through scheduled work were privileged over traditional psychoanalysis is the key to such important conceptualizations in the collaborative works by Deleuze and Guattari as transversal communication and transversality, assemblages of enunciation and desiring-machines, a-signifying semiotics and pre-personal singularity. As Genosko notices, these terms would not comprise a traditional philosophical universe of references. They constitute social tools for articulation of individual and collective affects and recomposing the components of subjectivity. The pragmatic effects consist in new kinds of responsibility that can be taken, new constructive and productive ways of seeing and living that can be accomplished; that is, all the objectives that are as important for therapy as they are for education.

Deleuze used the biological notion of a rhizome as a metaphor for multidirectional growth and diverse productivity. Noel Gough structures his essay

"Becoming-Cyborg: a rhizomANTic assemblage" as a narrative experiment inspired by Deleuze and Guattari's figuration of a rhizome. In Chapter 6 Gough deploys the conception of cyborg in popular and academic media to question some taken-for-granted assumptions of curriculum theory, teaching, and learning. He demonstrates how Deleuze's conceptual inventions can generate productive and disruptive agendas in educational research. Gough coins the term "rhizomANTic" in the manner of Deleuzian neologisms and connects Deleuze-Guattarian rhizomatic method with an actor-network theory, or ANT, as well as with Haraway's innovative metaphor of semantics. He elucidates the intertextual relationships between research texts and fiction by using Deleuze's philosophy as both a catalyst and a particular inflection. Gough's essay demonstrates how the explorations of the fiction genre in/for educational inquiry converge with Deleuze's philosophical concepts. Referring to *Difference and Repetition* (1994) where Deleuze states that a book of philosophy belongs to a kind of science fiction, Gough re-enacts a similar disposition by presenting and performing educational research methodologies in a variety of fictional modes.

Gough argues that understanding cyborgs as assemblages of socio-technical relations provides a generative conceptual framework for imagining and developing productive posthuman pedagogies, that is, approaches to teaching and learning hospitable to emergent cyborg subjectivities and corporealities. He presents cyborg pedagogy as an educational practice for science teachers. Gough places particular emphasis on the narrative construction of cyborgs within the experiential practices of intertextual machineries and explores their functioning as novel resources for transforming the discursive fields in which they circulate. A specific *Cyberantics* assemblage, Gough claims, can work as a Deleuzian figuration to inspire science educators, especially because *Cyberantics* functions as a complex system displaying the properties of what contemporary science calls chaos and complexity theories. Noticing that some cyberpunk science fiction narratives bring to mind the synergistic links between Prigogine's theory of self-organization and the cybernetic project of building intelligent artefacts, Gough relates *Cyberantics* to a postmodern science education text and imagines teaching and learning as assemblages of sociotechnical relations embedded in and performed by shifting connections and interactions among a variety of organic and textual materials. It is such a rhizomANTic assemblage that lives on and disrupts the manicured lawn of formal education. For Gough, the kinds of cyborgs that we and our children are becoming are shaped and reshaped by the pedagogical stories we mutually construct.

Becoming-cyborg is part and parcel of Deleuze's generic concept of *becoming-other*. Any becoming is always already *becoming-minor*. Nomadic tribes wandering in the smooth space of the steppe represent a Deleuzian minority. Zelia Gregoriou's essay develops this particular trope of Deleuze's in the context of educational philosophy. In Chapter 7, entitled "Commencing the Rhizome: Towards a minor philosophy of education", Gregoriou argues that an experimental encounter with Deleuzian thinking will liberate educational philosophy from being limited to established meanings, communicability, or an ideal speech act. The emerging image is that of what Deleuze would have called a *minor* philosophy of education, the latter in no way alleging, as Gregoriou points out, any inferiority or immaturity but instead carrying within itself a creative force of multiplicity and openness. Gregoriou follows up Lyotard's analysis of the postmodern condition, aiming to reclaim philosophy of education from its nuptial arrangement with the social sciences by means of "commencing the rhizome" and bringing Deleuze's novel concepts (of which rhizome is just one) into educational discourse. Referring to the apparent lack of communication between philosophers and educators addressed at a recent symposium, Gregoriou turns to the effects of *becoming-minor* as a possibility to deterritorialize philosophy in terms of creating an unformed philosophical expression for each of many singularities in the field of experimentation, including the field of the classroom, permeated by collective enunciations. She posits pedagogy as analogous to Deleuzian philosophy at the (n − 1) dimension: not a progressive build-up of knowledge based on firm unshakable foundations but respect for the singular, picking up multiple disparate ideas and linking them into future possibilities.

Deleuze and Guattari's *rhizome* exemplifies nomadic movements across spaces: as embedded in a particular situation, rhizome goes in diverse directions instead of a single path, multiplying its own lines and establishing the plurality of unpredictable connections in the open-ended smooth space of its growth. If Zelia Gregoriou has commenced one particular rhizomatic line in her essay, it is Chapter 8, co-authored by Eileen Honan and Marg Sellers, that *traverses* it with another rhizomatic line in their essay entitled "(E)merging methodologies: putting rhizomes to work". Rhizome, for Deleuze, is a multiplicity irreducible to a single root that would have represented a research methodology grounded in an orthodox scientific method. Using Deleuze's figuration of a rhizome as fruitful in/for education, Honan and Sellers explore two different approaches to the development of a rhizomatic methodology in educational research. In a rhizomatic fashion, Honan and Sellers map the connections and disconnections between and across different educational pathways. Three connections are described: first, writing a rhizomatic text, which is non-linear and deliberately designed to be a part of the research method itself. The authors reflexively and critically examine the construction of their essay as an illustration for, as well as a description of, the partial and transgressive nature of writing rhizomatically within the broad field of educational research. Second, the authors argue that using the rhizomatic image of thought in order to analyse the discourses operating within data requires a specific "rhizo-textual analysis" of the intersections and connections between various discursive *plateaus*. This type of analysis is undertaken to provide an account of how an individual child is constituted within policy texts.

The authors, finally, follow Deleuzian lines of flight that connect and link disparate forms of data to arrive at (im)plausible readings and interpretations constituting analysis of the multiplicity of writing, artworks, video, and interview transcripts. They follow and cross over the multiple rhizomatic lines to provide an (unlikely) account of the linkages between the construction of the individual child in a syllabus text devoted to the teaching of English, and the construction of what they call the rhizomatic child within moments of informal playing in an early childhood setting. Honan and Sellers assert that the multiplicity of various disconnections is provided as an illustration to the thesis of the impossibility of establishing some kind of formulaic methodology that would have neatly answered Ian Buchanan's question, in the context of social critique, of "how does it work?" Being aware of the dangers of what Sandra Harding called "methodolatry," the authors offer their essay as one particular and specific reading of the contributions that Deleuzian theories and his philosophical method can and should make to educational research methodologies.

David Lines' essay exemplifies a specific variation on Deleuze's thinking in the context of music, and art in general, and explores the theme, which is attuned to more improvisational images of thought. Chapter 9, titled "Deleuze, Education, and the Creative Economy", problematizes the current approach to education understood in terms of the knowledge economy that employs the reductive concept of creativity. What is habitually understood as "creativity" in our age is aligned with the production of capital, technical innovations, and the presentation of fast knowledge via digital communication channels. Deleuze's understanding of art and creativity is however, as Lines tells us, very different. Art is first and foremost creative; yet Deleuze's way of conceptualizing *creativity* differs noticeably from many recent performative projections of the concept of creativity that often manifest in a wide range of fields including business, management and education. Lines' essay purports to examine how creativity presents itself in different contexts, often as a part of a family of concepts in and around teaching and learning in the creative, cultural, and knowledge industries.

For Lines, the performative function of creativity is *machinic* (as Deleuze would have said) in its both repetitive and different role and considering its impact(s) on cultural change. Yet, in educational contexts these forces and images can cause difficulties, particularly if and when they simply help to reinforce dominant, normative educational practices that obscure emergent or *minoritarian* knowledge. Such notions and performative functions would stand in stark contrast with Deleuze's philosophical thinking as artistic! With this difference in mind, Lines presents Deleuze's ideas as providing an important insight into everyday practices of teaching and learning and the ways of conceiving specific teaching activities such as planning and assessment. Lines notices that the difficulties of working with economic discourse in educational sites still remain. He concludes his chapter by asserting that – as economic forces remain embedded in all forms of culture – it is not sufficient to say that a Deleuzian artistic-creativity on the one hand is superior to production-creativity on the other. The exploration of Deleuze's ideas, however, opens up possibilities of how art can be a force of change even within existing confining cultural forces in education. The artistic and creative potential in an image of a rhizome, or a deterritorializing impulse, is frequently used by Deleuze in order to, as Lines claims, describe an often-untimely line of thought that is strategically different in quality to representational or "captured" expressions of thinking. This movable and changing line is nomadic in its essence. Lines argues that Deleuze sees art in terms of a musical and improvisational creative force functioning as a catalyst for new directions in education and new modes of learning.

Todd May and Inna Semetsky's essay "Deleuze, ethical education, and the unconscious" addresses the ethical dimension of Deleuze's philosophy in the context of education and pedagogy. Chapter 10 proposes and explores several conceptual shifts important for education as derived from Deleuze's ethics and his unorthodox practical "epistemology". The authors suggest that it is what we do *not* know, rather than what we do, that is of educational significance. The corollary is that education is to be committed to experimentation rather than transmission of pre-existing facts or inculcation of given values in the classroom. Taking a metaphysical turn, the authors agree with Deleuze that Being (with a capital B) can be conceptually approached and contrast the logic of identity of Anglo-American philosophy with Deleuze's logic of difference and multiplicities. They refer to the Deleuzian *real* as comprising both the virtual and the actual; and make a conceptual shift to the level of the unconscious akin to the virtual, potential tendencies. Drawing from Deleuze's ontology of the virtual, May and Semetsky assert that much of our world, as well as our learning, are unconscious rather than conscious. They distinguish ethics from traditional morality and insist that ethical education in its actual practice is to be informed by Deleuze's larger ontology. Abandoning the idea of values as a set of identities leads, as the authors assert, to an important question of what we might be able to make of ourselves. For Deleuze, it is the evaluation of experience, and not a conformity to prescribed values, that characterizes our ways of being and modes of existence.

May and Semetsky insist that the learning process involves what Deleuze called the conquest of the unconscious, hence the process of thinking and learning is both cognitive and corporeal, therefore by necessity having its unusual origin in practice and not in theory. The authors bring into the conversation Deleuze's philosophy of language with its creative and expressive potential, which is capable of retrieving the structures of the unconscious and making us see, think, understand, and create! Pedagogical experiment and classroom experience involve both a teacher and a student whose roles become those of a creative artist or an inventive scientist and who would have abandoned the common sense in favor of experimentation. The authors make it clear that Deleuzian ethical education would involve not just our minds but our whole lives. Ethical education is creative because it takes us to places that are not there until they are created from the virtual out of which we live: values are produced in practice when we venture into unknown territory for which new concepts are to be invented. A thorough analysis of Deleuze's ontology, logic, and ethics allows the authors to propose that Deleuze's practical philosophy tends toward Nel Noddings' ethics of care in education.

There exists a question paramount to education: What is language as praxis, as both possible and actual transformation? This is a question with which Kaustuv Roy wrestles in his contribution to this collection. Noticing that the notion of communication historically presented itself in a troubled fashion, Roy remains pessimistic even of Habermas' efforts to work out its conditions of possibility. Instead, Roy turns to Deleuze's unorthodox philosophy of language and his approach to communication, making them the focal points (or should we say, lines? Lines of flight?) of his essay entitled "Deleuzian murmurs: Education and Communication". In Chapter 11, and thinking along with Deleuze, Roy presents Deleuze's argument that language is not just a medium but an ontological entity, which is constantly mixing itself up with physical materiality. What are the implications of this analysis of language for communication and educational practice, asks Roy. Can language directly enter into voice? And if so, how does it get beyond the slogans or what Deleuze and Guattari dubbed in terms of order-words with which language immediately orders reality? Starting his essay with the critique of communication based on the Deleuzian critique of representation, Roy aims to draw the distinction between language and code and explore the political and performative dimension of the communicative act. Roy makes it clear that any direct communication (that is, pure repetition without any intervening difference) is plainly impossible; instead there are two kinds of interchanges that occur between language and bodies and to which Deleuze refers as the incorporeal and corporeal transformations. The performative effect of an interchange is a becoming of part-subjects produced as a partial outcome of the existentializing function, as Felix Guattari would have called it. The existentializing function is akin to the expressive or performative aspect of language that, in its functioning as an experiential event, breaks down the schemata of certainty and representations. According to Roy-Deleuze, this function represents a direct challenge to the conception of communi-cation as simply a transmission of code(s). Instead there is a process described by Roy in terms of "an ongoing activity that is ever-present as differential murmurs between the order of things and the order of words". For education and pedagogy, a reciprocal relationship between physical bodies and language and their mutual transformation means, as Roy asserts, that we can escape the settled reality of order-words and begin to partake in the social production of being, thereby becoming able to micropolitically heal the private-public split.

Considering the pessimistic attitude towards Habermas' theory of communi-cative action taken by Kaustuv Roy in his chapter and that Deleuze himself used to denounce the so-called universals of communication, the essay written by Inna Semetsky and Terry Lovat represents a formidable challenge to such a perspective. Chapter 12 is entitled "Knowledge in action: towards a Deleuze-Habermasian critique in/for education". The authors construct a shared framework for Deleuze's philosophy and Habermas' critical theory by virtue of the common pragmatic dimension inherent in their approach to knowledge. For both, the value of knowledge lies in its practical import at the level of action. The authors explore three ways of knowing as articulated by Habermas and position them alongside Deleuze's method of nomadic inquiry which supplements strict analytical reasoning (akin to Habermas' first cognitive way) with a broader format of diverse forms of cartographies aiming at the mapping of new directions for praxis. Presenting the theory-practice nexus as defined by everyday engagements with knowledge production, Semetsky and Lovat specifically focus on the experimental and experiential dimension as providing an opportunity for the emancipation of the "nomadic subject" in terms of critical freedom.

Experience is rendered meaningful by means of exercising a specific self-reflective, or critical, mode of thinking and knowing, which the authors posit as the most significant for Deleuze and Habermas alike. Deleuze was explicit in this regard when he described such thinking in metonymic terms: entering an echo chamber and creating a feedback loop (Deleuze, 1995). Semetsky and Lovat also address a complementary aspect of critical thinking, namely its clinical or ethical dimension, and arrive at several important implications for moral, or values, education. They argue that a moral subject cannot be reduced to an individual agent but is always intersubjective or relational. Such a relational "self-other" agency must embody a creative thinker capable of evaluating new experiences and making sense out of/for problematic and conflicting experiences embedded in social relations. The analysis (and synthesis) of Deleuze-Habermasian critique leads Semetsky and Lovat to posit questions crucial for the actual educational process (How can education in the form of nomadic inquiry be implemented in practice? How can knowledge be enacted?). They imagine the three modes of knowing in the context of classroom discussions asserting that critical evaluations demand our self-reflection on past-present-and-a-possible-future; engaging with the most strange and unfamiliar others at the interpersonal level; as well as confronting ourselves. The authors' conclusion is like a musical chord in their saying that we become authentic selves while engaging in the practice of becoming-other.

Back in the 1990s, it was Elizabeth St. Pierre's pioneering qualitative research in education modelled on Deleuze's method of nomadic inquiry that introduced Deleuze's thought into educational discourse, even if not yet in a systematic manner. In her essay in this volume (Chapter 13) titled "Deleuzian Concepts for Education: The Subject Undone", St. Pierre emphasizes Deleuze and Guattari's approach to philosophy as the creation of new concepts. She employs and analyzes Deleuzian concepts to rethink the subject and explores the conceptualizations of individuation and subjectivity other than that of the individual of liberal humanism. The construction of subjectivity is effected by nomadic displacements, foldings, unfoldings, and refoldings; and educational research based on the methodology of the fold is presented by St. Pierre as science in its most provocative form. St. Pierre's chapter explores Deleuze's intensive way of reading a text as an experiential interaction with the field of *the outside* and demonstrates the extent to which Deleuze's concept of individuation is useful in educational theory and practice. St. Pierre says that Deleuze's early premonition of education as turning into business has indeed become a reality at the level of American federal policy that privileges a single model of educational research method with its top-down linear rationality and conformity to mandatory theory. She describes in detail a session at one of the annual meetings of the American Educational Research Association as, in effect, an erasure of the last fifty years' advance in qualitative research in education.

Addressing the ethico-political dimension of Deleuze's philosophy, St. Pierre focuses on the problem of the postmodern subject as a Deleuzian assemblage, both human and nonhuman, and on the pragmatic value of subjectivity. Positioning Deleuze's novel concepts in the field explored by Foucault, Butler, Haraway,

Derrida and Spivak, St. Pierre reminds us of the fragility of a subject situated within the conservatism of oppressive power relations in the educational community – yet it is precisely Deleuze's untimely memories of the future that help us in imagining a time to come in which the present struggle may change. St. Pierre asks an important question of how one can read a philosopher like Deleuze and not be transformed in some way. Her answer is unequivocal: once we start using in practice the *nomad, rhizome, middle, line of flight* to think about the world, we will live differently. St. Pierre notices that one form of resistance to the scientism based on the set of established norms involves accomplishing scholarship that would have upset the given order and presents her essay in this volume as a form of resistance aiming to create a critique of accepted values and, in the Deleuzian spirit, to indeed bring something new to life.

Each author who contributed to this collection did not write their essay with an Ego or merely Cartesian *Cogito* – but also with affect and desire, transforming and creating anew the nomadic space of education by this very experiment. For Deleuze, "[I]n the act of writing there's an attempt to make life something more than personal, to free life from what imprisons it" (Deleuze, 1995, p. 143). The philosophical/educational function is both critical and clinical: the *present-becoming*, by definition, has a re-valuative and untimely flavour. The future form of philosophy encompasses both a resistance to the present and a diagnosis of our actual becomings in terms of what Deleuze called becoming-woman or becoming-minor, but also in terms of becoming-revolutionary, becoming-democratic, becoming-pedagogical. Such is the role of the philosopher – including an educational philosopher – as a clinician or the physician of culture described as "an inventor of new immanent modes of existence" (Deleuze & Guattari, 1994, p. 113). In the passage from one milieu to another, each author in this collection contributed to the construction of meanings and concepts analogous to Deleuze's ingenious "immanent conception" (Deleuze, 1995, p. 144). This volume exemplifies the general principle of composition in music that cannot be given, according to Deleuze, in a directly perceptible or audible relation to that what it provides. Readers will enter into the multiplicity of folds which comprise this book, re-en-folding each chapter and marking new directions when taking zigzagging lines of flight into that what is yet to come so as to set conjunctions and conjectures free.

NOTES

[1] Acknowledgment: Chapter 1 is a reprint of Bogue, R. (2004). Search, Swim and See: Deleuze's apprenticeship in signs and pedagogy of images. In I. Semetsky (Ed.), Educational Philosophy and Theory, special issue Deleuze and Education, 36(3), pp. 327-342.

Chapter 7 is a reprint of Gregoriou, Z. (2004). Commencing the Rhizome: Towards a minor philosophy of education. In I. Semetsky (Ed.), Educational Philosophy and Theory, special issue Deleuze and Education, 36(3), pp. 233-252.

Chapter 13 is a reprint of St. Pierre, E. A. (2004). Deleuzian Concepts for Education: The subject undone. In I. Semetsky (Ed.), Educational Philosophy and Theory, special issue Deleuze and Education, 36(3), pp. 283-296. Thank you to Blackwell Publishers for permission to reprint.

² The oft-cited reversed Platonism of Deleuze should be taken with a grain of salt, in the opinion of the Editor. To remind the readers, "…there's no point at all doing philosophy the way Plato did, not because we've superseded Plato, but because you can't supersede Plato, and it makes no sense to have another go at what he's done for all time. There's only one choice: doing the history of philosophy, or transplanting bits of Plato into problems that are no longer Platonic ones" (Deleuze, 1995, p. 148).

REFERENCES

Deleuze, G. (1987). *Dialogues* (with Claire Parnet) (H. Tomlinson & G. Burchell, Trans.). New York: Columbia University Press.

Deleuze, G. (1994). *Difference and repetition* (P. Patton, Trans.). New York: Columbia University Press.

Deleuze, G. (1995). *Negotiations 1972–1990* (M. Joughin, Trans.). New York: Columbia University Press.

Deleuze, G., & Guattari, F. (1987). *A thousand plateaus: Capitalism and schizophrenia* (B. Massumi, Trans.). Minneapolis, MN: University of Minnesota Press.

Deleuze, G., & Guattari. F. (1994). *What is philosophy?* (H. Tomlinson & G. Burchell, Trans.). New York: Columbia University Press.

Peters, M. A. (2002, July–December). Geofilosophia, Educação e Pedagogia do Conceito. *Educação & Realidade, 27*(2). (Tomaz Tadeu da Silva, Trans., Portuguese, pp. 77–88).

Peters, M. A. (2004). Editorial: Geophilosophy, Education and the pedagogy of the concept. In I. Semetsky (Ed.), *Educational Philosophy and Theory*, special issue *Deleuze and Education, 36*(3), pp. 217–226.

Semetsky, I. (2006). *Deleuze, education and becoming.* Rotterdam, The Netherlands: Sense Publishers.

Inna Semetsky
The University of Newcastle
Australia

RONALD BOGUE

1. SEARCH, SWIM AND SEE:
DELEUZE'S APPRENTICESHIP IN SIGNS
AND PEDAGOGY OF IMAGES

Deleuze was a remarkable polymath, capable of bringing penetrating insights to a wide variety of disciplines. The number of topics addressed during his career was considerable, ranging from mathematics, biology, psychology, political science, and anthropology to logic, ethics, painting, literature, metallurgy, and the decorative arts. One might assume that as a lifelong academic Deleuze would have turned his attention to the subject of education with some frequency, but in fact he dedicated only a small portion of his energies to this field. He did, however, devote a few passages of *Difference and Repetition* (1969) to the relationship between thought and learning that are especially suggestive. These passages summarize the salient points he had developed in his 1964 study Proust and Signs, in which he approached Proust's massive *A la recherche du temps perdu* as an extended apprenticeship in the explication of signs. The question of teaching and its relationship to learning he left largely unexamined in these two works, but in *Cinema 2: The Time-Image* (1985), Deleuze spoke briefly of a "pedagogy" of images in the films of Godard, and from these remarks on Godard's treatment of sound and sight one can discern the outlines of what might constitute a Deleuzian theory of teaching. Taken together, Deleuze's studies of learning in Proust and teaching in Godard provide a map of directions one might pursue in developing a Deleuzian philosophy of education.

SEARCHING

Proust's *Recherche*, as its French title indicates, is a search for lost time, but Deleuze insists that this search is oriented toward the future rather than the past. Marcel, the hero of the *Recherche*, indeed explores memories of the past, but only as part of an apprenticeship that eventuates in his becoming an artist. His exploration of lost time is merely part of a search for the *truth* of time, which is one with the truth of signs. Signs for Deleuze are not transparent media for the communication of information. Rather, they are hieroglyphs, enigmas that point beyond themselves to something hidden. In this sense, the moon as sign is a bright surface gesturing toward its dark side. Every sign has something enfolded within it, something "other," that must be unfolded if it is to be understood. The interpretation of signs, then, is a matter of "explicating," or unfolding (from Latin *plicare*: to fold), that which is "implicated," or enfolded.

I. Semetsky (ed.), Nomadic Education: Variations on a Theme by Deleuze and Guattari, 1–16.

Deleuze identifies four kinds of signs in the Recherche: the worldly signs of polite society; the amorous signs of passion and jealousy; the evanescent sensual signs of involuntary memory; and the immaterial signs of art. Worldly signs are vacuous, with no genuine content, but they force Marcel to unfold their mysteries, to determine why one person is admitted to a given social circle, why another is snubbed, who belongs to which milieu, what constitutes the tone and relative prestige of a particular coterie, and so on. Amorous signs point toward the worlds hidden in the beloved, toward all those places the beloved inhabits when the lover is absent. The truth of these signs is revealed through jealousy, which compels the lover to unfold the mysteries of the worlds which are enfolded in the beloved and from which the lover is forever excluded. The sensual signs of involuntary memory are like the madeleine, whose taste suddenly fills Marcel with great joy as the unexpected presence of the Combray of his childhood comes over him. Such signs Marcel compares to tiny pieces of Japanese paper that, when placed in water, unfold and expand to reveal hidden landscapes imprinted on their surfaces. As Marcel observes of the savor of the madeleine he has just dipped in his lime tea, "in a moment all the flowers in our garden and in M. Swann's park, and the water-lilies on the Vivonne and the good folk of the village and their little dwellings and the parish church and the whole of Combray and its surroundings, taking shape and solidity, sprang into being, towns and gardens alike, from my cup of tea" (Proust, 1982, vol. 1, p. 51). The signs of art, finally, are signs of essences, manifestations of originary worlds that unfold within the material form of a given artwork but transcend that matter and reveal the truth of the cosmos as a dynamic process of self-differentiation.

Deleuze reads the *Recherche* as the record of an apprenticeship (*apprentissage* in French), or process of learning (French *apprendre*: to learn), and all learning, he asserts, proceeds via the interpretation of signs. "Everything that teaches us something emits signs; every act of learning is an interpretation of signs or hieroglyphs. Proust's work is based not on the exposition of memory, but on the apprenticeship in signs" (Deleuze, 2000, p. 4). By "learning" Deleuze clearly does not mean the mere acquisition of any new skill or bit of information, but instead the accession to a new way of perceiving and understanding the world. To interpret signs is to overcome "stock notions," "natural" or "habitual" modes of comprehending reality (ibid., p. 27). What often passes for learning is simply the reinforcement of commonsense notions, standard codes and orthodox beliefs. But the commonsense, conventional, orthodox world is ultimately illusory. Genuine learning, the learning through signs, takes us beyond the illusions of habit and common sense to the truths of what Proust calls "essences" and Deleuze labels "differences."

The usual assumption is that thought voluntarily seeks truth through the exercise of "good will," but what Proust shows is that the search for truth always commences with a disruptive event that compels thought into action. Philosophy's mistake, says Deleuze, "is to presuppose within us a benevolence of thought [*une bonne volonté de penser*], a natural love of truth" (ibid., p. 16). The ideas of the philosophical intelligence "are valid only because of their explicit, hence, conventional, signification," and "explicit and conventional significations are never profound; the only profound meaning is the one that is enveloped, implicated in an external sign" (ibid., p. 16). Philosophy's intellectual truths are "abstract and conventional" (ibid., p. 30) whereas the truths of signs are "fortuitous and inevitable" (ibid., p. 16). Only through a chance encounter with an unsettling sign can thought be jolted from its routine patterns, and only through such an encounter will the object of thought cease to be arbitrarily selected and attain the necessity of something that itself chooses thought, that constrains thought and sets it in motion.

Common sense organizes the world according to fixed identities and stable spatial and temporal coordinates, but for Proust and Deleuze the dynamic unfolding of the world is a process that escapes common sense and defies its set categories. That process is a ceaseless becoming in which things perpetually metamorphose into something else and thereby elude identification and specification, but it is also one informed by a virtual domain of "essences" or "differences" that are, in Proust's words, "real without being actual, ideal without being abstract" (Proust, 1982, vol. 3, pp. 905-06). It is through signs that Marcel learns the truth of essences, and that truth is disclosed initially through revelations of the different forms of time related to each kind of sign.

Worldly signs exhibit the "lost time" of frivolous activity, inevitable decline and universal alteration and annihilation. Amorous signs reveal another type of "lost time," that of "wasted time" [*le temps qu'on perd*, literally, "the time one loses"] (Deleuze, 2000, p. 21), a time of deception and disappointment which can only be absorbed in retrospect, after the love relationship has come to an end. To an extent, such forms of "lost time" may be accommodated within traditional temporal schemas, but not so the time that emerges in the sensual signs of involuntary memory. The time evoked through the madeleine, the uneven paving stones of Venice, and other such sensual signs is "time regained" [*le temps qu'on retrouve*, literally "the time one finds again"], which in Deleuze's reading is a version of the time of Henri Bergson's virtual past.[1] Bergson argues that a memory is not simply a faded or less complex version of an experience that once was present, but something that is qualitatively distinct from any present experience. The past is a single domain in which all past events coexist with one another. This domain is real, though it is virtual rather than actual. At each present moment time splits in two, into a dynamic actual present thrusting toward a future, and a "memory of the present," a virtual double of the present moment (something like a virtual mirror image of the present) that immediately forms part of the single domain of all past events. According to Bergson, when we try to remember something we leap into the virtual past as if entering a different medium. Once we find the memory we are seeking, we bring it back into the present, but usually in such a way that the memory is made to fit in with our actual, commonsense purposes and activities. As a result, the virtual character of the memory tends to escape our awareness. Only in dreams, moments of déjà-vu and other unusual experiences are we able to perceive the virtual past as it exists in itself.

Deleuze insists that Proust's moments of involuntary memory are not mere reminiscences but experiences that disclose such a Bergsonian virtual past. In the case of the madeleine, a common quality—the taste of the madeleine—links a present and a past moment, but in such a way that an "essence of Combray" is released, a virtual Combray that has never been present, save as a virtual "memory of the present." The great joy that fills Marcel comes from this sudden chance encounter with what Proust calls "a fragment of time in the pure state" (Proust, 1982, vol. 3, p. 905), time outside the ordinary coordinates of temporal succession. Yet Marcel's accession to the virtual past teaches more than a simple lesson about time, Deleuze insists, for in the experience of the madeleine Marcel encounters *"internalized difference, which becomes immanent"* (Deleuze, 2000, p. 60). The virtual Combray is embodied in the taste of the madeleine, made internal to that taste, immanent within it, and in this sense the madeleine internalizes something different, but that virtual Combray itself is an unfolding difference, an entity whose paradoxical kind of time is merely one aspect of its being as essence.

It is only in the signs of art that Marcel learns the full truth of essences and their relationship to time. The time of art is "recovered time" [*le temps retrouvé*, literally "time found again," the title of the last volume of the *Recherche*] (ibid., p. 24). Recovered time is the pure form of time, an unspecified temporal medium within which various temporal experiences may be actualized. Its time is like that of the verbal infinitive—"to work," "to sleep," "to dream"—a floating time unmoored from any tense, person, mood, or direction, an essence of temporality that serves as a generative medium from which different specific temporal configurations may issue ("I had worked," "she was to have slept," "we will have been dreaming," etc.). Such time, says Deleuze, is "complicated" (ibid., p. 45), a term he takes from certain Neoplatonic philosophers who speak of the cosmos as an enfolded, implicated One that unfolds, or explicates itself in the multiple, the originary state of which, before any explication, is a *"complication*, which envelops the many in the One and affirms the unity of the multiple" (ibid., p. 45). The time of art is a pure essence of time, a perpetual origin of time, as if with each work of art the world were once again coming into being for the first time.

The *time* of art, however, is only one dimension of essences, which are enfolded virtual differences that unfold themselves in the actual world. To a certain extent Proust is Leibnizian, Deleuze claims, in that "essences are veritable monads, each defined by the viewpoint to which it expresses the world" (ibid., p. 41). Leibniz's logic of "expression" is one of explication and implication, the whole expressing itself by unfolding itself in individual monads, each monad in turn expressing the whole by enfolding the whole as a specific vantage on that totality. In this sense, the world is like a city (to take a Leibnizian figure), which unfolds itself in particular places, each place enfolding the city from a given point of view. Yet in Proust there is no preestablished harmony coordinating all points of view, and hence each monad-site reveals a different city. And each such city is the expression of "difference itself, the absolute internal difference" (ibid., p. 42). What Deleuze means by absolute internal difference is perhaps best understood through the example of a single-cell ovum, which I discussed in Chapter One. Before fertilization, the ovum is crisscrossed by multiple gradients, zones of surface tension and lines of possible division. Of these virtual lines of potential division only one becomes actualized upon fertilization. At that point, a process of differentiation begins, whereby the one cell splits into two. Rather than regarding this process of meiosis as the mechanical construction of a preformed whole, Deleuze sees it as the unfolding of an internal difference that differentiates itself in an ongoing cascade of divisions. As the one cell divides into two, a process of individuation takes place, but the individuals formed—the two cells—are the result of the process, not its cause. Individuation precedes individuals, and individuation is a process of metamorphosis and becoming, one that produces individuated entities but always continues in further metamorphic activity.

"The world is an egg" (Deleuze, 1994, p. 216) in that the world is a dynamic process of metamorphosis through which virtual difference differentiates itself into actual multiple entities while itself remaining immanent within each of those entities. Everywhere difference explicates itself in multiple entities, and difference remains immanent within each entity, implicated within it. Hence, if the world is a city, it is also an egg, not a static collection of edifices but a living entity in formation. Further, it is neither a single city nor a single egg. Each locus looks out on a different city in formation, and there is no single originary ovum from which the city-organism arises. Differentiation proceeds in all directions at once, and wherever one finds oneself, there a different city is in a process of dynamic emergence. What Marcel ultimately learns through art is that the world is a city-egg in metamorphosis, each locus of which enfolds a difference that is actively unfolding itself. Common sense grasps the world in terms of stable entities and fixed relations, thereby misunderstanding difference in two ways, both as it manifests itself in the metamorphic process of becoming (the passage of the virtual into the actual) and as it exists in itself, as a virtual immanent within the actual. What art reveals is that immanent virtual domain, the domain of difference in itself, something that is "real without being actual, ideal without being abstract," something that exists outside temporal markers, in a perpetual infinitive of multiple potential temporal unfoldings.

Marcel's apprenticeship in signs proceeds in two stages and two directions, the first stage leading him from worldly through amorous and sensual signs to the signs of art, the second following a reverse order as he learns to interpret all signs as varying manifestations of internal absolute difference. In the first stage, Marcel must overcome two illusions, those of objectivism and subjectivism. The first is the illusion that the object emitting the sign holds the secret of the sign, as if, for example, the madeleine itself somehow possessed the virtual Combray within its physical being. To make such an illusory attribution is unavoidable, for "Everything encourages us to do so: perception, passion, intelligence, even self-esteem.... We think that the 'object' itself has the secret of the signs it emits. We scrutinize the object, we return to it in order to decipher the sign" (Deleuze, 2000, p. /27). Yet once Marcel overcomes this illusion, he falls into a second, the belief that the secret of the sign is merely a matter of subjective association. The problem here is that with subjective associations, anything goes. Any object may be associated with any other object, in which case signs are merely symptoms of their interpreters. What Marcel must finally learn is that the truth of signs is neither in the objects

5

that emit them nor in the subjects who interpret them but in the differences that are immanent in objects and subjects alike. Art leads Marcel to this truth since in each great art work a unique world is disclosed from a specific point of view, but in such a way that the artist-subject is *produced* by the point of view rather than himself or herself bringing the point of view into existence. Hence, if the world revealed by the great art work is a city, its revealing point of view is like a tower from which an anonymous and apersonal "one" views the dynamic unfolding of the city *and* the artist-subject below, and that "one" is difference itself in a process of self-differentiation.

Once art has taught Marcel the truth of signs, he is able to reinterpret the signs of sensual experience, love and the world and see that all are manifestations of differences, though in varying degrees of materiality and generality. The signs of involuntary memory, such as the madeleine, are close to the signs of art, in that they unfold a world (such as the virtual Combray) and a non-chronological time (the virtual past of the madeleine being a subset of the "complicated" pure form of time of difference). Yet such signs are contingent on circumstances for their emergence, since they are thoroughly enmeshed in the matter in which they appear, unlike the signs of art, which manage to "dematerialize" the medium—the physical paint, sounds, words—in which they are embodied. The signs of love and the world are likewise contingent and embedded in intractable matter, while the worlds they disclose are even less specific than those brought forth in sensual signs. Marcel's love of Albertine forms a series with his love of his mother, Swann's love of Odette, and other loves, such that Marcel comes to see all these loves as the general unfolding of a "theme," an anonymous structure of love that plays through the various heterosexual and homosexual liaisons of the *Recherche*. The signs of the world, finally, disclose social laws, broad regularities of thought and behavior that the sophisticates of the Recherche unconsciously reproduce as they themselves are structured and produced by these regularities.

SWIMMING

Proust's *Recherche* traces the path of a very specific apprenticeship, that of a young man discovering his vocation as a writer. His training proceeds via dinners and receptions, unhappy loves, unsettling recollections, and performances of powerful works of art—hardly the standard curriculum of what is generally thought of as an education. Yet in this aesthetic apprenticeship Deleuze finds the essence of learning, which "is essentially concerned with *signs*" (Deleuze, 2000, p. /4). Signs are enfolded differences that impinge on thought and force thought to unfold those differences. Encounters with such signs are fortuitous yet necessary, chance moments that defy common sense and choose the interpreter rather than themselves being freely chosen as objects of interpretation. In the course of explicating signs, the interpreter necessarily passes through two illusions, that objects possess the truth of signs, and that their truth arises from subjective associations. Once beyond these illusions, the interpreter discovers the virtual domain of differences, which unfold themselves within the actual through a process of metamorphic self-differentiation, while at the same time remaining immanent within the actual.

In *Difference and Repetition*, Deleuze incorporates many of the points raised in *Proust and Signs* within an extended treatment of what he calls the orthodox "image of thought," or the unstated preconceptions of thought implicit in traditional philosophy, and what might be called an "imageless," genuine thought. As in his earlier study of Proust, Deleuze here observes that the standard assumption in philosophy is that thought voluntarily, with a free and good will, pursues truth. Good sense protects thought from nonsense and leads thought in the proper direction (*sens* in French having a possible meaning of "direction"), while common sense provides for a common functioning of the faculties, a *sensus communis* whereby the senses and mental processes are coordinated in their mutual apprehensions (as when, for example, the sight, touch, sound, memory, and analysis of a given experience confirm that they are related to a single and same object of experience). Implicit in this notion of common sense is the model of thought as a form of recognition, recognition being defined through "the harmonious exercise of all the faculties upon a supposed same object" (Deleuze, 1994, p. 133). Recognition in turn grounds the notion of thought as representation, every representation presuming a unified perspective and stable objects governed by the complementary principles of "the Same and the Similar, the Analogous and the Opposed" (ibid., p. 167). Thought's goal in a world of recognition and representation is to eliminate problems and find solutions, to pass from non-knowledge to knowledge. Learning in such a world is simply the passage from non-knowledge to knowledge, a process with a definite beginning and ending, in which thought, like a dutiful pupil, responds to pre-formulated questions and eventually arrives at pre-existing answers.

What escapes orthodox thought is difference, or the genuinely "new," which can only be engaged through an "imageless thought." Rather than arising from a conscious exercise of good will, genuine thought must be forced into action through the disruption of ordinary habits and notions. That which is new is not orthodox but paradoxical, and hence its sense seems nonsense, not good sense. Its paradoxes include those of becoming, the virtual past, and the pure form of time, in which time's arrow is reversed or destroyed and thought as a result proceeds not in a single, right direction but in all directions at once. Rather than reinforcing the common functioning of the senses and faculties, difference splits them apart and pushes each sense or faculty to its limits, no single and selfsame object confirming the unified operation of a *sensus communis*. The object of an imageless thought defies recognition, for "the new—in other words, difference—calls forth forces in thought which are not the forces of recognition, today or tomorrow, but the powers of a completely other model, from an unrecognized and unrecognizable *terra incognita*" (Deleuze, 1994, p. 136). Such an object is understood not through representation but through explication, for the object is a sign, an internalized difference pointing toward something other than itself. Rather than eliminating problems, the thought of difference is itself a thought of problems, and learning, rather than occupying the gap between non-knowledge and knowledge, is the process whereby thought explores the domain of problems.

Many of the characteristics of such an imageless thought we have already encountered in our examination of Marcel's experience of the madeleine. Marcel is jolted from his routines by the taste of the madeleine. Its savor paradoxically enfolds a virtual Combray, whose time is an a-directional coexisting past. That virtual Combray is something different within the madeleine, and itself a difference engaged in a process of self-unfolding. The virtual Combray differs from any seen, heard, or touched Combray, for it is a pure object of memory, one that memory alone can grasp and that divides memory from the other faculties as the object is apprehended. The madeleine defies ready recognition and representation, signifying only by pointing beyond itself to something other and without resemblance to itself. But in what regard does the madeleine disclose a domain of problems, and how is learning related to such a domain? This we can determine by looking a little further at Deleuze's discussion of problems in *Difference and Repetition*.

Often philosophers act as if "problems are given ready-made, and that they disappear in the responses or the solution" (ibid., p. 158), which perhaps accounts for dogmatic philosophy's frequent "puerile examples taken out of context and arbitrarily erected into models" and its "infantile" proceedings in which "the master sets a problem, our task is to solve it, and the result is accredited true or false by a powerful authority" (ibid., p. 158). Deleuze contends, however, that problems must be both invented and discovered, and that they produce the conditions under which solutions may be judged true or false. Hence, each problem is "at once both the site of an originary truth and the genesis of a derived truth" (ibid., p. 159). Problems must be evaluated not according to their "resolvability," as often happens in philosophy, but according to their importance, their ability to generate new questions and the solutions related to those questions.

But problems for Deleuze are more than mere Kuhnean paradigms, for they are differential events that "do not exist only in our heads but occur here and there in the production of an actual historical world" (ibid., p. 190). Problems exist in a virtual domain of difference, and each problem may be characterized in terms of its "differential elements and relations along with the singular points which correspond to them" (ibid., p. 209). Deleuze draws this vocabulary of differential relations and singular points from the language of differential calculus. He notes that the basic formula for the derivative of a function, dy / dx, allows one to describe a relation between elements without determining their separate identities or specifying their values. "In relation to x, dx is completely undetermined, as dy is to y, but they are perfectly determinable in relation to one another.... Each term exists absolutely only in its relation to the other" (ibid., p. 172). The elements of a given problem are like the x and y of the formula dy / dx, undetermined elements that become capable of determination (though still without having any specified values) through their differential relation with one another. Hence, each problem delineates "a system of ideal connections—in other words, a system of differential relations between reciprocally determined genetic elements" (ibid., pp. 173-74). Deleuze also observes that in the geometric interpretation of the theory of differential equations one may characterize different equations in terms of their singular points, the focus of a given parabola, for example, being the singular point of the parabola generated by that equation. What is crucial for Deleuze is that one may determine the *existence* of such singular points and their *distribution* within a field of vectors without specifying their precise values or even what figures they might determine—whether a parabola, a curve, an ellipse, etc.

A problem, then, is not an amorphous muddle, nor a kind of shadowy double of its eventual resolution within a specific solution, but a structured field of potential actualizations, a system of differentially related elements and their corresponding singular points. The system of reciprocally determinable relations of a given problem establishes its fundamental elements, and the singular points demarcate various zones of potential actualization. The problem is virtual—real without being actual—yet it is always engaged in a process of actualization, and it is immanent within its various actualizations. The problem of differential calculus consists of its elements (at the most rudimentary level, x and y as related through the formula for the derivative, dy / dx) and the singular points distributed within a field of vectors. The elements and singular points only have an actual existence in specific equations and solutions, which may be mapped in particular figures (a given parabola or curve, say) with precise values. But the problematic domain of differentially related elements and singular zones of potential actualization remains immanent within actual equations and solutions, each equation being a concrete manifestation of a generative zone of potential differentiation. If one considers the phonemic dimension of language, one may characterize its problem in terms of the broad field of reciprocally determinable phonemic oppositions that belong to all languages, and the particular set of pertinent differences, or singular points, that find actualization in a given language. Each enunciation of a given phoneme is a concrete and specific sonic manifestation of a zone of potential enunciations delimited by a given pertinent difference, such that variations in timbre, pitch, and pronunciation of a given phoneme by different speakers "count" as enunciations of the same phoneme. One may also regard the development of a biological organism as an actualization of a problem, the reciprocally determinable elements being the differential relations common to animals in general, the singular points being zones of potential differentiation that may be actualized in the components of a dog or a cat, and that have actual embodiment in this dog or that cat.[2]

As should be clear from these examples, problems are not simply mental, subjective entities, at least in the common sense of those terms. They are ideal, in that they are virtual, but they are manifest in human and nonhuman, organic and even inorganic, systems alike.[3] Problems are "ideal 'objecticities' possessing their own sufficiency and implying acts of constitution and investment in their respective symbolic fields" (ibid., p. 159). Human thought obviously involves human subjects, yet, though problems do not come ready-made, and hence must be created, at the same time they are not mere fabrications of the mind, for they have a real, albeit virtual, existence as "objecticities" that manifest themselves throughout the world. Thus, when Deleuze turns to the subject of learning, he says that "Learning is the appropriate name for the subjective acts carried out when one is confronted with the objecticity of a problem (Idea), whereas knowledge designates only the generality of concepts or the calm possession of a rule enabling solutions" (ibid., p. 164). Learning and problems belong to the domain of the virtual, whereas knowledge and solutions belong to the separate domain of the actual; and learning is a matter of opening thought to the virtual domain of problems, which has its own autonomous existence, not a matter of solving specific questions and securing a permanent body of knowledge.

At three different points in *Difference and Repetition*, Deleuze offers as an example of learning that of learning to swim.[4] In the most extended treatment of this example, Deleuze remarks first that "to learn is to enter into the universal of the relations which constitute the Idea, and into their corresponding singularities" (ibid., p. 165). In other words, one must immerse oneself in a problem, with its system of differential relations ("the universal of the relations which constitute the Idea") and their corresponding singular points. The sea may be considered one such problem. "The idea of the sea, for example, as Leibniz showed, is a system of liaisons or differential relations between particles, and singularities corresponding to the degrees of variation among these relations—the totality of the system being incarnated in the real movement of the waves" (ibid., p. 165, translation modified).[5] One may say that the problem of the sea in general, its universal problem, is that of differential relations between dynamically interacting water particles, and that the problem's singular points are the nadir and apex of diverse potential wave functions. Each concrete, physical wave is an actualization of one particular set of singular points, and the whole of the sea is an embodiment of the system of differential relations that constitute the problem of the sea. "To learn to swim," continues Deleuze, "is to conjugate the distinctive points [*points remarquables*, a synonym for singular points] of our bodies with the singular points of the objective Idea in order to form a problematic field" (ibid., p. 165). Through contact with the sea, then, the singular points which are incarnate in the swimmer's body are conjoined with the singular points embodied in the sea, and the complex of singular points belonging to swimmer and sea together form a virtual, problematic field. The swimmer, of course, possesses an actual body, the sea has an actual material existence, and the swimmer learns to interact with actual waves. But it is this conjugation of singular points that "determines for us a threshold of consciousness at which our real acts are adjusted to our perceptions of the real relations, thereby providing a solution to the problem" (ibid., p. 165).

Consciousness, however, does not afford us direct access to problems and their singular points. Consciousness operates via good will, good sense and common sense, all of which distort difference and reinforce an interpretation of the world in terms of ready-made questions and preexisting solutions. Only through an involuntary confrontation with something other does thought engage difference, and that which provokes the thought of difference is a sign (as we saw earlier in our examination of Proust). Hence, "problems and their symbolic fields stand in a relationship with signs," for signs are those entities "which 'cause problems' and are developed in a symbolic field" (ibid., p. 164). If to learn is to conjugate singular points "in order to form a problematic field" (ibid., p. 165), then we may say as well that "to learn is indeed to constitute this space of an encounter with signs" (DR 35/23). In the case of swimming, the encounter with signs leads to the discovery of singular points in both the swimmer and the sea. The singular points immanent within the swimmer's body become manifest through the body's disorienting, subliminal micro-perceptions of an alien element. Through that body's attempts to adjust its motions with those of the sea, thought unfolds the singular points that are enfolded in the sign-particles of the sea, and as the body and the sea together form an interactive system of motions, a problematic field emerges, one of differential relations and singular points that extend across swimmer and sea. Thus, though learning to swim entails a passage to "a threshold of consciousness at which our real acts are adjusted to our perceptions of the real relations [of the sea]" (ibid., p. 165), problems are "the ultimate elements of nature [those of the sea, in the swimming example] and the subliminal objects of little perceptions [i.e., micro-perceptions below the threshold of consciousness]. As a result, 'learning' always takes place in and through the unconscious, thereby establishing the bond of a profound complicity between nature and mind" (ibid., p. 165).

To learn, then, is to immerse oneself within an alien element and thereby open oneself to an encounter with signs. (Think here of Marcel's taste of the madeleine as analogous to the neophyte swimmer's initial dive into the sea.) Signs "cause problems" through their disorienting shock, forcing thought to deal with experiences that disrupt the common, coordinated functioning of the senses and faculties (Marcel's strange gustatory sensations resembling the swimmer's initial unorganized tactile micro-perceptions). Through this encounter with signs, thought discovers a problematic field of differential relations and singular points that exists both within and without (the reminiscence field of Marcel-madeleine-virtual Combray being like the fluid sensori-motor field of swimmer-sea). Though it is within the actual that thought participates in the dynamic unfolding of the differential relations and singular points of the virtual domain of problems, that virtual domain remains apersonal and pre-individual, an ideal structure of potential zones of individuation that establishes "the bond of a profound complicity between nature and mind" (ibid., p. 165).

SEEING

In *Proust and Signs* Deleuze notes that Marcel learns little from his teachers—indeed, in the encounter with the madeleine, he has no teacher other than the madeleine itself. In *Difference and Repetition*, Deleuze assigns the swimming teacher a rather limited role, for "the movements of the swimming instructor which we reproduce on the sand bear no relation to the movements of the wave, which we learn to deal with only by grasping the former in practice as signs" (Deleuze, 1994, p. 23). It would seem that for Deleuze the best that teachers can do is to invite their students to participate along with them in an activity rather than show them what to do or how to do it. "We learn nothing from those who say: 'Do as I do,'" says Deleuze. "Our only teachers are those who tell us to 'do with me', and are able to emit signs to be developed in heterogeneity rather than propose gestures for us to reproduce" (ibid., p. /23). There is finally a basic mystery to learning, in that "We never know in advance how someone will learn: by means of what loves someone becomes good at Latin, what encounters make them a philosopher, or in what dictionaries they learn to think" (ibid., p. 165). Still, although we cannot know in advance what paths learning will take, nor can we induce genuine learning through precept and example, there is perhaps a function for the teacher in this form of education, one that Deleuze hints at when he says that our only teachers are those who "are able to emit signs" (ibid., p. 23). Deleuze does not develop this insight any further in *Difference and Repetition*, but we might be able to discern the outlines of a pedagogy of sign emission by looking briefly at his treatment of modern film in *Cinema 2: The Time-Image*, and specifically at the practice of one of Deleuze's favorite directors, Jean-Luc Godard.

Deleuze divides the history of film into two basic phases, the classic cinema and modern cinema. Classic cinema is dominated by an organization of space and time according to a rational, commonsense, Newtonian/Cartesian "sensory-motor schema" (Deleuze, 1989, p. 26). Modern cinema, by contrast, is marked by the breakdown of the sensory-motor schema and the creation of images that no longer conform to a single unified spatio-temporal structure. In the classic cinema, images are linked through their ordinary, "natural" connections with one another, "according to laws of association, of continuity, resemblance, contrast or opposition" (ibid., p. 276), whereas in the modern cinema images are juxtaposed in such a way that the gap *between* images becomes primary, "the interval is set free, the interstice becomes irreducible and stands on its own" (ibid., p. 277). Modern directors, however, do not simply disconnect images from their orthodox, commonsense chains of association; they also re-link images, yet in such a way that a productive difference emerges between images. Godard is for Deleuze an exemplary director in this regard. "For in Godard's method, it is not a question of association. Given one image, another image has to be chosen which will induce an interstice *between* the two. This is not an operation of association, but of differentiation, as mathematicians say, or of disparation, as physicists say: given one potential, another one has to be chosen, not any whatever, but in such a way that a difference of potential is established between the two, which will be productive of a third or of something new" (ibid., p. 179-80, translation modified).

The modern cinematic re-linking of images, then, is not arbitrary, but guided by a principle of maximum interaction, whereby the interstice between images is emphasized while at the same time the juxtaposed images are themselves altered and something new emerges in each "image-interstice-image" unit as a whole. For audiences, such differentially related "image-interstice-image" sequences pose problems, since the sequences are not readily assimilable within standard interpretive schemas. Modern cinematic images must be "read," in the sense that they must be construed through an active interrogation of the forces connecting the images. For each sequence, the audience must ask, What specific difference motivates this connection? What new movement is created through this juxtaposition? How does this sequence interact with other sequences? How do the sequences form part of an assemblage of multiple "image-interstice-image" units that maintain a certain consistency, a specific cohesiveness of multiple parts in dynamic interaction? Such a "reading" of images is complicated by the fact that modern directors emphasize not only the gaps between images, but also the gaps of silence between sounds, the gaps separating sound effects, music, and dialogue from each other, as well as the gap between the visual and audio elements of film (such that there is in modern films a constant back-and-forth of the visual and the sonic in dynamic disequilibrium rather than a mutual doubling or reinforcement of sight and sound). As a result, "a whole pedagogy is required here, because we have to read the visual image as well as hear the speech-act in a new way" (ibid., p. 247) and interrelate sight and sound through their differential relations with one another.

Deleuze observes that over the course of his career, Godard develops "his own pedagogy, his own didacticism" (ibid., p. 248), one that combines a method of differentially juxtaposing images and sounds and a self-conscious reflection on that method within the film itself: "Godard's strength is not just in using this mode of construction in all his work (constructivism) but in making it a method which cinema must ponder at the same time as it uses it" (ibid., p. 179). The film that "marks a first peak in this reflection" (ibid., p. 179) for Deleuze is *Here and Elsewhere* (*Ici et ailleurs*), a collaborative effort directed by Godard, Anne-Marie Miéville and Jean-Pierre Gorin that began in 1970 as a documentary about the Palestinian struggle and ended in 1974 as a meditation on images, sounds and what the film's narrator calls the "uninterrupted chains of images enslaving one another," a chain that assigns us our place "in the chain of events in which we have lost all power."

Here and Elsewhere is a film about "and," about the links that combine images and sounds in associative chains. (The French word "*chaîne*," besides denoting various kinds of physical and mental links, has associations as well with consumer and media culture—*travail à la chaîne*: assembly-line work; *chaîne*: [TV] channel.) The film moves back and forth between images of the Palestinian camps and a French family watching TV, with interspersed sections presenting a complex of sights and sounds in various formats—blanks screens, screens with nothing but words (key words flashing), montages of stills (documents of the workers' movement, photos of Nixon, Breshnev, Hitler, Golda Meir, the Holocaust, advertisements, etc.), shots of one, four or nine television screen broadcasts, an extended shot of three slides side by side with a disembodied hand replacing one slide after another, comic didactic sequences demonstrating the nature of filmmaking, and so on. The film's sequences in some ways confirm well-worn chains of association, many of which are dominated by the binary oppositions recited by the narrator (victory and defeat, foreign and national, order and disorder, black and white, here and elsewhere). But the narrator's insistent enunciation of "and," the repeated flashing of "and" and "+" in the intertitle messages, and the several prolonged shots of two wood blocks forming the word "*et*" ("and") that fill the screen, all call into question such links while raising the possibility of other connections, other uses of "and," connections of one thing after another in an additive, non-totalizing fashion, x *and* p, *and* b, *and* y .... The juxtaposition of Palestinian fighters and the French family watching TV invites a propagandistic reading of this relation as one of an authentic, active, and natural culture versus a media-saturated, passive, consumerist culture, just as the alternating stills of Hitler and Golda Meir suggest a facile equation of the two figures. But as the narrator states, it is "too simple and too easy to simply divide the world in two," "too easy or too simple to say simply that the wealthy are wrong and the poor are right," for "there are no simple images, only simple people, who will be forced to stay quiet, like an image."

Midway through the film, the narrator offers an analysis of the "enchaining" of images whereby one image displaces another in a constant flow, and consumers of the images are invited to find their place in the flow. He also remarks on sounds—how one sound dominates another, and how sounds gain power by being represented by images. The film's critique of images, however, is not restricted to mass media images, for in the film's final section, a female narrator subjects the directors' own Palestinian footage to a critical interrogation. As a close-up sequence of a Palestinian woman occupies the screen, the female narrator points out that the woman is a young, beautiful actress chosen by the directors to play a pregnant woman, though she is not pregnant herself. Footage of another woman haltingly reciting lines fed to her by an off-screen prompter is accompanied by the narrator's remarks on the woman's initial enthusiasm at participating in the Palestinian cause and her evident boredom and unease as the recitation continues and she seemingly longs for a humbler, less elitist role in the struggle. As we watch a young girl loudly declaim a patriotic poem, the narrator comments that the girl may be innocent but her theatrical manner is not, for it echoes the poses of a revolutionary theater whose images are tired and clichéd.

Besides providing a direct verbal critique of images, though, the film also offers an implicit rethinking of images through their isolation, their disconnection from conventional chains, and their reconnection in unorthodox series. The sequences of the "pregnant" actress, the stuttering reciter, and the histrionic young girl cease to function within some revolutionary saga. Isolated from narrative chains of association, the sequences function as singular points, loci of potential development that are not pre-judged and pre-viewed. The stills and documentary footage of Palestinian corpses, workers' demonstrations, and Holocaust victims interjected in unexpected patterns throughout the film finally block ready assimilation within an ideological framework, but instead force a rethinking of the meaningful differences that pertain to the violence that extends from the Russian revolution to the present. By the close of the film, the juxtaposition of a circle of soldiers in quiet conversation and the French family watching TV has lost its clear ideological bearings. The insistent long takes of the two groups provide no new pre-digested information about the images, the undercoded shots asking the audience to make its own connections between the images. The male narrator finally comments that the filmmakers were unable truly to see and hear the Palestinians when they shot their footage because they sought elsewhere the revolutionary solution to problems they could not see and hear at home. The challenge, he concludes, is "to learn to see in order to hear elsewhere. To learn to hear oneself speaking, in order to see what the others are doing. The others, the elsewhere [ailleurs] of our here [ici]."

LEARNING TO THINK

Learning for Deleuze is a subset of what we usually mean by learning, just as thought for him is a subset of what generally passes for thinking. What Deleuze deems genuine learning and genuine thought belong to the domain of signs, problems and the virtual, a domain that is, in Proust's words, "real without being actual, ideal without being abstract." To learn is to encounter signs, to undergo the disorienting jolt of something new, different, truly other, and then to explicate those signs, to unfold the differences they enfold. As one does so, one passes through objective and subjective interpretative illusions until one grasps difference itself in its immanent differentiation within the actual. Then one sees the world as an a-centered city-egg engaged in metamorphic becoming in all directions at once, but one sees as well the virtual domain of difference in itself, which is not an amorphous chaos, but an infinite collection of structured problems. Each problem consists of a general set of differentially related elements and their corresponding singular points, or zones of potential actualization. Genuine learning involves an engagement with such problems, a re-orientation of thought following its initial disorientation, such that thought may comprehend something new in its newness, as a structured field of potential metamorphic forces rather than a pre-formed body of knowledge to be mastered. One cannot teach the truly new in its newness, but one can attempt to induce an encounter with the new by emitting signs, by creating problematic objects, experiences or concepts. Hence, the pedagogy of signs entails first a critique of codes and conventions, an undoing of orthodox connections, and then a reconnection of elements such that the gaps between them generate problems, fields of differential relations and singular points. Such teaching, however, is itself a form of learning, for it proceeds via an encounter with signs and an engagement with problems. To teach is to learn, finally, since for Deleuze genuine teaching and learning are simply names for genuine thought. The goal of teaching and learning is to think otherwise, to engage the force of that which is other, different and new. What Deleuze details in his accounts of learning and teaching is that dimension of education that inspires all true students and teachers—the dimension of discovery and creation within the ever-unfolding domain of the new. It is also the dimension of freedom, in which thought escapes its preconceptions and explores new possibilities for life.

NOTES

[1] For a detailed discussion of Bergson's virtual past, see chapter three of Deleuze's *Bergsonisn*, (B 45-70/51-72).

[2] In some regards, Deleuze's concept of the problem may be related to that of "structure" in some forms of structuralism. In "How Do We Recognize Structuralism?," Deleuze characterizes structures in terms of differential relations and singular points, and he argues that the structural analyses of Lévi-Strauss, Althusser, Lacan, Foucault and others may be understood in terms of this model (Deleuze, 1998). One should be cautious in assimilating Deleuze to this tradition, however, for he departs from most structuralists in his emphasis on the virtual, the positive nature of difference, and the generative force of self-differentiating difference within structures.

[3] It should be evident that Deleuze uses the term "Idea" in an unconventional way, drawing his concept of ideas from what he identifies as Kant's "profound theory of Ideas as problematizing and problematic" (1994, p. 161). Ideas for Deleuze are in no sense transcendent, essential or eternal entities, but instead virtual problems immanent within the real.

[4] Although Deleuze nowhere says as much, it seems likely that he draws the example of swimming from Bergson, who in *Creative Evolution* describes the effort to think something new in terms of learning to swim (Bergson, 1911, pp. 192-94).

[5] Deleuze's identification of the sea as a Leibnizian problem hinges on a rather unconventional reading of Leibniz's remarks about the sound of the ocean (as, for example, in Leibniz's Preface to *New Essays on Human Understanding* [1996, pp. 54-55]). Deleuze develops this reading of Leibniz in *Difference and Repetition*, (1994, pp. 213-14).

REFERENCES

Bergson, H. (1911). *Creative evolution* (A. Mitchell, Trans.). New York: Henry Holt and Company.

Deleuze, G. (1988). *Bergsonism* (H. Tomlinson & B. Habberjam, Trans.). New York: Zone.

Deleuze, G. (1989). *Cinema 2: The time image* (H. Tomlinson & R. Galeta, Trans.). Minneapolis, MN: University of Minnesota Press.

Deleuze, G. (1994). *Difference and repetition* (P. Patton, Trans.). New York: Columbia University Press.

Deleuze, G. (1998). How do we recognize structuralism? (C. J. Stivale, Trans.). In C. J. Stivale (Ed.), *The two-fold thought of Deleuze and Guattari* (pp. 258–282). New York: Guilford.

Deleuze, G. (2000). *Proust and signs: The complete text* (R. Howard, Trans.). Minneapolis, MN: University of Minnesota Press.

Godard, J.-L., Miéville, A.-M. (directors). (1974). *Ici et ailleurs*. France: Sonimage/INA.

Leibniz, G. W. (1996). *New essays on human understanding* (P. Remnant & J. Bennett, Trans.). Cambridge: Cambridge University Press.

Proust, M. (1982). *Remembrance of things past* (Vols. 1–3, C. K. Scott Moncrieff & T. Kilmartin, Trans.). New York: Vintage.

Ronald Bogue
The University of Georgia
USA

DAVID R. COLE

2. DELEUZE AND THE NARRATIVE FORMS OF EDUCATIONAL OTHERNESS

INTRODUCTION

I pull my copy of *Metrophage*[1] out of its battered pink paper folder. It is suitably badly printed, and the black and white stripes of the dysfunctional roller have left interference patterns running from the right to the left that distract the eye and make discernment of the faint courier words difficult and time consuming. I randomly separate the pages and start reading:

> He stood and Nimble Virtue tossed a packet of Mad Love at his feet. It came to rest by the toe of his boot, where the water was icing up over a flaking patch of dried blood. Welding marks, like narrow scars of slag. The slaughterhouse had been grafted together from a stack of old Sea Train cargo containers. A cryogenic pump hummed at the far end of the place, like a beating heart, pushing liquid oxygen through the network of pipes that criss-crossed the walls and floor. From the ceiling, dull steel hooks held shapeless slabs of discoloured meat. Jonny looked at the slunk merchant.

Kadrey (1995, part 3, p. 1).

When we read this passage, what is the tenor of the voice that we might deploy through the use of the third person narrative? In the examination of educational narrative forms, whether through qualitative research or self-evaluation exercises, one might discern many voices that could crowd one's analytical frame. The problem for education is straightforward, and has been neatly summarised by Inna Semetsky (2004) when she said, "[A] new non-representational language of expression, exemplified in what Deleuze (1994b) called a performative or modulating aspect, is being created by means of the language structure going through the process of its own becoming-other and undergoing a series of transformations giving birth to a new, as though foreign and unfamiliar, other language," (p. 316). This is happening as I speak or as you read these words through the immense structures and processes of the education systems of the industrialised West. *Metrophage* was born of these structures and now sits innocently in my office or on the internet or in the computer files of high school students studying for examinations to go to respectable colleges. The problem can be broken down into two parts that I shall explore throughout this chapter:
– What are the languages of otherness that can be produced through the action of educational processing?

I. Semetsky (ed.), Nomadic Education: Variations on a Theme by Deleuze and Guattari, 17–34.
© *2008 Sense Publishers. All rights reserved.*

- How can we use this otherness to set off new directions of educational practice and how does the philosophy of Gilles Deleuze relate to these practices?

LEGITIMISATION

The first language of otherness that is perhaps the most readily discernible in the structures of education and the most widespread - is that which subverts legitimacy. When we speak about education, we load the language that we use with knowledge statements, power concerns and rules with claims to universality. This practice is derived from the values and normative conditioning of science. Jean-François Lyotard (1984) in *The Post-modern Condition* designated the grand or overriding narrative of knowledge as being that of legitimisation. This is scientific knowledge - the legitimacy of which Lyotard (1984) indissociably linked to the legitimisation of the legislator since the time of Plato (p. 8). Thus the language called science has been strictly inter-linked with those called ethics and politics. Importantly, they both stem from the same perspective, that of the Occident, which uses various strategies to dominate other perspectives and their multiplicity of minor narratives. The development of an integrated state system has incorporated the language of scientific knowledge as one of its legitimising principles, and codes the practices of science as being its own. The state uses the procedures of science: e.g., falsification and verification, in order to maintain its authority and presence in the various language games that are played out in order to control and manipulate society. Lyotard (1984) has advised that the public have free access to the memory and data banks of the state, so that the language games may be played out with as much information as possible, though they would be, as he terms it, "non-zero-sum games," (p. 67). Michel Peters (1996) has admirably dealt with many of the political and social concerns that result from Lyotard's analysis, and has incorporated Foucault's normative historical processes into his understanding of the present educational situation. Peters (1996) indicates the ironic state of affairs that we find ourselves in, where the politicians of the liberal states continue with their grand narratives, yet social and pragmatic realities make the legitimacy of their statements almost universally untenable (pp. 79-91). For those of us caught in the middle, working inside the educational machine of Western democracies; it is as if the commands coming from the centre are being continually scrambled and dislocated by their journey into the particular localities where they are enacted. It is as if civil society (Habermas, 1999) is being continually turned upside down from its rhetorical description in government to its pragmatic maintenance through educational institutes.

What are the languages of otherness that question the legitimacy of the state and civil society and how do they relate to the philosophy of Gilles Deleuze?
- Criminal
- Revolutionary
- Punk
- Anarchist
- Fast capitalist
- Terrorist

I could probably carry on adding elements to this list, as the subversion of legitimisation of the state, civil society and scientific language is a widespread language game. These minor narratives appear as interwoven into classrooms in one form or another through the discourses of the children and the teachers and the media where they circulate freely. They relate to Deleuzian philosophy with respect to his formulation of minor literature (Deleuze & Guattari, 1986). In this work Deleuze & Guattari (1986) examined the role of Yiddish with respect to Czech and German through the writing of Franz Kafka. They found that it is a language where, "minor utilizations will carry you away," (p. 25). Something similar has been happening in the education systems of the West through the relationships that have developed with respect to legitimisation. However, there is another dimension to the production of minor educational narratives of otherness that challenge the legitimacy of the state, civil society and scientific language. This is semiology, and to get closer to Deleuze's position in this field of inquiry; it is worth briefly comparing his linguistic ideas with those of Wittgenstein.

LANGUAGE-GAMES

To understand how the languages of otherness that challenge legitimisation work according to Deleuze; it is useful to note that his account of language production and control parallels that of Wittgenstein in several ways. Firstly, a basic proposal that follows from the rejection of mentalist accounts of language and thought as adequate justifications in Wittgenstein; is that the meanings of words cannot be taken away from their use, a move Deleuze (1990) made in *The Logic of Sense* (p. 146). The idea that there is something that is the meaning of a particular word, that can be accessed in isolation from any direct use in a specific context, is thoroughly dismantled in the *Philosophical Investigations*: "only someone who already knows how to do something with it," writes Wittgenstein (1998), "can significantly ask a name," (section 31) and later, '[W]hen one says, "He gave a name to his sensation" one forgets that a great deal of stage setting in the language is presupposed if the mere act of naming is to make sense,' (section 257).

This stage setting and foreground work has been translated into the legitimizing principles of education and is immanent in the sense that teachers and educators play the language-games of legitimisation through their lesson design and implementation. It could be stated that educators are trained, disciplined and domesticated through the educational machine to such a point that they tend not to be particularly aware of the *abominable faculty* that has been instilled in them, "consisting in emitting, receiving and transmitting order-words," (Deleuze & Guattari, 1988, p. 76). This process of semiotics occurs through the inculcation of the rules of linguistic expression on the one hand; which has as much to do with gesture, body language and the significance of posture as it has to do with syntax, lexicon and the lessons of grammar. And on the other hand, semiotics works according to the networks of social practices - such as the way the day is divided up into work time and break time, or the differing and suitable modes of communication between colleagues, management and trainees that one may observe in

educational establishments. The western education system has produced social praxis that is divided and streamed into appropriate behaviours for each situation in the working day. Deleuze & Guattari (1988) call these two sides of the social machine:
- The machinic assemblage of bodies which is training and discipline.
- The collective assemblage of enunciation or the statements of order-words in circulation at a given point.

The difficulty of differentiating these educational strata replicates the problem in Wittgenstein of distinguishing between his corresponding terms for the machinic and collective assemblages: forms of life and language-games. We may read the two sides as mutually related, yet without directly representing one another, a relationship that Deleuze & Guattari (1988) describe as *reciprocal presupposition*. This means that neither side can be adequately understood except in relation to the other; neither is primary or foundational, they both appear at once - in the double articulation of the strata. In other words, the language-games of the education system do not represent corresponding forms of life – philosophy or educational theory as exemplary practices cannot create some special language that gets more deeply into the heart of things, nor can it use "some sort of preparatory, provisional one [...it can only] use language full-blown [...] this by itself shows that I can adduce only exterior facts about language," (Wittgenstein, 1998, section 120). Why is this the case? It is because language has no interior. As Deleuze and Guattari (1988) have said, "If language always seems to presuppose itself, if we cannot assign it a non-linguistic point of departure, it is because language does not operate between something seen (or felt) and something said, but always goes from saying to saying" (p. 76). Thus the languages of otherness that spring from the immense source of western legitimisation and that are enacted through the organisation of education (language-games or order-words that reciprocally presuppose the forms of life or assemblages); pass on their codes from word to word. In addition, these methods of semiotic dissemination are strengthened through the electronic methods of communication that are now available such as the internet and SMS messaging.

The analysis of Deleuze and Guattari (1988) gives us a battery of material relations, and an open-ended series of concepts that can be applied or ignored as the investigation dictates; as we explore ever further into the narrative forms of educational otherness. The pivotal notion for them is *double articulation*, the separation of material flows of bodies, events and signs into two reciprocally-presupposing levels. Do Wittgenstein's terms *language-game* and *form of life* designate the double articulations of the social machine, which Deleuze and Guattari (1988) call respectively the collective and machinic assemblages? On either side, two opposing tendencies can be observed, one towards stability and regularity, and the other towards creation and change. In Wittgenstein's terms, the former would be speech-actions in accordance with grammar - or on the larger scale, unproblematic and smooth social functioning in the educational machine - while the latter is seen in his various examples of the inability to apply grammar rules correctly, and of attempts to misuse language in this context that would seem to encapsulate narrative forms of otherness. Wittgenstein presented the possibilities of language malfunction as peculiarly illogical practices; that have greater significance than just getting words wrong. However, by emphasising this ever-present possibility; he has taken the focus away from separate, exclusively linguistic problems. Furthermore, Wittgenstein has fused errors in with the complex and interwoven threads of language, thought and social behaviour that are inseparable, and indeed produced by the education machine; as it works to make disciplined and domesticated subjects that might be controlled through language in terms of getting the orders right. Perhaps this is just the common state of humanity, as Wittgenstein (1998) suggests when he writes:

> Suppose you came as an explorer into an unknown country with a language quite strange to you. In what circumstances would you say that the people there gave orders, understood them, obeyed them, and rebelled against them and so on? The common behaviour of mankind is the system of reference by means of which we interpret an unknown language (section 206).

Whilst taking the analysis further by squarely looking at the problem of otherness in terms of control - or the order-words and machinic assemblages that educators employ; Deleuze and Guattari (1988) do agree on the social nature of language and the resultant language-games. Wittgenstein leaves us hanging in terms of the relationship between language and the modes of existence that might help us to escape from these interminable games. It is for him an uncanny fact of language production that the use-value we ascribe to it is invariably tied up with the control and regulation of behaviour. I want to say that there is a way out of this conundrum, and it is through the philosophy of Gilles Deleuze, particularly when he has written in conjunction with Félix Guattari (1984, 1988). This escape route is located deep inside the heart of creating language. There the otherness that spreads immanently through the education system as educators enforce the principles of legitimisation through language-games is not apparent. It is a place wholly encapsulated by desire.

THE LANGUAGE OF DESIRE

This place of desire has been a site for serious intellectual and educational investigation. It has involved research into the hybrid, asignifying, non-linear narrative forms of otherness that are currently developing around the globe – and owes much to the interventions of feminist, cybernetic and experimental social scientists and their "common notions" (Parisi, 2004, p. 200). Their efforts have not developed immutable equations or formulas to structure research into the nature of desire; but they have extracted themes of a qualitative and local nature. These themes may have been hidden due to previous explorations that adhered to the disciplinarian codifications of power and not conforming to the perturbations of desire. This quote from Sandra Harding explains what to look for in our application of Deleuzian philosophy to education:

> Once we stop thinking of modern Western epistemologies as a set of philosophical givens, we can begin to examine them instead as historical

justificatory strategies; as culturally specific modes of constructing and exploiting cultural meanings in support of new kinds of knowledge claims (Harding, 1986, p. 141).

Deleuze sets up 'the other' as the focus of inquiry, Harding specifies the discourses to be analysed. One aspect this research into the narratives of otherness and desire has been characterised as *cyber-feminism*. It is the opportunity for the expression and elaboration of difference in opposition to any tyranny of the status quo, or the world-view of institutionalised structures of patriarchal control (Shields, 1996, p. 9). Studies such as those of Anne Balsamo (1996) or Veronica Hollinger and Joan Gordon (2002) have placed the cyborg figure of Donna Haraway (1991) at the leading edge of an interruption in male dominated knowledge and narrative. It could be said that to render the technological figure as feminine (but not a subject), is a tactical manoeuvre designed to impinge upon our perceptions and understanding of the processes that are being analysed in education and through creating otherness. In the case of investigating a language of desire, the questions applicable to contemporary narrative forms shift from those that feed into a categorical mechanism concerned with formulating a 3-dimensional structure that effectively co-ordinates the integration of language in society; to a flat perspective, where the paradigms of communication and data-inter-relatedness change from peripheral objects of the curriculum to central figures filled with desire (Parisi, 2004, p. 195). This feminist perspective strategically stays on the edge of educational discourse, where the difference opened up by the desire to be involved with narrative experimentation, may not be forced back into previously coded and recognised forms, but has a nomadic position (Deleuze & Guattari, 1988, p. 431).

This insight into creating a language of desire concurs with Sue Golding's (1997) collection of writings that have presented *eight technologies of otherness*. In this work she defined otherness as, "simply and only a cosmetic wound; a very thin, virtual, and in this sense 'impossible' limit," (p. 7). It could be stated that Golding's collection of essays sets out to rethink the notion of otherness. It is generally assumed that the other, or otherness, is something that does not fit in technically speaking. But then this supposition may lead to a slide, and that change in position turns into a human object, so otherness becomes, for example, woman, the black or Jew, or in our case the misbehaving child. This other is therefore the group that doesn't fit in with what was being framed in the first place; in education the normative concerns are the narrative forms of conformity, regulation and control that exclude otherness. In *the eight technologies of otherness,* otherness is strategically placed as a surface, and that surface is both the expression of the subject and that what is not part of the object. For example, to say that 'the thing' has pain in it is only accurate in as much as the object you are dealing with has pain in it, and the part that is otherness, the other entity is only comprehensible in as much as it is related to, in this case, a body. Otherness thus has this peculiar property to it, which is that it both frames something and simultaneously has no life on its own. Up until very recently most social scientists were dealing with otherness in the same way that physical scientists would look at atoms; and therefore they did not take into account the relational quality of otherness. It could be said that we require something different for contemporary society where information carries the load of relational forms and is characterised by fluidity and changes in nature. The technologies of otherness of which pain is one, though it is named by Sue Golding in her book as cruelty (Figure 1); fit in to the being or the entity, and could also be perceived as at the same time passing through 'the thing'. The technologies of otherness are part of the excess of the object, and yet they make up the thing itself. In so doing these technologies may produce a language of desire, or a non-representational language to use for the narrative forms of educational otherness.

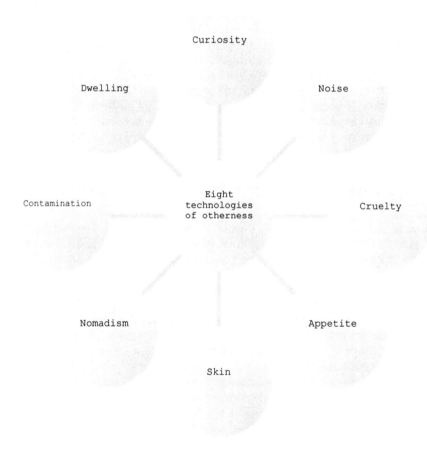

Figure 1. Sue Golding's (1997) eight technologies of otherness

This schema could be used as a way of understanding desire in language in terms of capturing non-representational otherness. It is worthwhile to point out that in 1977 Deleuze wrote a personal set of notes for Michel Foucault. In them he said, "...desire does not comprise any lack; neither it is a natural given; it is an assemblage of heterogeneous elements which function; it is process, in contrast with structure or genesis; it is affect, as opposed to feeling; it is haeccity (individuality of a day, a season, a life), as opposed to subjectivity; it is event, as opposed to thing or person. And above all it implies the constitution of a field of immanence or a 'body without organs', which is only defined by zones of intensity, thresholds, gradients, flux," (p. 11). One might see how a language of desire would be constituted through these statements about desire. In particular, the body without organs is a powerful figure to reconceptualise education working around sexualities, desire and the construction of the self. We might ask ourselves: do our educational practices enable this language? It is a paradox of otherness that it is defined by movement, yet there is also something 'in it' such as has been captured by the categories of the eight technologies of Sue Golding or the body without organs. To explore this element of educational narrative otherness further, we must examine Deleuze and Guattari's notion of nomadism and how it relates to language and education. Nomadism cannot be constituted through otherness or as a relative force against the sedentary power that is immanent in the state and civil society control of education in the West. Nomadism should be understood 'in-itself' to the extent that it may be used as a critical tool to enable a language of desire that may express otherness.

NOMADISM

To understand what Deleuze and Guattari (1988) mean by nomadism; we first need to state that the narrative styles, sources of information and types of knowledge claims change when we question the power structures that have been upheld and are indeed upholding the educational and administration systems of the West. For example, the writer and experimental artist Manuel de Landa, has posited the notion of *pandemonium* (cf. Selfridge, 1958) defined in terms of messages not being sent to specific locations, but when they are broadcast to concurrent independent objects. Therefore, control of the system is relinquished from a uni-directional (A-B) approach where A controls B and now spreads smoothly in the space of simultaneous message-recipient relationships. An example of pandemonium was the operation of numerous Jacquard looms during the Industrial Revolution (Landa, 1991, p. 164). As such, pandemonium is not exhausted by definition as a humanist-historical concept, or as a scientific-realist perception; it may be more appropriately defined as an [inhuman-chaotic-immanent procedure] - it is a counter strategy to the rendition of the loss of power by humans due to machines or the direct transfer of system control to simultaneous digital environments in the contemporary workplace (Murphie, 2005, p. 19).

Pandemonium has been happening through education in highly industrialised countries via the introduction of technology into the learning process (New London

Group, 1996). Technologies such as SMS or the internet are fast and beguiling forms of communication that enable learners to talk to each other immediately. Nomadism in this context is the fluidity and movement that is produced by this technology. It also simultaneously creates the conditions of otherness in that subjects and words of command and power may be emptied of meaning in an electronic and mediated state. The analysis of Deleuze & Guattari (1988, pp. 351-424) have named this tendency as the war machine; and they track it through history where technology has promoted new social forms such as armies and more recently the simulation of war games in virtual reality. The nomadism of contemporary society concerns the knowledge of control mechanisms, tracking immanent, nano and macro-tendencies, and should not attempt to undo societal and educational ruptures in favour of the rhetoric of government or the 'civilised' West. It could also be stated that pandemonium is a useful rubric for educational narrative research on otherness and a coherent formulation of Deleuze & Guattari's nomadism.

In contrast to Deleuze and Guattari's (1988) narrative perspective of the nomad that might be enacted through pandemonium; technological society was theorised by Jacques Ellul (1964) from a static historical-humanist perspective, through which he examined the political consequences of a society of technicians. As a precursor to Deleuze-Guattarian thought, this approach opens up the ways in which they have radicalised educational narrative forms by introducing nomadism into authorial legitimisation and the resultant language of desire. Contrariwise, Ellul tracked the development and placement of technique from a fixed position – and found it to be constituted by regimes of technical knowledge with useful applications that have been organised by social groups concerned with power. Technique was designated as being mobile, following the divisions of *Zweckwissenschaft* - the practical sciences - in order to lay waste to various moral and political regimes such as organised religion, usually to the benefit of a state system (Ellul, 1964, p. 317). In a similar way to Jünger (1949a), the question of whether technical disciplines are able to centralise in autonomous economic and political systems, does not preclude lateral communication between technical epicentres, as *techno-Zeitgnosse* – or technologised contemporaneity (p. 121). This contemporaneity fuses technical expertise with the ability to communicate the particular knowledge as an integral part of the activity. In this way, the medium for mediation is singularised (Jünger, 1949b); and it could be said that this is happening at a breakneck pace in the current globally inter-linked information world, where the narrative forms of education are evolving into new and mutated formats due to factors such as the internet and SMS messaging. The nomadic war machine (Deleuze and Guattari, 1988, p. 420) of *A Thousand Plateaus* is a schema whereby this mutation may be tracked, and integrated with a radicalised cyber-feminist analysis (cf. Parisi, 2004, p. 200). As such it is an important formulation that helps us to understand how the sedentary power of the institutions of the West is being undermined by the augmented regimes of movement that they are ironically producing. Yet to comprehend the breadth of this conjunction fully; we must understand how Deleuze constructed the nomadic war machine as a singular idea for technological movement through his engagement with philosophy.

SINGULAR OTHERNESS

The intellectual construction of the notion of the nomadic war machine starts with Deleuze's (1994a) reading of western philosophy in *Difference and Repetition*. According to Deleuze, the *diaphora* of Aristotle is a false transport. Deleuze argues that diaphora never shows difference changing in nature; we never discover a differenciator of difference, which would relate in respective immediacy, the most universal and the most singular. This is vital when describing the mechanisms of technological transformation. The differenciator for Deleuze differenciates difference in-itself, and is a component in his ontological exploration of generalised anti-Hegelianism and the Heideggarian philosophy of ontological Difference. Deleuze reverses the ontological methodology of positing *substance* or *being* as the grounds for asking the questions, "How does matter change?" (Aristotle), or "How can being gain determinacy?" (Hegel), or "How can being sustain its difference?" (Heidegger); instead, Deleuze asks the question, "How can difference sustain its being?" Michael Hardt (1993) has located the source of Deleuzian ontology in Bergson, where internal difference has been elevated to the level of the absolute (p. 7); in contrast to Mechanism or Platonism, where difference is thought of contingently (*per accides*). In attempting to think internal difference, Deleuze wishes to ground being in difference, whereupon the internal difference is not conceived as simple determination; but achieves 'substantial differences' (*per se*).

Deleuze pursues the philosophical point about difference to set up a new perspective on singularities. This relates to the construction of the war machine and otherness in education in that the technological regimes of intensity where nomadism is enacted is not a particular occasion of innovation or social instance of augmented peculiarity. It is characterised more definitely through the use of singularities. Singularity for Deleuze is beyond particular propositions no less that universality is beyond general propositions. Here the echoes of Deleuze's project resonate with those of Whitehead. Whitehead (1978) proposed propositions as hybrids of pure potentialities and actualities (p. 185). Singular propositions for Whitehead contain the potentiality of an actual world including a definite set of actual entities in complex reactions. Deleuze and Whitehead diverge to an extent at this point in that Whitehead wished to extend actual entities to set up relations with eternal objects or "predicates of the proposition," (Whitehead, 1978, p. 186). The singular proposition for Whitehead includes in its potentiality the complex predicate finding realisations in the *nexus* of reactions between logical subjects (the definite set of actual entities). Deleuze (1994a) pursued the argument by turning to problematic Ideas rather than remaining on the level of singular propositions. Problematic Ideas are not simple entities, but are multiplicities or complexes of relations and corresponding singularities. For Whitehead, the question of the problem is figured in relation to actual entities, each with their own formal existence, entering into objective relations with the actual entity in question. The answer for Whitehead (1978) is to posit the "creative action of the universe" (p. 56), always becoming one in a particular unity while adding to the multiplicity of the universe. This for Whitehead is the concrescence into unity, which every entity must enter into as a result of its creative action and the establishment of new relation, which Whitehead (1978) termed as *innovative becoming* (p. 79). Deleuze (1994a) characterised the problem of thought by the distribution of the singular and the regular, distinctive and ordinary points taking place within the description of a multiplicity in relation to the ideal events, which constitute the conditions of the problem (p. 189). The problem for western education is the production of otherness in its very folds.

It could be said that Deleuze and Whitehead both worked on the problem of otherness in a complementary manner. The work of Deleuze (1994a) and Whitehead (1978) is comprehensible as parallel yet distinctive projects that add philosophical detail to the action of singularities as nomadic others in technological environments; however, I would not wish to posit an identity or assemblage, such as Deleuze-Whitehead, in the manner that Alain Badiou (1994) does in his essay concerning *The Fold.* The creative difference of Platonic Forms in Whitehead, opposes the actual difference of singularities in Deleuze. Both thinkers are joined more definitely in their appropriation of Bergsonian notions of *durée* and intuition, and a dynamic relationship to science. In Whitehead's (1978) terms, temporal endurance (durée) depends on *subjective aim*; his expression for Bergson's intuition is *conceptual prehension.* This temporal endurance selected for any one actuality, determines how the extensive continuum is atomised by atomic actualities of a locus in the "unison of becoming" (p. 128). Whitehead's philosophy of the organism, which presents a coherent cosmology for science in terms of process, then establishes the foundations for mathematical expression of physical science. These complex categoreal conditions (Whitehead, 1978, pp. 219-283) consist generally in satisfying some condition of a maximum, to be obtained by the transmission of inherited types of order. Otherness in this sense is dependent on time concerns in the individual that might extend and create this sensation as working processes. Whitehead would therefore diagnose the narrative forms of otherness in the education system as deriving their nature from relative and interactive worlds of mediation that are being created through the technological and augmented regimes of change that have swept through highly industrialised countries.

Deleuze (1988), on the other hand, has highlighted the Bergsonian schema for time, which unites *Creative Evolution* and *Matter and Memory*, and is a contrasting way of examining the virtual transformations that are happening due to the post-modern nomadism in contemporary society. Deleuze worked by beginning with an account of a gigantic memory, a multiplicity formed by the virtual coexistence of all sections of a cone (p. 60), each section of the cone is a repetition of all the others and is distinguished from them only by the order of relations and the distribution of singular points. The one-whole point of unity in Whitehead and the Platonists is for Deleuze (1988), a *virtual point*, where duration is difference in kind, in itself and for itself. Differences in kind and degrees of difference coexist in a Single Nature through the virtual point, where Bergson spoke of different intensities and degrees in a virtual coexistence, in a single Time or simple Totality (p. 94). Actualisation of the unity take the form of divergent lines, each of which corresponds to a virtual section and represents the incarnation of the order of relations and distribution of singularities peculiar to the given section in differenciated species and parts (Deleuze, 1994a, p. 212). Singular otherness is therefore the workings of this virtual point according to Deleuze. It is not the idealism of the Platonic forms of Whitehead. On the contrary, the production of the narratives of otherness is a communal affair, based on the material condition for the war machine, such as the companies that produce software for virtual war games. It is in a state of heightened intensity due to global conflict and differing ideologies coming into contact through material concerns such as the need for oil. In terms of education, the Deleuzian perspective is to explore the workings of the virtual point and to disseminate strategies that make the singular otherness that is harnessed through virtuality real for the students. This approach corresponds to the recent ideas of James Gee (2004), in which he suggests that virtual reality games act as conduits for complex learning behaviours that would stimulate interest in mainstream literacy practices.

The direction of the Deleuzian argument leads against multiplicities conceived of as numerical, quantitative multiplicities, of the kind G.B.R. Riemann and Einstein (Einstein, 1920) have proposed. For example, when speaking about Freud's psychoanalysis of the Wolf-Man; "These variable distances are not extensive quantities divisible by each other; rather, each is divisible, or 'relatively divisible', in other words, they are not divisible below or above a certain threshold, they cannot increase or diminish *without their elements changing in nature,*" (Deleuze & Guattari, 1988, p. 31). The Bergsonian suggestion, in contrast to quantitative multiplicities, is of qualitative multiplicities and difference 'in kind' not "in degree". However, qualitative and quantitative multiplicities do not act dualistically, but given Bergson's *durée*, act from unity to multiplicity, virtuality to actuality. Deleuze does maintain ground for the ideal or transcendental in the virtual, but his process of actualisation is not a degradation or copy in the real: it uses the creative, immanent, explosive force of life itself.

Thus Deleuze came upon his "formula" for creativity through intense philosophical work. These explosive acts that he has used in order to constitute qualitative multiplicities may join together in libidinal action or in the form of desiring-machines. In the context of educational otherness and narrative forms, the rebellious and anti-disciplinarian discourses in our education systems are animated and driven by such forces. This is why Deleuze, perhaps resting heavily on Nietzsche and Spinoza, gives us the freedom to track otherness down to its root causes. The nomadic otherness (or war machine) that is set free by the internet and SMS messaging; is vitalised by the singularity of its expression and the sexual power that it evolves in concrescence. In addition, a "new transversal subjectivity emerges, which takes others as constitutive moments in the construction of a common plane of becoming," (Braidotti, 2005, p. 10).

RELATIVE AND CONSUMER OTHERNESS

If we dig deeper into the nomadic otherness that is produced by technologies such as the internet and SMS messaging, we find the commercial mores that characterise late or fast capitalism. It is all too easy, as Deleuze & Guattari (1988) put it, to get carried away with a kind of "science fiction" of micro-connectivity (p. 422). The retention of an exterior approach to the artefacts and processes involved with learning in contemporary global society is to construct a perspective of cyber-materialism. This complex position retains the exteriority of desire and its many connections (Murphie, 2005, p. 18), so that they may not hidden by the mind seeking knowledge in education or idealism – even if it is in a micro or local and qualitative sense. It is also in line with contemporary sociological investigations:

> ...the consumer takes on the role of the agent of aestheticization, or of branding. For example, the tourist consumes services and experiences by turning them into signs; by doing the semiotic work of transformation...it turns referents into signifiers. This is one sort of the demand-side of semiotic work that characterises what Featherstone calls the aestheticization of contemporary everyday life....this aestheticization leads to an endless profusion of space odysseys- subjects & objects travelling at increasingly greater distances and speeds. Objects are emptied out of meaning and material content (Lash & Urry, 1994, p. 15).

Deleuze and Guattari (1984) explored these processes most effectively in *Anti Oedipus*. In this work, the micro processes of integrated otherness are spread on a global economic and political plane. They are summarised through the conjunction, *desiring-machines*. This figure is still relevant today as the machinic qualities of fast information based capitalism mesh ever deeper into the languages of desire that we might formulate. As Claire Colebrook (2002) has expressed it, "Any practice, technology, knowledge or belief can be adopted if it allows the flow of capital," (p. 127). This is a serious point for education, as it puts any intellectual work under pressure, as Bronwyn Davies (2005) has vigorously explored in terms of neoliberalism. She signals at the end of her piece an escape route through desire, that constitutes as she puts it, "narratives and storylines, the metaphors, the very language and patterns of existence through which we are subjected and made into members of the social world," (p. 13). Deleuze does take us further into the language of desire as he opposes subjectification by positing desire in terms of the plane of becoming or immanent nomadism. In terms of education, there is no hiding place from fast capitalism in the human subject and the tendency to use emotional language; as it has been thoroughly and effectively hollowed out through marketing and the expression of desire for products. Immanent nomadism escapes such relative emptiness through the possibility of singular otherness and the formulation of a constitutive language of desire that is formed as Sue Golding (1997) has expressed it through the construction of a surface or immanent material plane of change.

This perhaps brings us close to the kind of desire that reflects the narrative forms that we find in contemporary educational otherness. The speedy circulation of objects emptied of meaning creates a type of aesthetic experience, which is thoroughly mediated. It is tempting at this point to make the conjunction constituted by Deleuze-Baudrillard, in that we have reached a similar level of 'object politics' (cf. McLaren & Leonardo, 1998, pp. 215-243), where the work of the two theorists may be joined. Yet Baudrillard does not leave an escape route from the submergence of multifarious sign-symbol relationships, and the ways in which consumer otherness may belittle and dominate education. Deleuze, on the other hand, does give educational theory credence, and the mapping out of the narrative forms of educational otherness that have been presented in this chapter provides the lines of flight for education (cf. Leach & Boler, 1998). Deleuze and Guattari (1988) originally used the phrase, 'lines of flight' in *A Thousand Plateaus;* where it signifies that social phenomena include escapes and inversions, and it is along these lines of flight that the escape from organisation and centralisation happens; it is a process of leaking between categories. The learning process in this context is condensed in time and extended through space - it communicates a sense of mutated and paradoxically unreal reality (cf. Ansell Pearson, 1999). The curriculum sits on this sense of unreal and accelerated reality as a hyper *site of mediation*, rather than a stable overlay of categories of learnt knowledge, skills or process that might depress this sense of unreality.

CURRICULUM OTHERNESS

It is a fact of any educational innovation that nothing will change in schools unless teachers are included and part of the new programme (Seaton, 2002). The most pressing issue for them is going to be in terms of curriculum reform that would incorporate the narrative forms of educational otherness into the production and functioning of their lessons. Important questions that should be asked to aid this incorporation include:
– How can teachers use the effects of legitimisation and the ways in which minor narratives are created that challenge meta-narrative status?
– What are the language-games that deal with otherness?
– How can teachers use the language of desire?
– How can nomadism help to generate engagement and interest in lessons?
– How does the notion of singular otherness infuse teaching practises?
– What are the lessons of relative and consumer otherness that would augment knowledge provision?

To help answer and structure these questions, and to put forward a Deleuzian curriculum of otherness, I have formulated these ideas into a knowledge curriculum diagram:
– The narrative form of history would embrace 'perspectivism' through the understanding and insider knowledges of multiple cultures and time periods rather than mono-culturalism (imperialism).
– Geographical narrative forms should extend from the study of 'natural processes' into urban space, discursive space and surveillance (Davis, 1990).

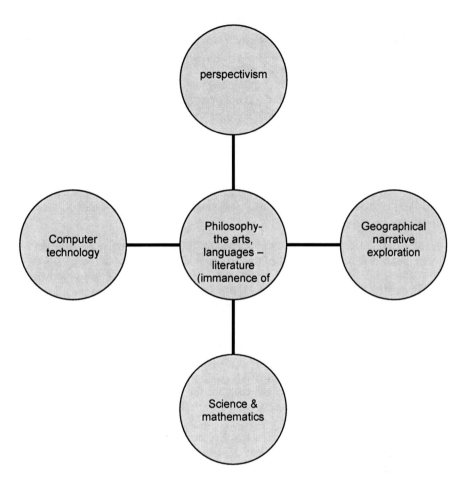

Figure 2. Deleuzian curriculum of otherness.

- The learning of science and mathematical narrative formats should act as a kind of intellectual buffer zone before embarking on creative application of these formats.
- Computer technology sits at the heart of the acceleration in the circulation of signs and emptied signifiers and should be immanently attached to cultural significance rather than merely learnt code.
- The narrative forms of philosophy, the arts, foreign languages and literature should be central to the curriculum and the way in which mediation is dealt with through educational research and organisation.

This simple curriculum framework for construction should act to enable teachers and students to explore otherness and the ways in which it is present in our narrative formats in education. It is by no means prescriptive or definitional with respect to the type of content material the teachers might look to insert into each part off the curriculum, as this will wholly depend on local needs and wishes. What this curriculum does is encourage substantial engagement with otherness, and what could be termed as, "the connection of a multiplicity of molecular desires…that should act to catalyse change on a larger scale," (Guattari, 1995, pp. 230-231). In our case it is through teachers capitalising on the narratives of otherness in education to build strong links between their curricula provision and the conceptual and affective growth of everyone in the places where they work.

CONCLUSION

In conclusion, I would like to take us back to the one of the sources of otherness in Deleuze, and that is the writings of Friedrich Nietzsche. In a lecture about the philosophy of Nietzsche, Fred Ulfers (1999) explains how he integrated otherness into being:

> When I said self-same, self-contained beings; the notion of being is important here because it's not an aspect of the 'given-ness' of a self but the result of the violence of simplification and falsification of the singular, whose otherness can never be reduced to the 'is', the self-presence of being, since it is radically temporal, event-like, constituting continual transitoriness and fleetingness.

As such the Nietzchean conception of otherness built a picture of the self that may act as a springboard for Deleuze's singularities and nomadism. In education these are non-foundational moments; that may come along during class time or more likely as we consider our teaching strategies and results, and ruminate about the ways in which we may improve and enhance the student's experience. Otherness leads away from the social and cultural perspective of education; that may be vaunted as a means to giving students social justice and egalitarian rights (McLaren, 1989). This does not mean that concentrating on the narratives of otherness excludes the social/critical elements of education, but that it does enhance and perhaps capture many of aspects of mainstream provision that have previously 'slipped beneath the radar' in the western educational machine. As David Geoffrey Smith (1999) has put it in dramatic terms, "In the ocean of wisdom, the moment Self and Other have been identified they have disappeared, or been transformed or mutated into yet another unfolding of the drama in which all things, all people regardless of race, gender or class participate," (p. 24). I am reluctant to put it in those terms, but certainly this statement resonates with Deleuze and Guattari's (1984, 1988) work on otherness.

The point here is that Deleuze gives us a means and focus to deal with otherness in education. In his early work, *Nietzsche and Philosophy* (1983), he signalled this intent by exploring multiplicity, becoming and affirmation. These three factors represent a politics of difference, through which we may integrate otherness into education. It is an ethical stance that takes the passion and desires present in educational contexts and proposes a way of working that does not suppress, hide or sublimate these forces, but indicates points of contact through change and narrative forms so as to make education better.

NOTES

[1] *Metrophage* was a cyberpunk novel that was published in 1988 by Ace Books. Richard Kadrey also put it up for free distribution on the internet, where it garnered an underground following. I chose this piece to represent a narrative form of educational otherness due to the technologically eerie and rebellious landscape that it creates.

REFERENCES

Ansell Pearson, K. (1999). *Germinal life: The difference and repetition of Deleuze*. London: Routledge.

Badiou, A. (1994). The fold: Leibniz and the Baroque. In C. V. Boundas & D. Olkowski (Eds.), *Gilles Deleuze & the theatre of philosophy* (pp. 43–73). London: Routledge.

Balsamo A. (1996). *Technologies of the gendered body: Reading cyborg women*. Durham, NC: Duke University Press.

Braidotti, R. (2005). Affirming the affirmative: On nomadic affectivity. *Rhizomes, 11/12*(fall 2005/spring 2006). Retrieved July 19, 2006, from http://www.rhizomes.net/issue11/braidotti.html

Colebrook, C. (2002). *Understanding Deleuze*. Crows Nest, NSW: Allen & Unwin.

Davies, B. (2005, March). The (Im)possibility of intellectual work in neoliberal regimes. *Discourses: Studies in the cultural politics of education*, 26(1), 1–14.

Davis, M. (1990). *City of quartz: Excavating the future in Los Angeles*. London: Vintage.

Deleuze, G. (1988). *Bergsonism* (H. Tomlinson & B. Habberjam, Trans.). New York: Zone Books. (Original work published 1966).

Deleuze, G. (1994a). *Difference & repetition* (P. Patton, Trans.). New York: Columbia University Press. (Original work published 1968).

Deleuze, G. (1997). *Desire & pleasure* (M. McMahon, Trans.). Retrieved October 21, 2004, from: http://www.arts.monash.edu.au/visarts/globe/issue5/delfou.html (Original work written 1977).

Deleuze, G. (1994b). He stuttered. In C. V. Boundas & D. Olkowsky (Eds.), *Gilles Deleuze and the theatre of philosophy* (pp. 23–33). London: Routledge.

Deleuze, G. (1983). *Nietzsche and philosophy* (H. Tomlinson, Trans.). London: The Athlone Press. (Original work published 1962).

Deleuze, G. (1990). *The logic of sense* (M. Lester & C. Stivale, Trans.). New York: Columbia University Press. (Original work published 1969).

Deleuze, G., & Guattari, F. (1984). *Anti-Oedipus: Capitalism & schizophrenia* (R. Hurley, M. Seem, & H. R. Lane, Trans.). London: The Athlone Press. (Original work published 1972).

Deleuze, G., & Guattari, F. (1988). *A thousand plateaus: Capitalism & schizophrenia Part 2* (B. Massumi, Trans.). London: The Athlone Press. (Original work published 1980).

Deleuze, G., & Guattari, F. (1986). *Kafka: Toward a minor literature* (D. Polan, Trans.). Minneapolis: University of Minnesota Press. (Original work published 1975).

Einstein, A. (1920). *Relativity: The special and the general theory: A popular exposition* (R. W. Lawson, Trans.). London: Methuen & Co Ltd.

Ellul, J. (1964). *The technological society*. London: Jonathan Cape. (Original work published 1954).

Gee, J. P. (2004). *What video games have to teach us about learning and literacy*. Palgrave: Macmillan Press.

Golding, S. (1997). *Eight technologies of otherness*. London: Routledge.

Guattari, F. (1995). *Chaosophy: An ethico-aesthetic paradigm* (P. Bains & J. Pefanis, Trans.). Bloomington: Indiana University Press.

Habermas, J. (1999). *The structural transformation of the public sphere: An inquiry into a category of bourgeois society* (T. Burger, Trans.). Cambridge, MA: MIT Press. (Original work published 1962).

Haraway, D. (1991). A cyborg manifesto: Science, technology, and socialist-feminism in the late twentieth century. In *Simians, cyborgs and women: The reinvention of nature* (pp. 149–181). New York: Routledge.

Harding, S. (1986). *The science question in feminism*. Milton Keynes: Open University Press.

Hardt, M. (1993). *Gilles Deleuze: An apprenticeship on philosophy*. London: UCL Press.

Hollinger, V., & Gordon, J. (2002). *Edging into the future: Science fiction and contemporary cultural transformation*. Pennsylvania: University of Pennsylvania Press.

Jünger, F. (1949a). *Die perfektion der technik*. Frankfurt: Klostermann.

Jünger, F. (1949b). *Maschine und eigentum*. Frankfurt: Klostermann.

Kadrey, R. (1995). *Metrophage*. Retrieved December 6, 2002, from http://www.speed.demon.co.uk/kadrey/metro3.txt

Landa, M. (1991). *War in the age of intelligent machines*. New York: Zone Books.

Lash, S., & Urry, J. (1994). *Economies of signs & space*. London: Sage Publications.

Leach, M., & Boler, M. (1998). Gilles Deleuze: Practicing education through flight and gossip. In M. Peters (Ed.), *Naming the multiple: Poststructuralism and education* (pp. 149–172). Westport, Conn: Bergin & Garvey.

Lyotard, J. (1984). *The post-modern condition: A report on knowledge* (G. Bennington & B. Massumi, Trans.). Minneapolis, MN: University of Minnesota Press. (Original work published 1979).

McLaren, P., & Leonardo, Z. (1998). Jean Baudrillard: From marxism to terrorist pedagogy. In M. Peters (Ed.), *Naming the multiple: Poststructuralism and education* (pp. 215–244). Westport, Conn: Bergin & Garvey.

McLaren, P. (1989). *Life in schools: An introduction to critical pedagogy in the foundations of education*. New York: Longman.

Murphie, A. (2005). Differential life, perception and the nervous elements: Whitehead, Bergson and Virno on the technics of living. *Culture Machine* (EJ). Retrieved August 25, 2005, from http://culturemachine.tees.ac.uk/Articles/murphie.htm

New London Group. (1996). A pedagogy of multiliteracies: Designing social futures. *Harvard Educational Review, 66*(1), 60–92.

Parisi, L. (2004). *Abstract sex: Philosophy, bio-technology and the mutations of desire*. London: Continuum.

Peters, M. (1996). *Poststructuralism, politics and education*. Westport, CT: Bergin & Garvey.

Seaton, A. (2002). Reforming the hidden curriculum: The key abilities model and four curricular forms. *Curriculum Perspectives, 22*(1).

Selfridge, O. G. (1958). Pandemonium: A paradigm for learning. In *Mechanisation of thought processes: Proceedings of a Symposium held at the National Physical Laboratory*. London: HMSO.

Semetsky, I. (2004). Becoming-language/Becoming-other: Whence ethics? *Educational Philosophy and Theory, 36*(3), 313–325.

Shields, B. (Ed.). (1996). *Virtual spaces, real histories, living bodies*. London: Sage Publications.

Smith, D. G. (1999). *Pedagon: Interdisciplinary essays in the human sciences, pedagogy, and culture*. New York: Peter Lang.

Ulfers, F. (1999). *Nietzsche's ethics beyond good and evil: A lecture by Fred Ulfers*. Retrieved August 02, 2006, from http://www.egs.edu/faculty/ulfers/ulfers-nietzsche-beyond-good-and-evil-1999.html

Wittgenstein, L. (1998). *Philosophical investigations* (G. E. M. Anscombe, Trans.). Oxford: Blackwell Publishers. (Original work published 1953).

Whitehead, A. N. (1978). *Process & reality: An essay in cosmology*. New York: The Free Press. (Original work published 1929).

David R. Cole
University of Technology, Sydney
Australia

CLAIRE COLEBROOK

3. LEADING OUT, LEADING ON:
THE SOUL OF EDUCATION

In Muriel Spark's *The Prime of Miss Jean Brodie,* Miss Brodie reminds her
students of the etymology of 'education,' which, she insists, derives from the Latin
educere, to lead out: 'The word "education" comes from the root *e* from *ex,* out,
and *duco,* I lead. It means a leading out. To me education is a leading out of what is
already there in the pupil's soul.'[1] This reference to leadership is emphasised by
the picture on Brodie's wall of Mussolini's soldiers: and it is the image and visual
power of leadership, the affect and lure of power that dominates Spark's novella.
Brodie's leadership of her girls is enticingly enigmatic. Like Plato's Socrates in
The Symposium Brodie insists that she is not pouring in content, but leading
students out. If there is something worthy and enticing about an education that is
not the imposition of some already given truth but the formation of those selves
who must grasp the truth, there is also something dazzling and beguiling about the
leader who insists that there is no external content or body of knowledge that the
student must grasp or receive. It is the student's soul that grounds the educational
journey, and that soul bears a proper potentiality while waiting for the experience
of education. Beyond the relation of leader to lead there is only the path or passage
to fulfilment, no truth other than that of self-formation. If education is a leading,
what is the student being led towards? Is there a truth to which the leader must also
submit, or is education nothing more than a relation of self-formation, in which the
student repeats, in order to make her own, the movements of mastery? Spark's
novel raises the question of the tyranny, seduction, allure and affect of truth, along
with the seduction of the 'master' who supposedly holds the way to truth. Brodie is
well aware that leadership requires image, and that education is not just the
communication of content, the transfer of information, but is inextricably tied with
the force and affect of the *way* in which the self passes beyond itself to what it
comes to know.

   For Brodie, of course, what the student invests in and comes to know is nothing
other than Brodie herself: '"It is because you are mine,' said Brodie. 'I mean of my
stamp and cut, and I am in my prime.'[2] Spark's novel, like so many other texts of
the twentieth-century suggests that if education is only formal, if it only has to do
with development and mastery – and not some exposure to truth – then all we are
left with is captivation by image. How then do we avoid the crude notion of
education is a 'pouring in' or simple conveyance of information without allowing
the life of learning to become nothing more than an exercise in self-formation?
Sparks' suggestion in the enigmatic *The Prime of Miss Jean Brodie* lies in the
transfiguration of the commonplace. If the world is not already given as so much in

I. Semetsky (ed.), Nomadic Education: Variations on a Theme by Deleuze and Guattari, 35–42.
© *2008 Sense Publishers. All rights reserved.*

terms of manipulable information, then the 'leading out' of the soul has to exceed the soul of the enclosed human subject – the leader, master or image of man – and concern itself with all those 'souls' or micro-perceptions of which the world is composed. Souls are not potentialities waiting to be unfolded, but are potentials for creating relations, responses and perceptions – or *folds*:

> The tiniest of all animals has glimmers that cause it to recognize its food, its enemies, and sometimes its partner. If life implies a soul, it is because proteins already attest to an activity of perception, discrimination, and distinction – in short, a 'primary force' that physical impulsions and chemical affinities cannot explain ('derivative forces'). Thus there can be no reactions ensuing from excitations, but from outer organic actions that in the soul are proof of an inner perceptive activity. If life has a soul, it is because it perceives, distinguishes, or discriminates, and because a whole world of animal psychology is first of all a psychology of perception.[3]

In his preface to *Anti-Oedipus* Foucault points out that the task of Deleuze and Guattari's work is to guard against the 'micro-fascisms' in us all.[4] How is it that we are seduced, enslaved and captivated by an image of man or humanity – an image which is historically produced, but which comes to seem as the underlying truth of our being? Foucault's own answer to this question suggested that the very idea of truth, as that towards which thought ought to be led, was responsible for a politics of normalisation. We no longer actively question what our life ought to become so much as aim to know, discover, manage and communicate the facts or data of life.[5] The allure of *not-thinking,* of being led by an image of man, of failing to think – all these symptoms are, for Deleuze and Guattari, tied up with the ambivalent structure of desire, and the imbrications of affect with concept.[6] Thinking *is* desire; an approach to what is other that is also affected by what is other[7]. In striving to enhance itself all life engages with what is other than itself, and each engagement produces a singular relation, altering knower and known. Foucault suggests that we abandon the politics of truth, or an ethics of knowledge where we strive to *know* what we ought to do, and recognise the discursive forces and relations that produce truth. Truth and selves are effects of the relations of power, and we can only be liberated from truth by thinking relations of power critically – in terms of what they do, and not some supposedly underlying substance.[8] Deleuze – in a way that is curiously Heideggerean suggests that we imagine the relation between truth and thinking differently. Truth is not some external substance that thought may adequately represent, but this does not mean that truth is nothing more than an effect of relations. Indeed, for Deleuze there is a truth or power of life that *insists* and produces relations, relations that cannot be reduced to a single network of power. Thought is not the grasp or apprehension of truth, and truth is not a correct idea or content. Striving for truth is still an education, a leading away from the present and self-evident, but this is not towards some already present content, but to *problems*. Like Heidegger before him, Deleuze is critical of a truth that thought must simply represent adequately, and is critical of an education, which would consist of the formation of a correct method.

According to Heidegger the essence of truth is tied to the passage of education. Truth is not what is immediately visible but requires a transformation of the self, a turning away from everyday opinion and the self-evident towards something that needs to be un-hidden or removed from concealment. For Heidegger, this is made most evident in Plato's cave allegory, where those who are captivated by the shadows cast on the wall initially believe that they see being itself; when taken into the blinding light they still prefer the visible shadows. Only when they become accustomed to the light, and then return to the cave do they realise that the images they see and take for real are made visible by another source, the sun, which stands in the allegory for the essence or true being of all that is visible. The importance of education for Heidegger, and its intimate relation to truth, lies in the necessity of the passage. The true is what requires a distance or difference from everyday opinion, and in this necessary distance of truth there is also a resistance. The readily visible and immediately grasped shadows are easier on the eye, requiring no transformation of the self. The cave's prisoners have to be dragged into the light, and led to a source beyond a world they took as their own.

It is at this moment in Western thought that the essence of truth and education, according to Heidegger, marks a moment of decision. If truth becomes an idea – a correct way of viewing and grasping, then education becomes humanism, the production of the correct way or method of seeing. Truth becomes a fully revealed, present and adequate form, which allows us to grasp and encounter life 'correctly.' What is *lost* in this Platonic moment is the question of how ideas emerge: the genesis or emergence of thinking. Correct thinking is accepted in advance as a normative model. Truth and correctness become ideas that enable us to see the given, and the emergence of truth and thinking from the given – the genesis of truth, and the question of *what thinking is* – are forgotten. The educated student is given a model or method within which to think, led away from everyday illusions and granted a proper logic.

For Foucault it is just this leading away from the self-evident, this violent transformation of the given into a mere appearance and semblance, that marks the fall of Western thought into an 'ethic of knowledge.'[9] With the routing of the sophists, speech is no longer accepted in its force and power but is judged by some supposedly higher, but not immediately evident, truth. How is it that one voice or forceful utterance disavows its force and presents itself as nothing more than the innocent representation of a truth that lies in wait to be disclosed? The routing of the sophists is, Foucault insists, a 'logophobia' that fails to address the constitutive power of discourse, its capacity to produce relations, distribute fields, establish points of authority, and institute hierarchies. To a certain extent, Foucault follows Heidegger in his resistance to a normative model of thinking, and in his attempt to describe the historically different relations that produce various substances of knowledge or modes of truth. But whereas Heidegger wants to think the truth of being – that which gives itself to be thought, rather than truth as some correct method or logic, Foucault challenges the ethic of truth. His 'games of truth' describe acts of self-formation that are *normative* – governed by questions of how one ought to be – but not *normalising*, for they are conducted in the absence of any truths of reason. Like Deleuze, Foucault criticises the *depth* of truth, the idea that the field of language and appearance is grounded upon some transcendent truth – a truth that legitimates, underpins, and provides critical leverage against, mere opinion and the affective powers of rhetoric.

On the one hand, then, Foucault would be in line with an enlightenment critique of external authority or the invocation of a transcendent truth. Criticism of opinion is *responsibly* achieved, not by the appeal to a mystical or privileged outside, but by looking at the ways in which various statements achieve and institute relations of authority. On the other hand, Foucault is critical of a pedagogical imperative shared by both Platonic and enlightenment discourses of truth. The idea that truth is *other than* the self-evident, the idea of a transcendental condition that can be discerned *from* the what can be said but which is itself not reducible to that what can be said was crucial to Kant's call to enlightenment.

Enlightenment is not just freedom from external authority and imposed tutelage, it is also the recognition and intuition of a source beyond experience that makes experience possible. For Kant, the criticism of everyday opinion occurs, not by the imposition of a higher authority, but through recognition of how opinion is possible. If there can be disputes regarding the immortality of the soul, the freedom of the will, the limits of space and time, then this is both because we can *think* of what lies beyond the experienced, material, caused and limited world, and because we cannot know or definitively answer such questions. That disputes of this type cannot be settled, and that they devolve upon opinion, reveals that there is a power to form questions beyond what can be given through experience and verification. The authority of Kant's appeal to truth, therefore, does not just subordinate opinion and present itself as one more authority; it asks opinion to take itself seriously, to assess its own possibility of being expressed. Everyday experience is led away from itself and being exposed to the light, but this light is no longer an external idea so much as the reason's own power. Enlightenment education is not the revelation of a higher ground or truth, but a turn towards the self's own conditions for everyday experience.

Now for Foucault, these supposed conditions of the sayable are not reason's own, and the critique of the field of the sayable does not look to hidden conditions: not to that which produces relations, but to the always singular or historical distribution of relations at any one time. There is no truth to be discerned behind the field. Authority is achieved through the distributive effects of power, but there is no power itself awaiting apprehension when one's gaze is deflected from the surface of appearances. Indeed, this is just where Deleuze marks his difference from Foucault. Foucault's ontology remains dualist. Power distributes, regulates, orders and establishes the hierarchy in the field, but Foucault does not question what it *is* that power acts upon and, in Kantian fashion, suggests that power is known only in terms of its effects as produced relations and not as it is in itself.[10] For this reason, any appeal to a luminosity or source of truth beyond the field of power can only take the form of an ethic of knowledge: the construction of a putative ground or truth that subordinates and disavows the force of discourse. Both Foucault and Deleuze resist the idea of some ground of being behind appearance and difference, some truth *behind* appearances, and they both set themselves against a certain enlightenment injunction to turn back to the transcendental and universal ground from which opinion emerges. Both want to recognise the force of opinion, stupidity, malevolence, contingency and the violence of concepts – the connections of thought that cannot be explained by reference to some good image of thought or reason. Foucault, however, remains critical: we can play with the field of relations, context it critically from within, but because power is known in its effects and relations we cannot ask about the truth of power.

By contrast, Deleuze insists upon the monism of his ontology: that relations are not produced by the distribution of a field. Rather, life is composed of powers to produce relations, and it is the task of thinking *as learning* to intuit the powers that compose relations. The concept of desire describes a life of differing powers, each point of life grasps and connects with another point across different planes; there is no power or field of relations within which singularities are distributed. Rather, there are just powers to differ – singularities – with each power producing relations from itself. We can explain this difference by going back to Kant. For Kant, whatever properties things in themselves may have, we only know them through relations, and these relations establish a lawful and knowable field of experience.[11] For Foucault, similarly, we study what something is through its relations, the ways in which truth is established through institutions, procedures, bodily comportments and the connections of statements. If we want to ask how sexuality comes to be posited as our truth, then we have to understand the ways in which statements about sexual acts become articulable with statements about what it is to be human, and in turn we have to see how the 'truth' of humanity is produced as a knowable object in prisons, hospitals and courtrooms. The gaze and question produces itself a distribution between examining authority and the viewed object as its substance. The idea of what precedes or lies outside power can only be effected critically from within power, and the call to enlightenment can only be a demystification of all those supposed substances – such as sexuality – that might act as external guarantors for, or substances of, truth.

By contrast, Deleuze insists that relations are external to terms; what something is, the power it has to differ, produces a specific relation from itself, and this relation will differ according to just what each power connects with or encounters. Desire is positive, striving to become what it is, but also differing with all those desires that it crosses. In more concrete terms we can say that the field of appearances, of statements, of opinions and possibilities is always *more* than established relations. Texts, for example, have a power to provoke new relations; bodies – not just human bodies – are powers to provoke images, depending on each new connection and relation, but the body is not reducible to the ideas or images we have of it. If we take thought as a mode of desire this leads to two consequences. First, thought becomes differently according to the problems it approaches. Second, true thinking moves beyond established relations and constituted terms to the *other* desire it encounters. We should, for example, look to the sense or force of a text, to the *problems* of history, to the genesis of the concepts – and not just to the constituted discursive field. Pedagogy is, then, a leading away from appearances and opinion, from the already defined and unremarkable, not to some underlying ground, but to a desire that will never be presented in itself, but will always differ according to the questions we pose, and will in turn transform the very being of the question.

We can make sense of this, I think, from the notion of Socratic pedagogy, which is tied to desire, or Eros, but is also directed against the sophists' reduction of truth to force. Indeed, Deleuze's overturning of Platonism deconstructs the opposition between truth and sophistry: there is a truth of appearances, an ability to think the truth of what appears, not as some hidden content, but as the life or difference of appearances. In Socratic pedagogy, for example, Socrates' interlocutor is often not led towards some content, but is exposed to the movement of dialogue *and* to a sense of the limited nature of already constituted terms. Socrates does not offer a definition of justice, love or beauty but shows – through dialogue – that current concepts are rigid and finite, incapable of moving with the possibilities of life. On the one hand, in Socratic pedagogy, truth cannot be reduced to the relation of power; one does not accept as true what has been given from authority, nor what has been forcefully said. Even more importantly, truth is not affect; it is not the allure or seduction of persuasion, not the ease of the readily repeated and consumed, and even less is the true this or that desired and valued thing. Socratic pedagogy is erotic because it produces itself through a relation. This relation is not one of force or power, not the quantitative or skilful victory of force, but the seduction of personality. What one desires in Socrates is not the answers he offers, nor the being that he is, but his desire: his difference from any already given opinion, his distance from what he says or presents himself to be. Truth, here, is hidden, is other than the already said and readily perceived, but it is not some idea that one can grasp and set against the visible, it is a power to disrupt, question and think beyond the visible. To desire Socrates is, further, to move away from the passive acceptance of definitions and opinions, and to transform oneself, not into what Socrates is, but a potential to question, to *not* know.

Socratic pedagogy, with its intensification of Eros, poses one of the major problems of the politics of critique and enlightenment. How does the criticism of already given experience avoid becoming a tyrannical authority, and enslavement of life for the sake of some invented higher world? Without such a critique, how do we avoid the mere circulation of the already sayable, the domestication of knowledge to the management of information, and the reduction of pedagogy to the training in merely formal and critical knowledge?

The answer in Deleuze's own thinking can be found in the related concepts of intuition, schizoanalysis, problems and desire. To read a text or learn from a philosopher is to aim to think or intuit the problem that provides the force of their work. And if we accept that thinking is a mode of desire, a striving or impulse of life, then each attempt to encounter a work's problem will itself open a new problem, depending upon the desire of the thinker. On the one hand, then, the truth of the work is always more than the work itself; it is the field of sense or possibility from which a work emerges. Approaching the problem of a text will result in a series of articulations depending upon the field of sense we inhabit. The art of reading is neither the retrieval of information, nor the adoption of a method, nor the description of a text's produced effects. To learn or to be led out from oneself require that one does not grasp or recognizes an object as given but rather encounters a problem and intuits the desire as that striving from which any text emerges.

Further, as Deleuze and Guattari make clear in their notion of schizoanalysis, and Deleuze makes clear in his notion of 'image of thought,' we all too readily remain captivated by affect. The 'fascism' in us all goes beyond the easy passage from affect to opinion. Whereas a concept produces a series of connections and enables us to think – for example, we can think of the concept of 'the subject' grounded in the mind or a separate realm of disembodied ideas as opposed to the world – affects are singular and propulsive. An image can make us weep, vomit or shiver, without judgement. Even if affects and concepts are always, in experience, infolded within each other, the task of thinking requires their disengagement. Perception forms unities or identities from flows of signs, and produces images and bounded wholes. Such production can be explained as an *investment*; the energy of thought grasps an object that gives it form: say, the visual image of the brain, which seems to provide a symbol for the unity of thinking. Thought strives for the genesis of the images and concepts within which we move; opinion remains at the level of captivation and constituted relations. Opinion is the unreflective passage from affective perception to judgement. In *What is Philosophy?* Deleuze and Guattari cite the example of the opinionated consumer of cheese who passes from a sensible revulsion, to a generality, from 'I don't like this,' to 'this is no good.' But affect can also paralyse thinking in deeper ways, such as the image of man as a rational animal, or the easily consumed, palatable and anodyne image of the mind as a storehouse of transferable skills, well-formed methods and communicable concepts. Thought is all too easily seduced by opinion. Leading thought away from opinion is not the imposition of a higher truth, nor the revelation of a proper logic; it is the provocation to problematise, and to think first of all the truth of problems rather than solutions.

For Deleuze, there is no learning or thinking without truth, without the desire to encounter the sense or genesis of a problem, but this truth – though it exists in itself, and must be thought of as existing in itself – is the power to disclose itself differently with each new encounter. If, for example, we ask ourselves about the problem of *Paradise Lost* – why Milton wrote a theodicy, why he felt that life required justification, and why this justification could be answered by an image of paradise – then we also provoke who we are. Today, we *don't* feel the 'compromise' of earthly existence, or the capacity of the people to choose subjection, to be a universal historical problem. To teach this text one needs to get a feel for the questions it asks, and a sense of the problems we inhabit. This sounds very much like good old-fashioned Heideggerean hermeneutics, and there are many similarities. But there is also a difference: if thought is desire, and desire lives by encountering, connecting, transforming and differing, then the sense of a text or problem is not the way it discloses the world or being; it is a provocation, a violation of good sense, an assault on method and consensus; it is a non-transferable irrelevance that at the same time transfers a potentiality for relevance. Learning to swim is not replicating the movements of the swimming teacher; nor is it feeling the waves that the teacher herself is responding to; it is imaging the response to new and other waves.

NOTES

1 Muriel Spark, *The Prime of Miss Jean Brodie,* Harmondsworth: Penguin, 1965, 36.
2 *Prime* 97.
3 Gilles Deleuze, *The Fold: Leibniz and the Baroque,* trans. Tom Conley, London: Athlone, 1993, 92.
4 Michel Foucault, 'Preface,' Gilles Deleuze and Félix Guattari, *Anti-Oedipus: capitalism and Schizophrenia,* trans. Robert Hurley, Mark Seem, and Helen R. Lane, Minneapolis: University of Minnesota Press, 1983, xiii.
5 Michel Foucault, 'Subjectivity and Truth,' *The Essential Works, 1: Ethics,* ed. Paul Rabinow, 87-92.
6 Gilles Deleuze and Félix Guattari, *What is Philosophy?* trans. Hugh Tomlinson and Graham Burchell, New York: Columbia University Press, 1994, 197.
7 Deleuze, *The Fold,* 132-33.
8 Michel Foucault, 'The Will to Knowledge,' *The Essential Works 1,* 11-16.
9 Michel Foucault, *The Archaeology of Knowledge,* trans. A. Sheridan Smith, London: Tavistock, 1972.
10 Gilles Deleuze, *Foucault* trans. Séan Hand, Minneapolis: University of Minnesota Press, 1988, 140.
11 Rae Langton, *Kantian Humility: Our Ignorance of Things in Themselves,* Oxford: Clarendon Press, 1998.

REFERENCES

Deleuze, G. (1988). *Foucault* (S. Hand, Trans.). Minneapolis: University of Minnesota Press.
Deleuze, G. (1993). *The fold: Leibniz and the Baroque* (T. Conley, Trans.). London: Athlone.
Deleuze, G., & Guattari, F. (1994). *What is philosophy?* (H. Tomlinson & G. Burchell, Trans.). New York: Columbia University Press.
Foucault, M. (1972). *The Archaeology of knowledge* (A. Sheridan Smith, Trans.). London: Tavistock.
Foucault, M. (1983). Preface. In G. Deleuze & F. Guattari (Eds.), *Anti-Oedipus: Capitalism and schizophrenia* (R. Hurley, M. Seem, & H. R. Lane, Trans.). Minneapolis: University of Minnesota Press.
Foucault, M. (2000). Subjectivity and truth. In P. Rabinow (Ed.), *The essential works: Ethics* (Vol. 1, pp. 87–92). Harmondsworth: Penguin.
Foucault, M. (2000). The will to knowledge. *The Essential Works, 1,* 11–16.
Heidegger, M. (1998). *Pathmarks* (W. H. McNeill, Trans.). Cambridge: Cambridge University Press.
Langton, R. (1998). *Kantian humility: Our ignorance of things in themselves.* Oxford: Clarendon Press.
Spark, M. (1965). *The prime of Miss Jean Brodie.* Harmondsworth: Penguin.

Claire Colebrook
Edinburgh University
UK

JACQUES DAIGNAULT

4. PEDAGOGY AND DELEUZE'S CONCEPT OF THE VIRTUAL

An illustration of a "machine à détonner" in the analysis of free software

INTRODUCTION

Deleuze died in 1995. It was before the explosion of the Internet, yet nothing indicates that he would never become interested in the effects that the Web could have for pedagogy. The manuscript (Deleuze, 1996) on which he was working at the time of his death would have developed the question of the virtual. The conception of the virtual that Deleuze proposes invites us to question the phenomenon of the Internet not only in terms of a controlled society (Deleuze, 1990) but also in the declension of the concept of virtuality as a *machine à détonner*[1], where the pedagogical parenthesis would constitute an example *par excellence*.[2]

In order to illustrate this conjunction of the pedagogical parenthesis and the virtual, we propose two ways of linking them: through an analysis of free software[3] as an example of a *machine à détonner* and through a reference to Giorgio Agamben's (2005) messianic time. But above all, the reference to Deleuze's unique method allows us to maintain that pedagogy *is* creation – as are the arts, philosophy, and the sciences – the creation of creators faithful to Common (*Commun*) enrichment. Pedagogy is not just a profession, but also a vocation in the sense of being faithful to the Common. There are at least three complementary propositions that follow from Deleuze's legacy:
– all creators, no matter what their discipline, play with the frontiers of perception, that is, at the limit of the virtual;
– all creators have in common that they contribute to the Common;
– free software and pedagogy constitute two examples of this double activity.

THE VIRTUAL

We live in an age of electronic surveillance, of over-consumption, of the widespread transformation of immaterial and common goods into merchandised goods, and of the impotency that is becoming more and more manifest with respect to nation-states in their abilities to impose limits on environmental destruction and the impoverishment of a growing number of people in the world. This list is obviously not exhaustive, and the different positions facing the Internet are as contradictory as they are diverse.

I. Semetsky (ed.), Nomadic Education: Variations on a Theme by Deleuze and Guattari, 43–60.

The virtual versus the real

Many authors think that the Internet contributes to the de-realization of the world, to its ontological impoverishment and, by implication, to the indifference or impotency of those who – mainly in good faith – battle against abuse and violence. We are alerted to a general demobilization facing the responsibility of citizens, which the Internet contributes to feed. This in turn provokes an escape from reality, the relativity of values, the loss of confidence in democracy and the announcement *ad nauseum* by postmodern eulogists of the death of utopias, history, and ideas.[4] They hide, on the one hand, a nostalgia for reality behind the distressing spectacle of a hyper-real society and, on the other hand, the indignant call of resistance, for the regulation of the entertainment industry, and the cultural, moral, and political impoverishment of which the Internet would be designated, in legal jargon, an important witness. The left and the right often confront one another on the nature of new technologies, but less often on what is to be done. The irritable left would rather wish that we took a distance in the face of new technologies, while the right prefers that we control its usage by censoring its contents and its fields of application.

We can just as easily sing a different tune. The Internet can revive and renew democracy on a global scale by allowing millions of individuals, who were until now deprived, to actively participate and contribute to making the world a better place through free and open discussion on the Internet. Yes, there are utopians of the Internet.[5] Several projects are devoted to "doubling" many of our institutions, such as virtual schools (especially at the university level), large virtual libraries and museums, electronic trading, consulting firms and services, etc. Many of these projects, according to the eulogists of progress, can make up for past delays, particularly in education and in matters of commerce. The left and the right find themselves on the same side to celebrate the promises of the Internet, even if they await completely different and often contradictory results.

Lastly, we can find innumerable nuances between these extreme positions. We can easily find testimonies to this on the Internet itself, notably through blogs, discussion forums, chat spaces, and interactive news sites. Not everything is clearly cut, and we discover rather quickly that everything that is said about the world "as it turns" can be said just as well about, and on, the Internet itself.

What the extreme positions nevertheless have in common is that they ascribe to technology a power that it may not have, as though the problems and promises of the Internet were linked to the technological age. This presents new challenges, both terrifying and promising, that await us today with the arrival of new technologies, and particularly those associated with the virtual. But above all – and this holds for the greater majority of authors and users of the Internet – the virtual is usually opposed to the real because it is held to be but a poorly defined copy or a substitute that doubles a disenchanted (deception), untouched (indifference), or revived (enthusiasm) real.

The virtual is in fact often considered the rival of reality. It is here that a reference to Deleuze becomes most important because, for Deleuze, "[T]he virtual is opposed not to the real but to the actual. *The virtual is fully real in so far as it is virtual*" ([1968] 1994, p. 208). In fact, it is the possible that opposes the real.

The virtual is real

We need to understand in what sense Deleuze establishes his equation and, in particular, which problem he is addressing when he denounces the opposition between the real and the virtual. We also need to show how the Internet inscribes itself as an extension of this problematic.

The oldest, and most easily recognizable, virtual "machine" is the world itself. Our relation to the virtual is our relation to the real world. But why do we multiply the names of the real? Why do we sometimes call it real and at other times virtual? What is it about the concept of the virtual that is necessary for Deleuze? Does he only use the real for a dual purpose?

"The philosophy of Gilles Deleuze," Jean-Luc Nancy writes, "is a virtual philosophy, in the sense that we use this word today when we speak, in an uncanny manner, of the image or of virtual reality – where we designate by this a universe formed entirely of images, and not only of images that are illusions of the real, but rather in the sense that there is no longer a place for the opposition between the real and the image. The 'virtual' world (in the English sense of this word) is a universe of effectivity-images" (1998, p. 118).

The image here responds to questions relative to problems of *perception* and *representation*. Deleuze's main effort, in philosophy, has been to do away with representation, that is, transcendence that he associates with negation and even with the refusal of the world. Virtual philosophy, as we shall see, relies on an immanent view of the world and life. If the Internet and cyberspace can be called virtual in the sense of such a philosophy, it has to be because everything *cyber* belongs to the world – to be defined "as strictly part of the real object" (Deleuze 1994, p. 209) – instead of opening onto another world. The cyber constitutes but another stratum of this world. The virtual does not oppose the real, but is constitutive of it.

It is an old philosophical question that asks whether the world is One or Multiple. The question is central to politics (the question of the ideal) and religion (the question of a supreme Being), but we should also add pedagogy and education by way of their historical and conceptual affiliations. These are areas where the confrontation between the two positions is very much alive. The two concepts that best summarize the issue are immanence and transcendence. To revive the Ideal, Deleuze thinks, would be clinging to a transcendental view. It would mean adopting either an idealist perspective, which gives the world a Platonic model to imitate, or a dialectical, Hegelian, perspective, which introduces in the world its own negation as a condition of its movement.

Representations

The problem of representation – from a political perspective at least – consists in presenting an ideal, which it would be possible to realize. Deleuze finds the origin of this problem with Plato and his paradigm of the model and copy which presents a view of the world as split in two: the perfect world of Ideas (that of the model) and the imperfect world of matter (that of the copy) ([1969] 1990). The originality of Deleuze's reading – and the specificity of the problem that he draws – is that Plato's true problem is in the rivalry located between different pretenders relative to the status of the copy. We therefore need a criterion for separating the true copies or simulacra from the false. Plato's true intention is to exclude simulacra by chasing from the Republic all of those who fabricate and value simulacra, notably the sophists and poets. The Platonic solution of posing the existence of a universal model as a measure for the evaluation of copies is unacceptable, in the eyes of Deleuze, for at least two reasons.

First of all we would have to assume another world in comparison to which our own is dull and miserable. There is therefore a devaluation of our world, a sadness in dwelling in it, as well as the promise – by exchanging renunciation for the free and experimental exercise of thought – of acceding to universal truths through a philosophical or theological conversion. The consequences come next: hierarchies are dispersed throughout the world and its social organization. These hierarchies are founded on a presupposition according to which the privileges are given to those who, like the philosophers, make themselves out to be smugglers between the two worlds and thus function as absolute judges of truth and falsity, insofar as they are the only reliable witnesses of the very idea of truth. These hierarchies result in tainting the very idea of justice. Deleuze does not reproach Plato for his search for the truth but rather for prescribing a method of division (model-copy, true-false copies, true-false pretenders, etc.) that, although resting on a legitimate presupposition from the point of view in the exercise of thought, nonetheless proves dangerous in its dogmatic consequences: not only does the world find itself cut in two, but it also finds itself cut into an order of vertical values, with all of the inequalities that it imposes and legitimates.

The political space opened by representation thus becomes this game of realizing an ideal as we imagine it. The passage to the virtual/actual pair is not a substitution for the possible/real pair, where the legitimacy is not reconsidered within certain limits, but instead comes to support and frame it, so as to precisely prevent the death of the possible. "We need the possible! Otherwise I'll choke," wrote Deleuze, *à propos* of May 1968 (Zourabichvili, 1998, p. 340). It is therefore not so much the relation of the model to the copy that worries Deleuze, but rather the consequences of a neat division of the world on the basis of all the copies "other" than those finally *authorized to represent* the model.

Perceptions

For Deleuze ([1969] 1990) the idea of simulacra is like a "power": he simultaneously refutes the model as the good copy, contests all hierarchies, and stitches together the "two" worlds. Like all philosophers of immanence, Deleuze sees but one world, yet he conceives that we can represent it as multiple – as well as deduce a transcendental origin – since this is what thought does: it represents the world, and gives itself possible images or ideals with respect to disciplining action such that the realization of these ideals becomes the sole political program. He suspects that the imaginary of representation anaesthetizes the body and its power to be affected. But in fact the body has no problem in perceiving simulacra. It is only when the mind attempts to interpret them from the point of view of images (instead of leaving the image to affect the body directly and its capacity to perceive) that it imagines all the horrors that are assigned to it as the cause of humanity's misfortunes.

Instead of dividing the world in two, Deleuze carves the world into strata or layers and proposes some thresholds of perception. He "separates" the world into the virtual and the actual, both real. We humans are rather slow and fragile beings, and our perceptual thresholds give us relatively stable and permanent images of the world and ourselves. But the body never stops sensing and registering countless micro-perceptions on the basis of which our macro-perceptions, our images, and our "human" affects all synthesize (this holds for all of our images, including those of ourselves, landscapes, animals, rocks, the sun, pension funds, love fantasies, the ideal of justice, etc., without which human life would be impossible). These "synthesized" images are said to be actual, but their vapours, on which the body never ceases to nourish itself along the plane of micro-perceptions, plunge permanently into the virtual.

All that appears thus pulls its ground along with it, even if it detaches itself from this ground. Thus, that which appears clearly distinguishes itself from its ground. But this (back)ground is pulled along, in a certain manner, as that against which appearance affirms itself as difference. Yet this ground, which is thus always already is being pulled along, is not really distinct from it, but rather dissipates like a vapour just beyond our usual threshold of perception. The virtual is in this vapour, in every layer and every circle, forever dissipated. There is an open totality there. That which appears is thus the actual: it is distinct from the virtual, but in only one direction. This is what Deleuze calls a *unilateral distinction,* ([1968] 1994), which summarizes the relation between the virtual – the irrecoverable and dissipated ground – and the actual – the zone of rather clear distinctions, surrounded by the virtual's imperceptible mist. Therefore, although the virtual and the actual address two parts of the real, the separation or division does not cut the world in two but rather poses the distinction from a single side of the separation. The real is thus never completely divided. That's why it is immanent.

Is it possible to perceive the virtual, the mist itself? The answer is not so simple. Deleuze defines two movements between the virtual and the actual. The first movement espouses that which we have just come to describe: "an actual perception surrounds itself with a cloud of virtual images, distributed on increasingly remote, increasingly large, moving circuits, which both make and unmake each other. These are memories of different sorts, but they are still called virtual images in that their speed or brevity subjects them too to a principle of the unconsciousness" (Deleuze, 1996, pp. 179-180:6) According to this first movement, it is impossible to perceive virtual images without changing the thresholds of perception, without moving the frontier of the unconscious. But the circles can just as well become more and more dense to the point where all that subsists is the actual object and its virtual image: "actual perception has its own memory as a kind of immediate, consecutive, or even simultaneous double." (1996, p. 183) This is Bergson's theme of the specific memory, of which an experience of "déja vu" is the most common paradigm. Here the virtual image is perceived at the same time as the actual object and forms with it a crystal at the heart of which the one and the other have become indiscernible: "each relating to the role of the other." (Deleuze, 1996, p. 185).

What need to be disentangled are the processes at play. In the first movement, that which leads to the principle of the unconscious, the actualisation is itself called a singularity insofar as the constituted actual appears in the form of an individuality. In the second movement, that of indiscernibility, there is no actualisation but only individuation into a crystal. These distinctions are important because they apply to Time and because they define what is at stake in a virtual philosophy: a non-teleological vitalism on the basis which we can, a little later, construct a politics of "means without ends," in the manner according to Agamben (1995). For it is towards this that we are heading: to think of "citizenship" or the human community according to the exigencies of the virtual, as well as to show that the table is set for this task by certain regions of the Internet, such as where free software reigns.

What are we then to make of this relation to Time and of these distinctions between actualisation and individuation (we must also remember that this consists of two possible relations between the actual and the virtual)? We cannot simply think of the virtual in terms of space alone, for the virtual is primarily pure duration. The virtual is not a place or space, but the single duration of the whole of the past contracted into each present that actualises itself. It is on the line of time that the Deleuzian divisions are found, divisions that are close to those that he denounces in Plato but whereby the fundamental difference is perhaps in the passage of space to time as the source of thought. One must learn to pose limits to time according to the parameters of movement: contracted and fast, or relaxed and slow. The virtual/actual distinction will thus be of two sorts: at the most contracted point of time, when the present passes, and at the most relaxed and dilated point, when the past endures. "Duration is [...] *virtual coexistence*: the coexistence with itself of all the levels, all the tensions, all the degrees of contraction and relaxation." (Deleuze, [1966] 1991, p. 60). There are not many worlds, but many regions of the real, each corresponding to levels of the contraction/dilation of the past. A really contracted past does not consist of any less of the whole past than any other level of the same past, even if it is more dilated.

The actual is certainly deployed in space. However, the limits that it draws are inevitably cleanly cut from the side of the actual and blurry from the side of the virtual. Thus we discover once again a unilateral distinction. And yet one would have to admit that this concept would be difficult to imagine if there was only space, for where the unilateral distinction passes there also passes the limit between space, populated with actuals, and time, as the virtual coexistence of all of the past. Actualisation arrives from the side of the movement of time: the distinction blurs till chaotic non-distinction would have rendered the distinction void. Individuation, on the contrary, arrives on the side of space and makes a crystal with time: a clean distinction, but unilateral.

Let us now return to the question of the perception of the virtual: can we perceive it directly? The answer is becoming more clear: the body perceives a bit like the memory recalls. Plunging into the virtual is thus to exercise the memory with all of the body. To explore the memory of the world – to make the experience of the real as though it were a gigantic non-personal memory – purports to extract, in this very act, the new that invents itself as the present passes and the past endures.

To create

The introduction of the temporal dimension is significant. A virtual philosophy is in some sense a vitalism that Deleuze takes to its limit to the very concept of inorganic life (cf. Agamben, 1998). The world itself can be called virtual, that is, understood as dynamic evolution in all regions of the Real. The future is to be created, at all levels. Nothing is lost in duration, for all is created in the becoming of the world.

On several remarkable pages inspired by a book by D.H. Lawrence, Deleuze and Guattari portray creators as the courageous beings who risk their lives by stealing a piece of chaos from Time and by reporting on their work, according to the methods and forces of their discipline, by which they demonstrate their mastery (Deleuze and Guattari [1991] 1994, p. 203). If the work of art, a philosophical concept, or a mathematical function is not chaotic it is because it constitutes the development of a response or solution to a problem – itself posited, like an enigma, by the piece of chaos – which the creator has sought to formulate by working on it, even at the risk of his or her equilibrium and sometimes his or her life. It is the realm of problems where the actual always constitutes a tentative response or solution. We are, however, too slow and too fragile to inhabit the more turbulent and chaotic zones where problematic Ideas reside. Still, how do we gain access?

To virtualise

Few authors have tackled this question directly. Lévy (1995) approached it when he defined virtualisation as a movement that rises [remonte] from a solution back towards its problem. He showed how the deployment and development of cyberspace problematized entire regions of our spaces of life that had been stabilized in actual forms for a long time. He showed how the text, the body, and the economy were transformed by the virtualisation that operated on them through the development of virtual reality and the Internet in particular.

What we object to with Lévy is not his optimism or utopianism. No, what is a little troubling is the idea that virtualisation is sudden – a function of "new technologies" rather than of the "abstract machine" that constitutes the world as unlimited virtual "power". It is as if the new technologies themselves operate on virtualisation, or instead as if they themselves problematize the domains of virtuality. If this were the case we could certainly conclude that new technologies think by themselves and rival in power the best creators of the world. We are not yet there, however, and this derivation is only possible through the confusion between technology and virtual machines. The word "machine" is regularly used by Deleuze to designate the devices or abstract organizations by means of which creators (who are themselves collective organizations) come to think.

Bergson had the habit of saying that a well-posed problem is already resolved. He also said that problems have only the solutions that they merit. The first step in thinking is in the art of posing a problem. The unfolding of solutions (the development of actuals) is not any less demanding inasmuch as it is a creative act but it certainly depends on the quality of the problem and on the manner in which it was posed. Lévy's usage of the word virtualisation is appropriate insofar as he designates the process that rises from a solution back towards the problem that it resolves. This return, however, is not the fruit of new technologies, but an act of thought that is reserved exclusively, according to Deleuze, for creative spirits. This does not exclude the existence of creative organizations at the heart of which complex and powerful technologies are found; still, technologies do not think or create by themselves. An example of virtualisation is found in the second age of the concept. Deleuze and Guattari recognized three "ages" of the concept: there is the encyclopedic age with its universal heights, the commercial age tied to marketing and even the commerce of ideas, and finally, between the two, a more modest task that alone "can safeguard us from falling from the heights of the first into the disaster of the third" (Deleuze and Guattari, [1991] 1994, p. 12): the *pedagogy* of the concept.

There we have it: *pedagogy is virtualisation* inasmuch as it is an art of going back toward the problem, of explicating the issues and difficulties relative to the problem, of showing what other problems could have been raised through certain elements of the solution, etc. This is an essential point concerning pedagogy – pedagogy as creativity – to which we will return after the analysis of free software.

Virtual operators

Murphie's (2002) directly tackles the link between virtual reality and Deleuze's thought. Murphie's approach is quite different from Lévy. Murphie conceives of virtual technologies as *operators* that allow us to play directly with our perceptual thresholds. He thinks that virtual reality (VR)[7] produces a shock, as if it is the immanent nature of metaphysics itself that hits us head-on.[8] Little by little VR brings an end to the regimes of representation that have until now successfully suppressed, behind the emergence of the stable images of bodies and the states of things, the interactive nature of the virtual and the actual. Murphie partially agrees with Lévy when he acknowledges that VR accentuates – in comparison with other non-technological organizations – our means of acting on perception: they are tools that we control, that act on perception itself and with which we can amplify the effects. VR contributes, by giving us power over our perceptions, to a radical change of our conception of the world.

There are essentially two characteristics that allow us to identify a virtual "machine": it draws attention to itself in its modulation of perceptual thresholds and it is fully interactive. Take the case of a remote control that changes television channels. The fact of "flipping" transforms our experience of television. Navigating the Internet and interacting with sites lead to at least five types of threshold: the *territorial* (distances become relative), the *informational* (information flows between minds just as well as it does between mind and electronic chips or between the chips themselves), the *body/machine* relation (it suffices to mention the cyborg), the *representational* (where the frontier passes between representation and that which it represents), and finally *perception* itself (where the limits are subjected to plunges within the virtual). In sum, VR gives us knowledge of the power of modulation.

The relation between VR and virtual philosophy, and the means of reaching the virtual, become now clear. It is through a particular perception that we reach the virtual. And it is on perception that VR directly plays. The virtual properties of VR designate the virtual operators, what Murphie calls *the modulation of modulation*. Let us try to test this idea in the field of free software. And from now on we will call every virtual operator susceptible to opening a pedagogical parenthesis a "*machine à détonner*".

THE COMMON

The question of the common good often appears in discussions on the topic of free software. How does the relation play out between free software and the virtual in comparison to the Common and in terms of pedagogy? We address some economic issues, such as piracy and gratuity. The exchange networks on the Internet of digital files pose puzzles for the industries that believe themselves to be swindled and robbed by these practices. It is for this reason that the "entertainment" industry lobbied the States to make private copying illegal; it has now been given political and legal tools in order to respect copyrights in court, as well as technological means to block copying. The fight is very much alive between the industry and the "pirates."

The free position concerning the copying of software is clear: copying and diffusion are liberties guaranteed by all free or open source licensing. And in the case of other cultural products, the free software movement encourages authors to publish their works under licenses that authorize copying, at least for non-commercial usage. The free software movement does not contest the legitimacy of copyright but serves to assure the liberties that it defends. It would be an error to associate the free software movement with piracy. In a certain manner the crisis provoked by the exchange networks help the free software movement to sensitise consumers to the existence and quality of free products, which they invite the consumer to test and evaluate with respect to the owner's own comparable products.

There are, in addition, more and more articulate opinions making themselves heard to the effect that it is copyright itself that has gone too far. The main arguments are along these lines: the distinction between content and expression is highly problematic; content is never the fruit of one person alone, but always results from a common heritage; copyright only serves to defend monopolies[9] for the distribution of culture; and finally, it is the authors, in the name of whom all of this is negotiated, who bear the expense. Finally, there are opinions that defend copyright but question the economic argument posed by the industry that maintains that digital copying loses a lot of money for authors and editors. The main argument is that the electronic copying of a work does not touch the material stock of copies ready for sale. But the argument that each illegal copy translates as one less copy sold, as held by the industry, is false. The stock of copies to be sold always constitutes the same potential for sales (a digital copy is not one copy less, but one copy more). Some even go so far as to claim that illegal copies stimulate sales by giving greater visibility to the product via the Internet. To maintain that every illegal copy is a lost retail sale is to claim – and, according to certain analysts (Latrive, 2004), the proof is far from established – that everyone knows and desires the product prior to their copying. This is false since there are few potential customers. Besides, some "pirates" who engage in illegal copying end up "regulating" their situation when they really like the product.

À propos of the expression "free software," Stallman[10] has the habit of saying: free as in freedom and not free as in free beer.[11] The ambiguity is not present in French, but the fact that Stallman insists on the distinction implies that the question of the difference *between free and gratis should be posed.* The free software movement never set out to do away with the computing business, but only to transform it. Competition is affirmed as valuable and as a regulating mechanism; computing is considered an important industry capable of creating many quality jobs. What is put in question is the access to a source code that, considered as a known good, generates no economic value – in the sense that we cannot attribute any price to it – on account of its ownership. Corsani and Lazzarato (2004) sum it up by suggesting that knowledge is an intelligible good (immaterial), and it is in-appropriable, *non-exchangeable*, and non-consumable. Given that the very logic of exchange constitutes the foundation of liberal economy, a non-exchangeable good poses some evaluative problems. Corsani and Lazzarato state: "The transmission of knowledge does not impoverish the one who has it. On the contrary, its diffusion, instead of 'depriving its creator', contributes to an increase in its value. Invention (and knowledge) is therefore not consumable according to the criteria set by political economy. Only the exchange of material goods aims to satisfy the desires through the 'destructive consummation' of exchanged products."[12]

The authors agree on the necessarily *gratis* character of free software, that is, the very nature of knowledgeable goods (*biens de connaissance*) – common goods, as we shall see shortly – is beyond price. They insist that the source code is not only *free* (free as in freedom) but *gratis* as well (free as in free beer). We will draw, further on, an important philosophical consequence of this equation of freedom and gratuity with respect to source codes: gratuity will become aligned with a secular version of grace. From the point of view of economic thought, it is the distinction between invention and innovation that is at issue. In fact, many economists support the importance of a system that protects copyright because it is an incentive measure for innovation: "in the absence of monetary incentive nobody would be motivated to personally invest in a creative activity" (Corsani and Lazzarato, 2004).

The free software movement gives rise to a new work ethics (Himanen, 2001) where financial security, obedience to authority, the sense of responsibility, and self-sacrifice are replaced by a certain carelessness concerning financial security, the free sharing of knowledge, collaborative work, the care for equality and, above all, the joy, always the joy and pleasure in creating. Thus, the free software movement presents values constitutive of a new ethics that forces economics to review many of its models, particularly the monetary incentive towards invention. The theme of gratuity only concerns software in its electronic, and thus immaterial, version. It engages in the business of by-products (manuals, the distribution of well "packaged" and selected software, promotional products, etc.), advisory services, and lucrative training, which give even more reason to the claims of the free software movement to the effect that the free circulation of source codes will not kill the computer industry but will only point it toward a greater diversity of the market.

We can draw an initial conclusion from the new hacker ethics in its association with the free software movement: if the political project of the FSF (Free Software Foundation) appears too radical in the eyes of the computer establishment, one would be forced to admit that the revolution is not yet economical. On the contrary, free software flourishes rather well in the current liberal regime. Economists seem to be inclined in favour of the notion of common good in the dual sense that it has in the two grammatical genres of French.[13] Benkler (2003) classifies commons into four types based on two parameters. The first is to know whether goods are open to all (for example, air) or only to a defined group (for example, the traditional organizations of pastures). The second consists in asking whether it is regulated or not. "The most important resource we govern as an open commons," Benkler (2003) writes, "without which humanity could not be conceived, is all of pre-twentieth century knowledge and culture, most scientific knowledge of the first half of the twentieth century, and much of contemporary science and academic learning." Benkler proposes a strategy to construct a core common infrastructure alongside proprietary infrastructure. He sides with the philosophy of OSI (Open Source Initiative[14]) just like the majority of economists. But he demonstrates that OSI as well as all the other groups that develop software with open source coding have no other choice but to concern themselves with commons as well, and not only with technological efficiency. Economic success itself depends on it.

Behind Agamben's (1993, 2002) concepts of "whatever singularity" and "the Common" is found the expression of free usage, no rights, no property, an *usus pauper* of great wealth for the free community. The free software community has a few lessons to learn from the literary one. Language obliges, period. It obliges one to respect grammar, the precise meaning of words rooted in a long history, conventional usages, syntax, and all elementary rules of logic and rhetoric. One also has to respect the institutions, such as editors, the circles of readers, the critics, etc. An author knows the limits of language and submits to them voluntarily. Language invents its own silences and unique, piercing cries – terrifying and splendid at the same time – but they are always on the way, in one fashion or the other, toward outcomes that respect linguistic norms and obligations. For Deleuze, language is always tied to signification, denotation, and manifestation, the three main linguistic functions. Yet, there is a fourth dimension of language – the expression of sense – around which Deleuze ([1969] 1990) constructed an important part of his work and which he related to the virtual. Sense, Deleuze says, is an extra-being, a singularity that inheres in language: it does not exist, only subsists. Whereby time is that of an event, it inheres in language and subsists in the states of affairs.

This curious supplement, which is defined as a paradoxical moment, strangely resembles Agamben's idea of gratuity. It is a remainder. And, as an extra-being, it isn't obliged to anything, but abolishes all obligations without yet compromising that to which an obligation is obliged. What has arrived, when the author finishes his literary work, is sense, unpredicted and always unpredictable, still unique and irreplaceable source of the author's faith in textuality. Sense, without the author or language held accountable for it, suspends the laws of language, and renders them inapplicable. And yet, precisely for this very reason, sense nevertheless constitutes the tool or instrument that fulfills the work anew: there is no law of sense, but only its free use. Copyright obliges just as much as language. Copyleft obliges no less. But with a difference.

THE SYLLABUS

The syllabus has become a contract. From the outset, we do not see this contract as different in kind from the point of view of respecting a moral commitment or fulfilling a legal obligation. On the one hand, there is my word and my good faith, and on the other hand, there is the translation of the very object of my word into a norm and obligation. We can see how we might complain about this notion of a contract that, technically speaking, translates into an obligatory right that to which my word and my faith already holds me obliged, and often with a weight far superior to the command of the law.

We plead, instead, in favor of a difference in kind between faithfulness and the law, between the promise and obligation, and between ethical commitment and the respect of norms. It is not that one ought to oppose the law, one's obligations, or the norms, any more than one ought to change or reformulate them under the double pretext of a bad translation or the changing of course. Nor ought one to back away from them voluntarily. In the effort to fulfill the contract, the pedagogical contract, both morally and legally, distractions will arrive which are often no more than little tremors on the line of the contract, but that little by little dig away at the line to the point that the obligation is inapplicable. The law is suspended and becomes inoperative, without yet compromising the success of the project.

There are at least three ways to look at this. It could be that a contradiction appears between the law and morality. This is the classic case, which we might call the "Antigone complex": one's moral position, faith in a higher order (divine law, for example), or simply being faithful to personal convictions, allow one, under certain forces and circumstances, to maintain one's position right to the very end, even if this means breaking with the law in an illegal act. We could imagine all sorts of academic disobedience that, in the same manner as civil disobedience, might manifest itself in political controversy or open conflict with academic authority, as in the case of instructors with respect to the aims of the school and teaching. Examples might include the wearing of religious symbols within public schools, telling every student that they are performing "excellently" regardless of their performance on exams, the open criticism of the material being taught, and so on.

The second case is more conservative. It consists of what we might call "parliamentary" dissatisfaction – where all legitimate authority is incumbent on the one with the task of legislating – which generally translates as the task of continually adjusting the letter of the law to the obstacles it encounters, such as political changes or changes of course, or court decisions that invalidate the letter of the law. At one point school was optional, while it is obligatory at another. Or again, the constitution might say that by virtue of individual liberties, the ban against wearing skirts that are too short is invalid, let's say, because of a too restrictive definition of the word "short." Thus there is an infinite rewriting of laws with respect to the political plan.

Finally, the case that interests us the most: in a way it is nothing, or almost nothing. It is nothing other than the event of the cut or fracture between faithfulness – my given word – and the law. There isn't the slightest trace of a contradiction between my promise and the obligation that strictly holds me to it. There is no contradiction, but there is a paradox: it's as if the very object of the contract – that which the law also seeks to obtain, albeit through the formal channels of norms, commandments, or obligations – is realized paradoxically in the suspension of the contract. Something, which we are only learning to name, becomes the new instrument of fulfillment that faithfulness and the law have sought to realize together, but which only makes the law inapplicable. Examples of this are still to come since this constitutes the very object of this text. But we didn't simply invent this case either. It comes to us from another tradition, from the readings – few orthodox and completely secular – of the "mystery" of grace within messianic faith. It is a matter proposed by Agamben's reading of Paul's Letter to the Romans, in which Agamben recovers Walter Benjamin's intuition concerning messianic time, that is to say, of the time that remains to transform this world of ours into a Common space. Agamben's reading of Paul's Letter to the Romans is an expression of faith: a conviction, a calling, a hope, without doubt, that the world can become a more just and more respectful space for forms-of-life.

Rarely does it begin otherwise with politics, education, and the arts. We believe in something. What then does free software believe in? Stallman's answer is clear: in cooperation, in the sharing of knowledge, in the defense of source code as a common good, and in liberties that will assure future becoming. But this is but a point of departure. It's an expression still naïve in value and in the conditions of their fulfillment. Without the work of modulation on the still conservative thresholds from which the original ideas are conceived and expressed, without the particular attention to the vapours that inevitably surround all modulated thresholds, and without a faith in the unforeseen, the extraordinary, and the unknown that emerge without warning, as if to break the accord between moral commitment and legal obligation, the expression risks emptying itself of its vitality, of its virtuality. It would have been completely espousing the forms of obligation and thus following the path toward economic success, which is on the margins of this gratuity, this grace that history has given us as a gift: true gratuity, for which *nothing* obliges me.

It is interesting to note that certain authors, including economists and sociologists, contest the appeal to Mauss's paradigm of the gift to explain the logic of sharing within free software (cf. Flichy, 2002). Benveniste (cf. Agamben, 2005) comes to the rescue with a definition of gratuity with which we could believe that it might become the event towards which free software would attempt to show its loyalty. This gratuity is absolute: an absolutely free use, delivered from all obligations, and devoid of all pretensions of capturing rights or reclaiming properties. An immaterial gratuity, barely discernible, virtual, in excess only from the side of what it splits: from the side of faithfulness, as an instrument of the coming community, in order to accomplish what the law never had the means to realize, but which it allows, nevertheless, in becoming inapplicable.

CONCLUSION: ON PEDAGOGY

To what am I faithful as a pedagogue? In what have I chosen to believe? What values have I decided to incorporate? And how does the law, the academic law, the norms of communication, the social pressures that surround the processes of professionalism, how do all of these prove to be in keeping with my beliefs?

I'm fortunate since I'm able to avoid Antigone's dilemma (the violent confrontation between her faith and the law): that to which the law obliges me suits me just fine. I even take some pleasure in handling language skills, in developing citizen responsibility, a critical outlook, and the respect of cultural differences. All is well. I like my profession.

I apply myself, I invent examples (this is already an art worthy of at least another chapter...), and I open doors and passages for the students who discover a rich, complex, and often difficult heritage. I succeed in passing on to them a taste for effort. All is well.

I enter the classroom and we begin. I follow the course schedule to the letter. All is well. But I am on the watch, just like every other day, for a hint that, no matter how small it is, will allow me to open a parenthetical remark and take a step outside, with an example or paradigm. I give my lecture and follow the course schedule, but remain alert and on the watch, just like a cat, for the slightest hint. And it always arrives, in nearly every class: a distraction, a question from "out of left field," a slip of the tongue, anything that opens a parenthesis.

I have now left the textbook, and even left the course schedule behind. I am going in all kinds of directions: personal anecdotes, tangents that have nothing to do with the course material, judgments on governmental decisions, nothing, that is, that is prescribed to me, nothing to which I feel obliged by the profession. The parenthesis stretches. It's clear that I am taking more and more liberties with my professional obligations.

This lasts the whole year. The students have learned a few things and a few even tell me that they would like to follow and delve deeper into the questions that were left in suspense, into many the improvised examples, and into the seemingly trivial anecdotes. In fact they all say the same thing: it was the parenthetical remarks that touched them, and my faith in following and developing them on the margins of the course schedule that, paradoxically, gave them a taste for developing the prescribed skills. But it did so with something "extra," an immaterial excess, something absolutely *gratis*: a taste for creating, and for permanently "modulating" their relations to the world, to knowledge, and to others. In sum, to experiment with the virtual and to learn to become the creators of their lives in the patience of the free use of thought and faith in the Common.

Each time a parenthesis is opened it returns me to my original convictions and I have to laugh a little bit at myself each time because of the naivety that persists in my faith for the same old values that I inherited. But I find reassurance that, on the occasion of each new parenthesis and that with the more and more complex, problematic, and nuanced vapours and virtual layers that emanate from each new modulation, I am taking these old values less and less seriously, given all the good that they do, and the useless work that constituted the effort to rid myself of them, or worse, to change them.

I learn from the rhythm of my students to make the free use of thought in the faith of the Common, to invent concepts. If the creation of concepts is the object of philosophy, and if the creation of percepts and affects is the object of art, and if the creation of functions is the main activity of science, as Deleuze and Guattari (1994) say, we would like to suggest that the parenthesis, as well as the example, constituting a creative act, is the object of pedagogy. Above all we hope to have illustrated this through the long parenthesis (the example could have been used just as well) on free software, since it provides the political terrain where the future of the Internet, as a creative site, is being played out.

Can the Internet become virtual in, specifically, Deleuze's sense of the word? The creative pedagogical act and the political movement of free software clash (*détonnent*) together in a concert of the commercialization of the web, information, education, and culture. But it will take more than a detonator (*détonateur*) to re-engage pedagogy along the same lines as the virtual, particularly when e-learning and the commercialization of informational goods gradually reduces the entire actualised field of creation to that of simple entertainment.

Long live pedagogue-artists!

NOTES

[1] We are using this term in relation to Aristotelian "wonder." We cannot attempt to define philosophy without citing the definition that Aristotle gives in his *Metaphysics* because it is extraordinarily youthful and still corresponds with our own self-image. "It is owing to their wonder," Aristotle writes, "that humans begin to philosophize" (982b12-13). The word he uses is *thaumazein*, which gave us "thaumaturgy," a wonder or miracle worker, which we discover a little bit everywhere in teaching philosophy. For example, see the following page: http://www.grep-mp.org/cycles/moderne-2/philo-gerard.htm. [Trans: With the concept *"machine à détonner,"* Daignault is playing on the Aristotelian concept of wonder (*étonnement*), as well as calling attention to the musical notion of singing out of tune, or outside of tonality (*détonner*), and the notion of explosion and detonation (*détoner*). Deleuze had a passion for atonal music, and the notion of the "machine" is important in his thought. In order to maintain the different registers of Daignault's neologism, I have left it in its original French.]

[2] [Trans: The author's use of the term "parenthesis" in pedagogy refers to those moments in teaching when the lecture or course plan is momentarily suspended and opened up to the unknown and unpredictable. The pedagogical parenthesis is therefore not in one's control, but remains the possibility of learning through tangential and parenthetical remarks.]

[3] "Free software is a matter of the users' freedom to run, copy, distribute, study, change and improve the software." http://www.gnu.org/philosophy/free-sw.html

[4] Jean Beaudrillard (1981, 1996) is certainly a leader of this movement.

[5] Pierre Lévy (1997) has emerged as a dominant figure of this movement.

[6] The translation of this paragraph is from E. R. Albert and has been found on the Web. http://deleuzeatgreenwich.blogspot.com/2007/02/text-for-19th-february-workshop-on.html

[7] We will hereafter refer to virtual reality as VR.

[8] The word 'metaphysics' should not be heard as a synonym for the transcendental, instead it corresponds to the sense that Bergson gives it when he speaks of the "vapours" of the actual. Thus particular metaphysics is the discipline of the virtual.

[9] We turn the reader's attention to the interesting and relevant example of a minute of silence by Mike Batt. "Musician Mike Batt had paid a six-figure sum to settle a bizarre dispute over who owns copyright to a silent musical work. Batt, who had a number of hits in the 70s with UK children's characters The Wombles, was accused of plagiarism by the publishers of the late US composer John Cage, after placing a silent track on his latest album, Classical Graffiti which was credited to himself and Cage. Cage's own silent composition, 4'33", was originally released in 1952." http://news.bbc.co.uk/1/hi/entertainment/music/2276621.stm) .

[10] Richard Stallman is the founder of the Free Software Foundation.

[11] Stallman. [Trans.: English in the original. Daignault is calling attention to two different meanings of "free," which comes across in the terms *"libre"* (as in freedom) and *"gratuit"* (as in zero cost). In order to highlight Daignault's distinction I have opted to use "free" for *"libre"* and "gratis" for *"gratuit"* (and, likewise, "gratuity" for *"gratuité"*). This distinction between 'free' and 'gratis' is used within the discourse surrounding free software.]

[12] http://multitudes.samizdat.net/Globalisation-et-propriete.html

[13] [Trans: The French term *"bien commun"* has at least two meanings that Daignault draws on. One meaning is that of a "common good," namely the philosophical notion of a good that is good for all. The other meaning of "commons" is more specific to the free software movement, namely that of a space that is open and free to all. I have used both "common good" and "commons" where appropriate.]

[14] "Open Source Initiative (OSI) is a non-profit corporation dedicated to managing and promoting the Open Source Definition for the good of the community, specifically through the OSI Certified Open

Source Software certification mark and program.You can read about successful software products that have these properties, and about our certification mark and program, which allow you to be confident that software really is "Open Source." We also make copies of approved open source licences here." http://www.opensource.org

REFERENCES

Agamben, G. (1993). *The coming community* (M. Hardt, Trans.). Minneapolis, MN: University of Minnesota Press.

Agamben, G. (1995). *Moyens sans fins. Notes sur la politique.* Paris : Payot & Rivages.

Agamben, G. (1998). L'immanence absolue. In E. Alliez (Ed.), *Gilles Deleuze. Une vie philosophique* (pp. 165–188). Le Plessis-Robinson: Institut Synthélabo pour le progrès de la connaissance.

Agamben, G. (2002). *What is a paradigm?*. A lecture given at the European Graduate School Faculty. http://www.egs.edu/faculty/agamben/agamben-what-is-a-paradigm-2002.html

Agamben, G. (2005). *The time that remains: A commentary on the letter to the Romans* (P. Dailey, Trans.). Stanford, CA: Stanford University Press.

Baudrillard, J. (1981). *Simulacres et simulation.* Paris: Kawade Shobo Shinsha, coll. "Débats".

Baudrillard, J. (1996). Écran total. *Libération,* 6 mai.

Benkler, Y. (2003, June). The political economy of commons. *Upgrade. The European Journal for the Informatics Professional,* 4(3). http://www.upgrade-cepis.org (http://www.benkler.org/Upgrade-Novatica%20Commons.pdf)

Corasani, A., & Lazzarato, M. (2004). Globalisation et propriété intellectuelle. La fuite par la liberté dans l'invention du logiciel libre. In *Multitudes WEB.* http://multitudes.samizdat.net/Globalisation-et-propriete.html

Deleuze, G. ([1969] 1990). *The logic of sense* (M. Lester, Trans.). New York: Columbia University Press.

Deleuze, G. (1990). Post-scriptum sur les sociétés de contrôle. In G. Deleuze (Ed.), *Pourparlers* (pp. 240–247).

Deleuze, G. ([1966] 1991). *Bergsonism* (H. Tomlinson & B. Habberjam, Trans.). New York: Zone Books.

Deleuze, G. ([1968] 1994). *Difference and repetition* (P. Patton, Trans.). New York: Columbia University Press.

Deleuze G., & Guattari, F. ([1991] 1994). *What is philosophy?* (H. Tomlinson & G. Burchill, Trans.). New York: Columbia University Press.

Deleuze, G. (1996). L'actuel et le virtuel. In G. Deleuze & C. Parnet (Eds.), *Dialogues* (English translation by E. R. Albert). Paris: Flammarion. http://deleuzeatgreenwich.blogspot.com/2007/02/text-for-19th-february-workshop-on.html

Flichy, P. (2002). Les logiciels libres: Un modèle fécond. *Colloque 2001 Bogues.* Montréal: avril. http://www.er.uqam.ca/nobel/gricis/actes/bogues/Flichy.pdf

Himanen, P. (2001). *The hacker ethic and the spirit of the information age.* London: Random House.

Latrive, F. (2004). *Du bon usage de la piraterie.* Paris: Exils.

Lévy, P. (1995). *Qu'est-ce que le virtuel?.* Paris: La Découverte.

Lévy, P. (1997). *Cyberculture.* Rapport au Conseil de l'Europe dans le cadre du projet Nouvelles technologies: Coopération culturelle et communication. Paris: Odile Jacob/Éditions du Conseil de l'Europe.

Murphie, A. (2002). Putting the virtual back into VR. In B. Massumi (Ed.), *A shock to thought. Expression after Deleuze and Guattari* (pp. 188–214). London: Routledge.

Nancy, J.-L. (1998). Pli deleuzien de la pensée. In E. Alliez (Ed.), *Gilles Deleuze. Une vie philosophique* (pp. 115–123). Le Plessis-Robinson: Institut Synthélabo pour le progrès de la connaissance.

Zourabichvilli, F. (1998). Deleuze et le possible (de l'involontarisme en politique). In E. Alliez (Ed.), *Gilles Deleuze. Une vie philosophique* (pp. 335–357). Le Plessis-Robinson: Institut Synthélabo pour le progrès de la connaissance.
http://en.wikipedia.org/wiki/
http://www.gnu.org/philosophy/free-sw.html
http://www.opensource.org/

Jacques Daignault
Département des sciences de l'éducation
UQAR- Campus de Lévis
Quebec, Canada

Translated by Brett Buchanan
Laurentian University
Canada

GARY GENOSKO

5. FÉLIX GUATTARI AND POPULAR PEDAGOGY

INTRODUCTION: THE OURY BROTHERS

While many of us were excitingly entering the workforce for the first time as part-timer labourers in the tertiary sector, Félix Guattari was, already at sixteen years of age, on his way to becoming a militant. He was a child of the Liberation, and all of its "extraordinary wild imaginings," above all those of the youth hostel movement.[1] Radical pedagogue Fernand Oury (1920-1998) was instrumental in getting Guattari involved during the summer "caravans" from one hostel to the next that he organized in the Paris suburb of La Garenne-Colombes for suburban youth like Guattari, who grew up in the same department. Indeed, in his journal Guattari recalls a dream sequence in which there were "two different paths for going out of my house at La Garenne. One was towards Fernand Oury's house."[2] This chapter follows the path upon which Oury set Guattari.

Fernand Oury's influence was decisive for Guattari in both practice and theory. Guattari once remarked that "my presumed competence in this domain [setting up intra-hospital patient clubs at Clinique de Borde in the mid-1950s] was due to the fact that since the age of sixteen I had always been a 'militant' in organizations like the 'Youth Hostels' and a whole range of activities for the extreme left."[3]

The Guattari that we have received is best known for his collaborations: with Deleuze, Negri, Alliez, etc. Guattari's career path led him to take up psychoanalysis after abandoning the study of pharmacy, what he dubbed the "family business."[4] He was trained by Jacques Lacan, with whom he had a stormy relationship, and spent his career at La Borde, a place shrouded in myth and supercharged with as much intellectual caché as terror. In return for freedom to experiment with the institution's organization, Guattari offered, in a confessional mode, "constant fidelity to the local superegoism… ."[5] He also maintained his own practice. Jean Oury – another Lacanian superego - helped Guattari escape from an internship in pharmacy, a path not taken[6]; Fernand initiated Guattari into a militant's life that prepared him for what his brother had in store.

POPULAR PEDAGOGY

The picture of Guattari I want to draw in this chapter owes more to a little known schoolteacher in suburban Paris than the big names of post-68 French thought. Fernand Oury was best known as a key figure in the movement that updated the ideas of Célestin Freinet (1896-1966) for a new era of 'barracks schools' under the name of institutional pedagogy.[7] The new large urban (primary and secondary) schools of the 1960s were far removed from the one or two room, rural schoolhouses with

I. Semetsky (ed.), Nomadic Education: Variations on a Theme by Deleuze and Guattari, 61–76.

small numbers of mixed ages in the primary grades that defined the Freinet movement. Although Fernand's name is closely linked with the birth of the Institutional Pedagogy (IP) movement in the early 1960s, which was a sub-movement – a "recognizable strand"[8] - of Freinet teaching located in Paris, Freinet himself was not comfortable with IP's heavily theoretical discourse grounded in psychoanalysis, the "case studies" method of writing about children, and the creeping professionalization and desire for a pathway of accreditation (an idea alien to Freinet) of the teachers involved. In fact, the IP introduced an entirely new element into Freinet culture: academic research in education studies now had a role to play in Freinet activity.[9] Freinet's failed attempt to influence activities in the Paris group's journal (*L'Éducateur de l'Ille-de-France*) from his location outside of Cannes in the south of France led to the IP's expulsion from the Parisian Freinet group, the Institut Parisien de l'École Moderne.

Oury was not the only educator who influenced Guattari. Fernand Deligny (1913-1996) worked with psycho-socially marginal children, offering them an alternative to hospitalization. He also circa 1948 created a 'caravan' known as La Grande Cordée, "a network of lodgings for delinquents, pre-delinquents, and emotionally challenged children with the assistance of the Youth Hostels. Children impermeable to psychiatric treatment were welcomed by 'normal' adults."[10] Later, Jean Oury and Guattari invited him to bring the small group of children in his care to La Borde, where his film Le Moindre Geste was shot by Jean-Pierre Daniel in 1966.

Before Guattari coined the term schizo-analysis to describe his brand of psychotherapy, he worked under the rubric of what was known as Institutional Psychotherapy, that is, analysis undertaken by foregrounding the institutional context itself as a mediating object in collective life. This approach actively deconstructed the dyad of analyst-analysand and the familialism that perfused even the most avant-garde practices of psychoanalysis. Guattari focused on how an institution contributed to the creation of certain kinds of subjectivity; likewise, for educators working within the Freinet-inspired IP, the focus was on how the school itself created certain kinds of learning disabilities in its pupils. The organization, artifacts, fields of reference, and group life of an institution emerging through its collective self-invention was not empirical sociology or organization studies because the model was the psychoanalytic part object that was irreducible to its objective description. The "institutional object" could be known only through an analysis of a group's desire as it participated in and negotiated its creation. This gave to groups the ability to occupy the creative spaces of an institution and contribute to its ongoing elaboration in a kind of sculptural process. This would have been extremely difficult in a 'barracks' school with large numbers of children managed only through quasi-military routine. Institutional Pedagogy and Psychotherapy were grappling with very similar problems around how institutional objects were received, that is, introjected, by their denizens.

Guattari was learning the ropes of institutional experimentation in the course of his training as a young militant, first visiting Jean Oury at the small psychiatric clinic Saumery in the early 1950s. It was not until he joined La Borde a few years later and developed "the grid" – literally the tabular representation upon which the evolving schedule of work rotation in which everyone participated was inscribed - that he developed a portfolio of practices for gaining access to the ways in which complex institutional interrelations affected the psychical economies of actual groups. Guattari set about experimenting with ways to heighten and maximize an institution's "therapeutic coefficient" by unfixing rigid roles, thawing frozen hierarchies, opening hitherto closed blinkers, and modifying the introjection of the local superegoisms and objects. This role redefinition and displacement of fixed, hierarchical power relations and identities was scrambled micropolitically in a way that interrupted fantasies that would have otherwise bewitched the institution's denizens by trapping them in inflexible strata of authority and routines without any justification but their own continuation.

Jean and Fernand had been active in the IP and had therefore a working knowledge of the battery of Freinet techniques. Fernand had been a member of the Freinet movement since the late 1940s. Jean borrowed Freinet techniques and adapted them to new forms of group work at Saumery and then La Borde.[11] In a sense, then, Guattari was absorbing from the Oury brothers lessons in modified Freinet practices.

The notion that youth hostels could be lumped together with other far left experiments is hard to reconcile with the broad internationalist strokes of the hostelling movement. France was one of the original signatories to the establishment of the International Youth Hostel Association in 1932. Hostelling is a German creation dating from the early 20th century and catering to the country wanderer burdened only by a rucksack, with a foundation in educational experimentation – the elementary school hostel set up in Altena by Richard Schirrmann, widely considered as the founder of the Youth Hostel Movement, in 1909. While the politics of the IYHA may be appreciated through its actions over a number of decades – its successful resistance to National Socialist attempts to dominate the organization in the 1930s and, later, its steadfast refusal to permit South Africa membership and outright rejection of its proposed 'white' and 'black' hostel networks - the movement is centrist in its internationalism and valorization of youth travel, preferably in the country and on foot, and exposure to folk cultures in general. All the values of self-reliance and the benefits of fresh air and physical activity are found there, together with any number of restrictions (age limits for hostel use, division of the sexes in the dormitories, house parents, etc.). Organizationally, youth hostels are by-and-large voluntary bodies in the non-profit, NGO sector, organized around national councils with main executive bodies that conform to the basic standards set by the IYHA. Many national youth hostel organizations have direct connections with ministries of education and serve, in the manner of Schirrmann, as accommodation for traveling classes, a kind of "roaming school" or "school country house."[12]This is what Guattari suggests by the 'caravans' organized by Oury out of La Garenne, which used both schools and hostels as accommodation for roaming groups of schoolchildren during vacation periods. But what is the relationship between hostelling, far left militancy and popular pedagogy? What is the link between the youth hostels and Oury's Institutional Pedagogy and how did they contribute to Guattari's training as a young militant and influence his subsequent experiments with transdisciplinary groups?

THE FRENCH ANOMALY IN YOUTH HOSTELLING

In the history of the youth hostel movement, France is an anomaly. Although it was not uncommon for national associations to be divided and sub-divided along regional-territorial lines, in France competing associations emerged that were fractured along political and religious lines. This was a unique challenge for the IYHA. The original signatory for France was the Catholic wing of the movement, the Ligue Française pour les Auberges de la Jeunesse, long associated with the name of Marc Sangnier (1873-1950) and for its pacifist politics, not to mention conservative attitudes toward sexuality.[13] The first French youth hostel was established in Sangnier's country home in Bierville, south of Paris, and opened its doors in 1930.

In 1934 another French hostelling organization appeared, the Centre Laique des Auberges de la Jeunesse (CLAJ). According to one historian: "it drew on the latent anti-clericalism in French educational circles and gave political allegiance to the Popular Front Government; it emphasized the need for the young hostel-users to take a part in constructing and controlling their youth hostels, and large numbers of hostels sprang up all over the country like mushrooms… . Every group of hostel-users established its own journal which discussed in serious terms the mystique of youth-hostelling – the liberation of youth from the 'stuffy' tradition of the older generation. The movement could boast its own poet (the Provençal writer, Jean Giono) and its own collection of songs (Marie-Rose Clouzot's *La clé des chants*)."[14] There are several important points here that allow us to situate Guattari and Oury in this lay hostelling tradition. The first is the emphasis placed on the socialist politics of the Léon Blum's Popular Front (Front Populaire), which had come into power in 1936 behind a left unified in the face of the threat of fascism. The Front's emphasis on cultural enrichment through leisure, and the secularization of education, gave impetus to the formation of many new organizations, but most importantly provided funding for many existing organizations including the Centre Laique and the Ligue. Leo Lagrange was the minister in charge of the Ministry of Leisure at the time and he later assumed the presidency of the CLAJ.[15] The lay hostels multiplied faster than those of the Ligue largely because of government policies that saw in them places where workers, who for the first time enjoyed paid holidays, could vacation. A mythic status has accrued to the 'Communist' summer camps for children, *the colonies de vacances*, and the body that was charged with training its leaders (Centres d'Éntrainement aux Méthodes d'Éducation Active). Followers of Freinet were members of this body and Freinet's own school, which had room for boarders, participated in this scheme. At the time the government supported a wide-range of programs geared toward youth organizations. Under the Popular Front hostels, schools and other facilities became points of intersection for popular education, new opportunities for leisure, and the valorization of youth travel, and consensual political ideology machines within civil society. This enthusiasm was rekindled in the post-war years. Just as significant was the character of self-organization attributed to the hostels within the Centre Laïque, which underlined self-reliance through worker's control. This extended to the actual construction of the facilities, thus regaining the original mandate of cooperative labour that animated the hostelling spirit and which accelerated in the post-war years in the face of the considerable task of rebuilding and repair. It may be added that some of the remote hostels in unoccupied France during the war became "centres of resistance."[16]

However, it is the central role given to a self-produced collective publication that cements the relationship between Guattari, Oury, the youth hostels and institutional analysis. A key feature of Oury's Freinet-inspired pedagogy was the self-produced school journal and the collective responsibility assumed for its editing and distribution. While many national youth hostel associations had their own periodicals, including in France the Ligue's *Information et documentation*, these were not constitutive of the institution and stood apart from the project of its permanent reinvention. While many of these journals had so-called "romantic names such *as Au devant de la vie, Route joyeuse, Viens avec nous* and *l'Aube se lève*,"[17] publishing was not an activity separable from a hostel group's self-management. It constituted a key piece of institutional matter.

The IYHA would have preferred that the French organizations voluntarily merge into a single national body – a matter decided artificially during war under the occupation government in France. The international body encouraged this end by denying a splinter group from the Centre Laique separate membership rights in the postwar years (1947-48), after a third group, the Union Française, had joined the Ligue in 1947 as the Fondation Française des Auberges de la Jeunesse (FFAJ). The 'lay' movement had suffered its own split as the Movement Laïque (MLAJ) set its own course.[18] It was not until 1955 that unity was achieved in France in the form of a Fédération Unie des Auberges de la Jeunesse.

INSTITUTIONS IN QUESTION

Fernand's Institutional Pedagogy paralleled Jean's and Guattari's efforts at La Borde in the milieu of Institutional Psychotherapy. What both approaches appreciated was that the institutional context itself had to be analyzed. To this end, around 1960, a diverse group of therapists and educators gathered around the Ourys to discuss the problems of institutions, their production, and modification through creative organizational solutions, etc., under the name of the Work Group on Institutional Psychology and Sociology [*Groupe de travail de psychologie et de sociologie institutionnelles*, GTPSI]. Groups of this sort proliferated: in 1965 the Federation of Study Groups and Institutional Researchers [*Fédération des groupes d'études et de recherches institutionnelles*, FGERI] was founded and, later, in 1968, FGERI would develop sub-groups such as CERFI, Centre for Study and Research into Institutional Functioning [*Centre d'études de recherches sur le fonctionnement des institutions*], which published the journal *Recherches*, organ of institutional psychotherapy that Guattari directed. The followers of Freinet aligned with Fernand organized the Group for Therepeutic Education based in Nantes [Groupe d'éducation thérapeutiques, GET], which participated in FGERI, and found themselves in the company of psychiatrists, anti-psychiatrists, philosophers, architects, urbanists, activists … . Jean Oury brought to GET psychoanalytic models like the idea of writing case studies about specific students in the context of their class.[19] The Federation of Study Groups was nothing less than a transdisciplinary experimental research assemblage that Guattari described as a "*detour* through other disciplines that allowed false problems to be overcome (relative to functions of space: volumes, levels, communications, and the institutional and micro-political options of instigators and participants)."[20] The confluence of militancy and transdisciplinary experimentation had the goal of creating scenes of subjectification - and this was how Guattari characterized F. Oury's efforts - that overcame the "encasernée scolaire" (school-as-barracks) subjectivity, for an appreciation of collectivity sensitive to heterogeneous components as well as local conditions that would be otherwise steamrolled if one arrived with prefabricated interpretive grids."[21]

I want to emphasize the critique of the institution in the pedagogical context taken up by F. Oury and his colleagues in the Freinet movement. This perspective will help to explain some of the basic principles and influence of institutional psychotherapy and acknowledge Guattari's ongoing interest in the Group for Therapeutic Education, especially the role played by the importance given to singularization, a self-organizing process involving the constitution of an assemblage of components (intrinsic references), relations with other assemblages, and the analysis of their effects on subjectivity. For Guattari, this was "constitutive of finitude and authenticity."

The principles and program outlined in Oury's the classic co-authored statement on institutional pedagogy *Towards an Institutional Pedgagogy* (*Vers une pédagogie institutionnelle*, with Aïda Vasquez)), picks up on themes vital to Guattari's concept of the group. Oury and co-author Aïda Vasquez emphasized the act of writing as an individual and collective project that not only allowed for the expression of meaning and character by individuals, but realized success in communication, that is, being read or heard by one or more others (classmates, parents, correspondents beyond the school itself), like a subject group that speaks and is heard.

For Guattari the subject was a group or collective assemblage of heterogeneous components whose formation, de-linked from monadic individuality and seemingly bottomless interiority, not to mention abstract, universal determinations like Oedipus, could be seen through critical analyses of the actual vicissitudes of collective life in which persons found themselves. Guattari favoured a Sartrean-inflected theory of groups, distinguishing non-absolutely between subject (actively exploring self-defined projects) and subjugated groups (passively receiving directions), each affecting the relations of their members to social processes and shaping their potential for subjectification.

Pedagogical scenarios of subjectification were organized that guaranteed the certainty of writing in order to be read through the circulation of published, reproduced texts. The pillars of this process were the individual and collective school journal, inter-school communication and exchange of school journals, and the school printery. Correspondence was established between individuals, between individuals and groups (entailing reading before the class, but only from those sections of one's personal "free text," in the language of Freinet, that would interest the group, and upon which they would pass a certain kind of judgement, making corrections, suggestions, editing, toward its inclusion in a collective publication), and geographically diverse school groups exchanged collectively written manuscripts (refocusing attention on otherwise overlooked everyday situations that would appear unique to other readers). For Oury, the "school journal [composed of free texts] is a privileged technique"[22] in the constitution of a third object (that is never just a thing but always more than merely an object) that opens the students to multiple networks, breaking down the rigid teacher-student dyad in which the former superior *teaches* the latter inferior. Oury echoes a great chain of psychoanalytic objects - part[ial], transitional, institutional, *objet a* - that would become less and less typical (representational and/or non-significantizable) and progressively singular, that is incomparable, with this third object of the published text and other mediators. These third objects are held in common by a given group and focus the attention of its members. This Gutenbergian realization of the collective around the school printery and collectively 'perfected' (not corrected) text in the real work of cooperative production may sound today somewhat narrow in the age of networked virtual communities and real time blogging, but the machinic dimension of the mediating third term remains intact since it opens the class to the world as relations between class and community serve pedagogically as a focal point for lessons about grammar, reading, and writing. This theorization of basic operating principles along psychoanalytic lines is beyond the concrete, classroom focused thought of Freinet himself. Suffice to say that Freinet found the heavily psychoanalytic language of some of his Parisian followers to be alienating. Yet Freinet introduced at the material level mediating objects like the school journal, printery, and cooperative counsel that proved influential and indispensable for the Ourys. As F. Oury relates:

> The introduction of a *mediation* between therapist andpatient is, at least in the first instance, the necessary condition of the cure. It is the characteristic, if one can schematize it in the extreme,of institutional therapy. Apparently mediations may be objects (tools or goals) or persons, or institutions, but these alwaysprove to be more than objects or persons. At the Congressof 1957 Freinet said that a statue should be erected to the little printing press and not to him.[23]

The printing press is not a technofetish; its introduction into a school situation is not original with Freinet. What is original is its role as a mediation, a trans-versalizing space in which materially hierarchy is restructured, responsibilities are assigned and assumed, functions and transformations of those functions are managed, and existing institutional structures at all levels from the classroom through the school to the board, are called into question. Moroever, the printery is but one of many mediations, adequate to the specificities of the situation, by Freinet and his followers. Let's now look more closely at the school printery.

THE SCHOOL PRINTERY

Freinet was a great believer in trial and error learning and the École Freinet (the first of which opened in 1935 in Vence, France) was a school without lessons in which language (writing and reading) was acquired naturally but non-passively through technological mediations. The use of technologies of reproduction was at the heart of what Freinet called *L'imprimerie à l'école* – the school printery – also the name of the journal he began publishing in 1926. A few years later he added subtitles: cinema, radio, phonograph, etc. The Freinet School had one room devoted to a print shop housing then current technologies of engraving (linoleum and wood), movable type, and/or stencil and hand-turned Gestetner drum. Freinet had, in fact, designed a small press for school usage and marketed it to fellow travelers. Technology was put in the service of the school's communitarian life and was the means by which students made it their own school. Freinet and later Guattari thought that technology could be flush with molecular revolutionary activity, that real struggles were being staged by the deployment of a printing press towards the production of a newspaper as a source for lessons as opposed to the importation of a state-sanctioned reader, and a soldering gun, in the case of homemade pirate radios. In other words, the subjectivity of the militant makes the connection between technical and political choice.

As Oury notes above collective autocritique was embedded in the process of creating school journals for inter-school correspondence within and beyond France, as these were assembled from otherwise free texts created by individuals as they passed from drawing into language. The only school books were those created in the printery. For all of his focus on mechanical reproduction, Freinet refused to see the printing press as a "panacea." It constituted a "technique of free and creative work" and not a method.[24] Freinet's originality was not in selecting the use of printing, or even in emphasizing the production of a "free text," but in embedding these in an egalitarian and democratic atmosphere that began very simply with the removal of the teacher's raised platform and the refusal of a standard school reader.

A good deal rested upon this technique, however, for it was in mechanical reproduction that reading and writing both found for Freinet their justification and motivation (not the creation of interest as such but the deepening of interest). For schoolchildren there was something magical about them and he wrote of the "eternal enchantment, a permanent magic, which fires all the possibilities of expression, doubling the reach of new communications which totally integrates the scholarly effort into the complex process of contemporary life."[25] Beginning with the fixing of expression in drawings and the wonderment of their perfect reproduction as stencils in black and white (with the option for hand-colouring) or in colour,[26] Freinet observed the excitement and empowerment of young author-artists as they created their own books by adding new drawings daily as well as integrating works by their fellows. Some copies were sent to parents, while others made their way into the school journal, which was sent by post to other schools in exchange for their collectively produced journals. These kinds of activities were for Freinet "efficacious stimulants of the child's desire to create, possess and communicate a work which is their own."[27] These books are form and content: at first, letters to corresponding schools were "written by the teacher as dictated by the children, recopied by them, and all this will lead the students toward the well-founded practice of writing independently of drawing."[28] Copying gives way to independent writing: "the miracle occurs: the cycle is resolved: the manuscript text that the child perfectly understands in its role of expression, is composed and then printed. It is now, black on white, a majestic page that has been illustrated and added to the book of life."[29]

COOPERATIVE COUNCIL

Oury picked up Freinet's emphasis on democratic organization in the classroom through the weekly event called the *conseil de cooperative*, the cooperative council directed by the students themselves. It is adapted from Freinet's plan for a weekly meeting of the *cooperative scolaire*, the highlight of which was the reading and discussion of the mural journal containing under three columns - Criticisms/Congratulations/Requests - the week's record of non-anonymous student feedback.[30] This is far from the anodyne feedback or solicited comments popular in many schools under the cover of anonymity (the 'suggestion box') and discretionary bureaucratic responses. Each issue is discussed; positions are explained, defenses are mounted, students are reassigned to different tasks, when necessary: "Nothing is as moral and as profitable as this common examination at once critical and constructive, of the life of the class."[31]

In Oury's work with Vasquez, an institution is defined by "the places, moments, status of each according to his/her level of performance, that is to say according to his/her potentialities, the functions (services, posts, responsibilities), roles (president, secretary), diverse meetings (team captains, different levels of classes, etc.), and the rituals that maintain their efficacity … ."[32] An institution is, then, composed of these activities; these are its matters, not all of which leave behind well-formed, archivable substances. In the meeting the teacher is one among many participants and, although s/he may at times veto motions, the class remains active as a self-directed group, like Guattari's sense of a subject group that formulates its own projects, speaks and is heard, and puts itself at risk in pursuing its own ends and taking responsibility for them; indeed, the council is sometimes silent, faced with tumult, until it finds language. No one knows precisely how or where it will find it, just as in at La Borde the emergence of local jargon derived from the laundry and which Jean Oury dubbed "lingistique' (lingerie/li[n]guistique).[33] There is always a risk of disappearing, or simply being ignored, in both cases where young students and psychiatric patients are concerned, upon their insertion into the broad socio-economic-politico fields of normal child/adulthood. The *conseil* was for Oury the eyes of the group (witness of each persons' transgressions, successes...), its brain, as well, and heart, a refining machine: it is the "keystone of the system since this meeting has the power to create new institutions, and institutionalize the milieu of communal life."[34] In short, it helped to produce the institutional matter which could either be formed into semiotically well-defined substances or sidestep substance altogether by an a-signifying connection between form and matter that did not have a meaning effect (signified). The artifacts of this process of giving form to institutional matter are quite few since this semiosic articulation bypasses substance, if by this is meant concrete remainders. Much of effort to bring form flush with matter remained on the cutting room floor or unrecorded in the minutes of the school council, as it were, because it did not accede to semiologically well-formed substance.

The *conseil* is the pedagogical equivalent, on the organization level, of the collective bodies of *grilleurs* and *grilleuses* that arose as monitors of the work rotation schedules; a vehicle, then, of autocritique following from autoinvention, with all of its shocks, especially in our era of privacy when it would be unthinkable for patients' dossiers to be open for discussion as they were at La Borde.[35] The system put into place had to safeguard against favouritism (parachuting people into certain positions), remain sensitive and adaptable to emerging resistances, implosions, and exploitations (i.e., the fear of staff hired to work in the kitchen to take on healing tasks), allow for the segmentation of tasks, always complexifying itself along the way. The seductions of authoritarianism were always present for doctor or teacher.

PSYCHOANALYSIS IN/OF CONTEXT

The mediating third object is a fundamental principle of the institutional situation, following upon a critique of the dual therapeutic situation of psychoanalysis and the alleged neutrality of analysts. The red psychiatrist François Tosquelles, who had trained Jean Oury in the late 1940s, looked beyond the dual analysis at the openings provided by "multiple impersonal networks of the symbolic order ... [toward] a form of group therapeutics that is often established, with the doctor's knowledge, in psychiatric hospitals as a result of the material organization and the psycho-social interactions between patients and between patients and doctors."[36] For Oury, "the introduction between the therapist and the patient of a *mediation* is the necessary condition for the cure at least at the outset, and is also the characteristic, if one can schematize it in the extreme, of institutional therapy. The mediation may be apparently an object (tool or aim) or a person or an institution that always proves to be more than an object or person."[37] Such mediations may take diverse forms and, in the pedagogical milieu, the school journal, published by the class, a collective assemblage of enunciation, together with the *conseil*, is an organizational institution created, reinvented and maintained by the group over time. A mediating third object exists outside of one-on-one contact, and upon which work is done cooperatively, and for which responsibility is collectively assumed, through a series of obligatory exchanges (one speaks of the journal, apropos of a resolution, within a meeting defined by rules of order, etc).

Less psychoanalytically, institutional experimentation in the tradition of Freinet is based on the principle of "education by work." Freinet's conception of work is arrived at through his deconstruction before the letter of the work/play distinction. He writes work-play together to indicate his idea that it is not manual work at issue, but a material and intelligent activity imbued with the spirit of integration. It is not imitative like playing at working. He did not deny that "education by work" had "potential for an ulterior social production, but he put the emphasis on the excitement it generated for the children without producing in the end "a product directly useful to society."[38] Guattari often had to defend himself against the claim that he was offering at La Borde a series of fixed tasks, a form of social adaptation though labour.[39] Likewise for Freinet work-play was neither a species of technical apprentissage nor a corrective of some kind. These interpretations would give "prematurely a goal too directly utilitarian to childlike activity."[40] By the same token, work-play mixed joy with fatigue; timidity and surprise in a collective mode that organized the child's school world and did not permit a catastrophic distillation of play from work. Freinet refused to accept the separation, a "social duality" typical of his time, between intellectual and active manual work within the school's physical layout, the latter functioning as an annex.[41] Here, again, is a mediating third figure, the work-play of the school printery as deterritorializing the hard and fast dualism of its definition as either training in a profession (work) or art technique (play). It is a question, then, of giving a greater amplitude to the interactions of teachers and students. The dual-protagonist model no longer sufficed and was for all those involved in the institutional movement, extremely limited.

Students within the Freinet tradition are encouraged to become subject-groups actively exploring self-defined projects, as opposed to subjugated groups passively receiving directions and living a kind of empty seriality; each kind of group affects the relations of their members to social processes, shaping their potential for subject formation, the amount of risk they can tolerate, and how they can use such groups. The modification of alienating fantasies of inferiority and failure, of stripping away the armor that many wore against encounters with otherness, would encourage creativity with imperfection. This was not an exercise in remodelling subjectivities but, rather, in producing new forms of subjectivity through restless, almost baroque micro-sociological variations. A key medium for this dynamic refashioning is, as we have seen from the example of the youth hostels forward, the collectively produced journal embedded in "the institutional matter engendered throughout the tangle of workshops and meetings, as well as in daily life in the dining rooms and bedrooms, in sports, games and cultural life"[42] ; to which may be added, in the common rooms of hostels; and in the undertakings of the cooperative council. Guattari did not believe that the grid at La Borde was generalizable – "no single model being materially transposable in this way."[43] Still, the youth hostels and Institutional Pedagogy of Fernand Oury as well as the Institutional Psychotherapy undertaken at La Borde involved complementary forms of transversal experimentation.

Transversality "tends to be realized when communication is maximized between different levels and above all in different directions. It is the object toward which a subject-group moves. Our hypothesis is this: it is possible to modify the different coefficients of unconscious transversality at different levels of an institution."[44] In order for groups of students to realize their potential for transversality, they need to escape from the ghetto of passively receiving the experience and meaning of school; they are separated and largely segregated from this by layers of static administration and preformed semiotics (books, uniforms, gestures, etc). As a group, school children normally have little real power. Their transversality would remain latent to the extent that its institutional effects would be extremely limited by the lack of opportunities for manifesting it. In order to modify this situation, popular pedagogy reorganized the educational institution and redefined it through permanent reinvention by means of collective creation (in which the source of a group's unity has been internalized and shared as a common property) from the material to the cognitive level, bringing together roles and responsibilities hitherto held apart. A privileged institutional matter for the student's creation of their school experience was the school journal. This kind of collective publishing has been a constant in Guattari's life from the hostels through the journal *Recherches* by FGERI and then CERFI. It is important to observe the influence of the Freinet *journal scolaire* – the school magazine consisting of perfected free texts – on Guattari and also acknowledge how it differs from the school newspaper or yearbook, or even the militant broadsheet under the yoke of one or more editors (or meddling teachers). The collectively produced journal is a transversal tool used in subjectivity-production by a radicalized institution. Such a journal contributes to the collective creation of institutional matter and is not merely a product engendered by an institution (and into which it inserts participants); rather, the institution is in part a product of a journal's collective elaboration and refinement over time, including everything that befalls a project of this kind, even the plight of serial repetition as the production of the next issue or version handcuffs an editorial group with a penchant to rest on its laurels and nurture its transversality with opportunities for entropy – since it might really enjoy what it cannot get done! Freinet underlined the success of the school magazine/journal/periodical strategy by pointing to numerous international examples – in Europe and Mexico and South America.[45]

These reflections on collective autoproduction and the formation of institutional matter which give to artifacts of semiological substance such as journals a central role move in the direction of an interpretive strategy that sees in journal runs and editorial assemblages resources for the investigation of the processes of institutionalization. The journal-artifact is the key feature of the institutional matter engendered through editorial and other activities; indeed, not all the wide-ranging desiring productions, fantasies, positionings vis-à-vis a field into which a collective wants either to insert itself or whose main markers it wants to elude through creative transversal crossings, find such substantial formedness. However, perhaps simply because they survive as concrete resources, such publications are indispensable.

THE ROLE OF THE DAILY TIMETABLE

Historians of the Freinet Movement place much emphasis on its concern with classroom organization and scheduling, especially the daily timetable. Briefly, the day begins with the composition of a "free text" by each student, at the level of one's ability; this text is read aloud, and one is selected by vote, written on the board, and edited ("perfected"); after a short break class reconvenes for lessons required by the ministry, but which are delivered using the "free text" in conjunction with the information cards held in the school's "library" (fichier documentaire) consisting of essentially clippings and pedagogical materials produced by Freinet covering lessons on a variety of subjects; a vegetarian lunch (although students from the local area would go home for lunch) was followed by the printing process, each of several groups cycling in and out of the printshop from other activities such as listening to records or making handicrafts; a formal lesson was presented by means of either readings drawn from the card collection or from a text received from another school; after the short afternoon break the day ended with the so-called "stop-gap" – whatever else needed to be covered. The daily schedule was embedded in individual plans of work-play using the cards, the weekly cooperative meeting, and a variety of collective activities (gardening, crafts) as well as the need to cover certain subjects.[46] Here we see how democratic goals and rigorous scheduling of work and the rotation of activities dovetail in "the grid" adopted at La Borde; further, it is also evident how regular collective events provide a mechanism for feedback and the means for rebalancing the schedule. Guattari learned his Freinet scheduling from both Fernand and Jean Oury. Guattari described "the grid" as a double-entry table[47] for the management of time and task in daily, weekly, monthly, and even longer parameters, as well as on a rotating basis. "The grid" is first and foremost an instrument (evolving and increasingly sophisticated) for the management of personnel. The meaning of "militancy" in this context is far from the romance of revolution, and even agitation must take a back seat to manage skills. But this is no compromise: it is the very texture of the lessons about organization that Guattari learned in extra-curricular youth activities in the hostels movement and from Institutional Pedagogy. All followers of Freinet were, after all, known as "militants Freinet." And many self-styled militants were expelled from the Freinet movement because they sought to professionalize themselves and adopt the current trends of eduspeak!

CONCLUDING REMARKS

We can appreciate, then, the remarkable coherence in the transversalization of institutional life that runs from Freinet, the great organizer, through the Oury brothers to Guattari, as well as the constancy of tools like journal publishing from the school printery to *Recherches*. The key touchpoint is popular pedagogy and the collective autoproduction by various groups of institutional matter through publishing projects. This is not a traditional philosophical universe of reference. Just as Freinet democratized the classroom by rewriting the teacher-students relationship, Guattari desegregated the medical-non-medical personnel relation and rewrote existing doctor-patient scenarios. Institutional militants from Freinet to Guattari have forged transversal social tools for the communication and articulation of individual and collective affects through the creation of institutional matters. Such tools and their supporting techniques are the privileged means of recomposing the components of subjectivity so that new kinds of responsibility can be taken, ways of seeing and living may be favorably achieved, and ensure that constructive, anguish-free institutional matters are engendered.

NOTES

1 Guattari, Psychanalyse et transversalité, p. 154.

2 Guattari, The Anti-Oedipus Papers, New York: Semiotext(e), 2006, p. 303.

3 Guattari, "La Borde: A Clinic Unlike Any Other," in Chaosophy, New York: Semiotext(e), 1995, p. 189.

4 Anti-Oedipus Papers, p. 307.

5 Ibid., p.307.

6 Jean Oury, "Une dialectique de l'amitié," Le Monde (1 sept. 1992): 11. "He [Guattari] began studying pharmacy. That did not please him at all … I encouraged him not to continue."

7 See Tom De Coster, et al, " Emancipating a Neo-Liberal Society? Initial Thoughts on the Progressive Pedagogical Heritage in Flanders Since the 1960s," Education Research and Perspectives 31/2 (2004): 156-75.

8 Nicholas Beattie, The Freinet Movements of France, Italy, and Germany, 1920-2000. Mellen Studies in Eduation, vol. 74, Lewiston: The Edwin Mellen Press, 2002, p. 229.

9 Ibid., 232.

10 Catherine Bédarida, "Disparitions: Fernand Deligny – Un éducateur et un écrivain au service des enfants 'anormaux'," Le Monde (21 sept 1996).

11 Nicholas Beattie makes this point but limits Jean Oury's adaptation of Freinet techniques like the school printery to "work as a therapeutic tool," which is incorrect. See The Freinet Movements, p. 228.

12 Piet Kimzeke, "The Educational Function of the Youth Hostel," in The International Youth Hostel Manual, Graham Heath (ed.), 2nd Edition, Copenhagen: IYHA, 1967, p. 97.

13 Anton Grassl and Graham Heath, The Magic Triangle: A Short History of the World Youth Hostel Movement, Bielefeld, Germany: International Youth Hostel Federation, 1982, p. 47.

14 Graham Heath, "The Growth of the Youth Hostel Movement," in International Youth Hostel Manual, p. 19.

15 Grassl and Heath, Magic Triangle, p. 58.

16 Grassl and Heath, p. 85.

17 Grassl and Heath, p. 58.

18 Grassl and Heath, p. 105.

19 Jean Oury, "Finalités conscientes et inconscientes des institutions," in Onze heures du soir à La Borde: Essais sur la psychothérapie institutionnelle, Paris: Galiée, 1980, p. 259.

20 FFG ET09-26, pp. 135-6.

21 FFG I02-22, pp. 6-7.

21 FFG I02-22, p. 15.

22 Aida Vasquez and Fernand Oury, Vers une pédagogie institutionnelle, Paris: François Maspero, 1968, pp. 43 and 200.

23 Vasquez and Oury, Vers une pédagogie institutionnelle, p. 243.

24 Célestin Freinet, La méthode naturelle. 1. L'apprentissage de la langue, Neuchatel and Paris: Delachaux et Niestlé, 1968, p. 146.

25 Freinet, "L'éducation du travail," in Oeuvres Pédagogiques, Tome 1. Paris: Éditions du Seuil, 1994, p. 309.

26 Freinet, La méthode naturelle, p. 122.

27 Ibid., p.122.

28 Ibid., p. 123.

29 Ibid., p. 124.

30 Freinet, "L'École moderne Française," in Oeuvres pédagogiques, Tome 2, Paris: Éditions du Seuil, 1994, p. 59.

31 Ibid., p. 60.

32 Vasquez and Oury, p. 82.

33 FFG ET04-13: 6.

34 Vasquez and Oury, p. 82.

35 ET04-13 p. 9.

36 Vasquez and Oury, p. 242.

37 Ibid., p. 243.

38 Freinet, "L'Éducation du travail," pps.252-53.

39 ET 04-13: 3

40 Freinet, "LÉducation du travail," p. 252.

41 Freinet, "L'Ecole moderne Française," p.47.

42 Guattari, "La Borde: A Clinic Unlike any Other," in Chaosophy, p. 193

43 Ibid., p. 194.

44 Guattari, Psychanalyse et transversalité, p. 80.

45 See Freinet, "Rapid Growth of School Magazines in Various Parts of the World," in Cooperative Learning and Social Change: Selected Writings of Célestin Freinet, ed. and trans. David Clandfield and John Sivell, Toronto: OISE Publishing, 1990, pp. 34-5.

46 The schedule is presented by Beattie, Freinet Movements, pp.22-31.

47 Guattari, "La Borde: A Clinic Unlike Any Other," p. 190.

REFERENCES

Beattie, N. (2002). The Freinet movement of France, Italy, and Germany, 1920–2000. In *Mellen studies in education* (Vol. 74). Lewiston: The Edwin Mellen Press.

Bédarida, F. (1996, September 21). *Disparitions: Fernand Deligny – Un éducateur et un écrivain au service des enfants 'anormaux'*. Le Monde.

Clandfield, D., Sivell, J. (Eds.). (1990). *Co-operative learning and social change: Selected writings of C. Freinet*. Toronto: Our Schools/OurSelves and OISE Publishing.

De Coster, T., et al. (2004). Emancipating a neo-liberal society? Initial thoughts on the progressive pedagogical heritage in Flanders since the 1960s. *Education Research and Perspectives, 31*(2), 156–175.

Freinet, C. (1994). *Oeuvres pédagogiques, Tomes I&II*. Paris: Editions du Seuil.

Freinet, C. (1968). *La method naturelle 1. L'apprentissage de la langue*. Neuchatel: Delachaux & Niestlé.

Grassl, A., & Heath, G. (1982). *The magic triangle: A short history of the world youth hostel movement*. Bielefeld, Germany: International Youth Hostel Federation.

Guattari, F. (2006). *The anti-oedipus papers* (S. Nadaud, Ed. & K. Gotman, Trans.). New York: Semiotext(e).

Guattari, F. (1995). La Borde: A clinic unlike any other. In S. Lotringer (Ed.), *Chaosophy*. New York: Semiotext(e).

Guattari, F. (1987, January 29). *La grille* (ET04-13). Paris: Fonds F. Guattari, IMEC.

Guattari, F. (1985, November 23). *Du Zen aux galeries lafayette*. Interview with Jackie Beillerot (102-22). Paris: FFG, IMEC.

Guattari, F. (1983). *Molecular revolution*. Harmondsworth: Penguin.

Guattari, F. (1980). *L'intervention institutionnelle*. Typescript of an interview (ET09-26). Paris: FFG, IMEC.

Guattari, F. (1972). *Psychanalyse et transversalité*. Paris: Maspero.

Heath, G. (Ed.). (1967). *International youth hostel manual* (2nd ed.). Copenhagen: IYH Federation.

Oury, J. (1992, September 1). *Une dialectique de l'amitié*. Le Monde.

Oury, J. (1980). *Onze heures du soir à La Borde*. Paris: Galilée.

Vasquez, A., & Oury, F. (1968). *Vers une pédagogie institutionnelle*. Paris: Maspero.

Gary Genosko
Lakehead University
Canada

6. BECOMING-CYBORG

A RhizomANTic Assemblage

Make a rhizome. But you don't know what you can make a rhizome with, you don't know which subterranean stem is going to make a rhizome, or enter a becoming, people your desert. So experiment (Gilles Deleuze & Félix Guattari, 1987, p. 246).

So I shall. This paper is a narrative experiment inspired by Deleuze and Guattari's (1987) figuration of the rhizome. It is a textual assemblage of popular and academic[1] representations of cyborgs that I hope might question, provoke and challenge some of the dominant discourses and assumptions of curriculum, teaching and learning.

Emboldened by Deleuze's penchant for inventing new terms for his figurations,[2] I have coined the term 'rhizomANTic' (sometimes 'rhizomantic') to name a methodological disposition that connects Deleuze's rhizomatics, ANT (actor-network theory), and Donna Haraway's (1997) 'invented category of semANTics, diffractions' (p. 16, my caps.).[3] Diffraction is 'an optical metaphor for the effort to make a difference in the world' (p. 16), which Haraway (1994) also represents by the activity of making a 'cat's cradle' – a metaphor that imagines the performance of sociotechnical relations as a less orderly and less functionalist activity than the word 'network' often conveys. As my reference to Haraway's work suggests, my engagement with ANT leans towards those aspects of the theory that John Law (2003) characterises as 'after-ANT'. In an annotated bibliography on Law's ANT Resource Home Page, he refers to Haraway's (1997) *Modest_Witness@Second_ Millennium. FemaleMan©_Meets_OncoMouse™* as 'the best-known example of the different and partially related radical feminist technoscience alternative to actor-network theory. The "after-ANT" studies in this resource in many cases owe as much or more to Haraway as to ANT itself'.[4]

I also use the term rhizomantic because much of this essay is about ants.

WRITING CYBORGS

Writing rhizomantic as 'rhizomANTic' symbolically foregrounds my suspicion that ANT cannot wholly be accommodated by rhizomatics – it fits, but it sits a little awkwardly and uncomfortably. The extent of this fit (which improves as ANT segues into 'after ANT') can be demonstrated by comparing Haraway's and actor-network theorists' approaches to writing cyborgs with each other and with Deleuze and Guattari's (1987) approach to writing *A Thousand Plateaus*:

I. Semetsky (ed.), Nomadic Education: Variations on a Theme by Deleuze and Guattari, 77–90.

> We are writing this book as a rhizome. It is composed of plateaus. We have given it a circular form, but not for laughs. Each morning we would wake up, and each of us would ask himself what plateau he was going to tackle, writing five lines here, ten lines there. We had hallucinatory experiences, we watched lines leave one plateau and proceed to another like columns of tiny ants (p. 22).

Haraway (1985) writes cyborgs that chart the movements of some of those hallucinated columns of ants – maps of partial and dynamic connections between the material products of military-industrial cybernetics (and their violent and masculinised projections in popular media) and imagined possibilities for a feminist, anti-racist, multicultural and non-violent technoscience. Haraway's cyborgs exemplify Deleuze and Guattari's (1987) characterisation of the rhizome as a 'map' rather than a 'tracing':

> What distinguishes the map from the tracing is that it is entirely oriented toward an experimentation in contact with the real… The map is open and connectable in all of its dimensions… It can be… conceived of as a work of art, constructed as a political action or a meditation… [and] has multiple entryways, as opposed to the tracing, which always come back 'to the same' (pp. 12-13)

Haraway's cyborgs are 'an experimentation in contact with the real' – heterogeneous and multiple, but also historically located. Haraway (2000) emphasises that the term cyborg, as she uses it, 'does not refer to all kinds of artifactual, machinic relationships with human beings… I am very concerned that the term "cyborg" be used specifically to refer to those kinds of entities that became historically possible around World War II and just after' (p. 128).

Actor-network theorists such as Bruno Latour (1988a) initially traced machinic relationships with human beings in terms of 'mixing humans and nonhumans together'. To the best of my knowledge, Latour did not use the term 'cyborg',[5] but his insistence on the agency of non-human 'actants' is helpful in reading and writing cyborgs as hybrid sociotechnical entities. Key works in ANT, such as Latour's (1987) *Science in Action: How to Follow Scientists and Engineers through Society*, demonstrate a method more like Deleuze and Guattari's notion of 'tracing' than Haraway's imaginative mappings of possibilities. ANT as a method of tracing is particularly evident in *The Pasteurization of France*, Latour's (1988b) semiotic analysis of the network of arrangements and strategic mobilisations of different actors and entities that produced Pasteur as its spokesperson – as an effect, rather than as a primary agent or individual genius. These earlier versions of ANT represent networks in ways that centre on their functions and imply arborescent systems rather than rhizomatic messiness. Latour's more recent works move towards an increasingly rhizomatic sensibility, an urge to implicate as well as to replicate, as he demonstrates in *Aramis, or the Love of Technology* (Latour, 1996), a multi-vocal account of a failed transport technology in which he gives voice to a range of actors, including the technology itself, who debate the translations and negotiations that led to its final demise. Law (2000), writing in what he calls 'after

ANT mode', makes the convergence of ANT with Haraway's project explicit in his description of 'a cyborg-like or fractional version of relationality' that benefits from multiplicity and 'the privilege of a cyborg-like split vision'. He concludes that we live in 'a post-human world. There are no essential humans. People-machines, cyborgs, these are produced in the shifts and displacements of relations'. I would add that in a posthuman world there are no essential cyborgs either.[6]

I began to write cyborgs into my own stories of teaching and learning (see Gough, 1993d, 1994, 1995) by experimenting with connections between Haraway's cyborgs, the cyberpunk science fiction of William Gibson and others,[7] and the young people I encountered in homes, schools and universities who increasingly seemed to be taking the ambiguous kinships of organisms and machines for granted. Making these connections between material bodies and discursive formations helped me to question aspects of my practice that were occluded by the epistemological and ontological categories and dualisms that frame and permeate the humanist discourses of contemporary schooling and higher education, especially those that divide humans from others, such as human/animal and human/machine.[8] Although I also drew upon ANT in my work as a science educator (see Gough, 1993bc, 1998), I did not immediately connect it to my cyborg interests. Perhaps paradoxically, ANT had a decentring effect on my thinking, helping to shift my attention from more individuated notions of cyborg subjectivities and corporealities towards the relations that produce them. Now, the idea of rhizomANTically becoming-cyborg signifies my desire to imagine teaching and learning as material-semiotic assemblages of sociotechnical relations embedded in and performed by shifting connections and interactions among a variety of organic, technical, 'natural',[9] and textual materials. Such assemblages are rhizomatic in the sense that Patricia O'Riley (2003) describes as 'dynamic, heterogeneous, and nondichotomous; …they propagate, displace, join, circle back, fold... rhizomes like crabgrass, ants, wolf packs, and children, de- and reterritorialize space' (p. 27). I am especially interested in the narrative construction of these assemblages, such as the ways that the 'machineries' of texts (including this one) constitute sociotechnical relations, and the textual and intertextual effects of cyborg relations in transgressing and transforming the discursive fields in which they move. Through what narrative and textual strategies might we materialise the figuration of rhizomANTically becoming-cyborg as crabgrass in the manicured lawn of formal education?

To put it another way, if curriculum is, as Madeleine Grumet (1981) writes, 'the collective story we tell our children about our past, our present, and our future' (p. 115), then what are the ethical and material possibilities for becoming-cyborg in that story? Becoming-cyborg is not a matter of reducing the gap between the cyborg concept and the material cyborg body (which would be a mode of trans-cendent posthumanism) but, rather, affirms the perpetual immanence of the gap between the materialisation of the concept and its possibilities of future development. The kinds of cyborgs that we (and our children) are becoming are shaped and reshaped by the stories we mutually construct. Moreover, the generation and materialisation of these possibilities is as much a function of textual silences, denials, and refusals, as it is of whatever might explicitly be privileged by a text.

Rosi Braidotti (2000) suggests that 'fabulations'[10] can help to propel 'becomings' by bringing the unthinkable into representation, because 'undoing power relations in the very structures of one's subject position' requires 'awareness of the limitations as well as the specificity of one's locations' (pp. 170-1). Robert Scholes (1976) describes fabulation as 'fiction that offers us a world clearly and radically discontinuous from the one we know, yet returns to confront that known world in some cognitive way' (p. 47). Scholes (1976) adds:

> in works of structural fabulation the tradition of speculative fiction is modified by an awareness of the nature of the universe as a system of systems, a structure of structures, and the insights of the past century of science are accepted as fictional points of departure... It is a fictional exploration of human situations made perceptible by the implications of recent science (pp. 54-5).

I have found a fabulation that actualises some possibilities for rhizomantically becoming-cyborg in the context of the stories we tell our children.

It is the story of an ant.

A FABULATION FOR BECOMING-CYBORG: MAYAKOVSKY'S *CYBERANTICS*

If we are to believe Jerry Prosser (1992), then once upon a time a brilliant, eccentric and very controversial cyberneticist by the name of Stanislaw Mayakovsky built a cybernetic ant. This miracle of micro-miniaturisation, known as A7 (but named 'Ari'[11] by Mayakovsky), closely replicated[12] the structural and functional qualities of *Formica subsericea*, the ant species she was designed to resemble. She was equipped with a holographic memory and tiny (but very sophisticated) biotechnological systems that enabled her to communicate with other ants – she could decipher their semiochemicals and synthesise pheromones appropriate for her own use in virtually any circumstance. To test A7's capabilities in the field, Mayakovsky sent her into a nest of 'real' ants. Not only did these ants accept her, but she also played a significant role in ensuring the colony's continuity in the face of the accidental loss of its queen and an invasion by a related species of 'slave-making' ants (*Formica subintegra*).

One of Mayakovsky's eccentricities was that he did not present his findings in the usual way, that is, by publishing them in a scientific journal. Rather, he told the story of A7's construction and subsequent adventures by writing an illustrated children's book, *Cyberantics*, which became a best seller and won a major prize in the field of children's literature (see Figures 1 and 2). Many of Mayakovsky's colleagues were incredulous at what he claimed to have achieved – and scandalised by his means of communicating it – but he remained oblivious to criticism and, partly as a result, his work fell into disrepute in the artificial intelligence research establishment. Some years later, Mayakovsky disappeared under mysterious circumstances, and his work might have faded into obscurity were it not for the recent – and equally mysterious – reappearance of A7. This event prompted

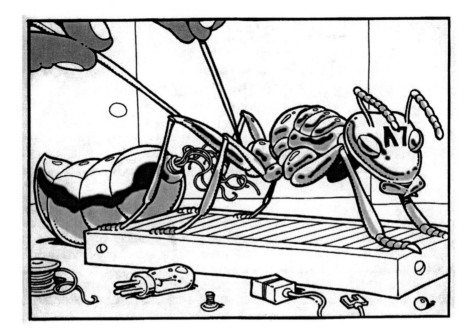

Figure 1: Mayakovsky assembling Ari (from Prosser 1992, p. 4, illustration by Rick Geary)

Figure 2: Cover of first edition of Mayakovsky's (c. 2172) Cyberantics *(Prosser 1992, p. 52, illustration by Rick Geary)*

Prosser (1992) to publish the annotated edition of *Cyberantics* (see Figure 3).[13] A particularly interesting note accompanies a drawing in the first edition that outraged both entomologists and cyberneticists. The drawing shows A7 vanquishing a spider many times her size and reveals that Mayakovsky had equipped her with a miniaturised cold plasma laser weapon.[14] As Prosser (1992) writes:

> He gave an ant a gun and presented his findings as a children's book. He once replied to criticism…by saying: 'It is only the limited imagination that takes refuge in the banal structures of formal science. A childlike sense of wonder and curiosity transcends these limitations and is more faithful to the aims of science than academic dogma and conceit. This is why I wrote for children' (p. 30).

I have no quarrel with Mayakovsky's assertions, but (from the standpoint of one of my present subject positions as a science teacher educator) I am more concerned with the 'banal structures' and simplistic textual practices of formal science education. Like Mayakovsky, I am interested in generating and sustaining alternatives to these structures and practices. As I argue at much greater length elsewhere (Gough, 1993a, b), much fiction (including children's fiction but especially science fiction) is 'more faithful to the aims' of education than the 'dogma and conceit' of many contemporary education texts.

Figure 3: Cover of Prosser's (1992) annotated edition of Mayakovsky's Cyberantics (illustration by Rick Geary)

Nevertheless, *Cyberantics* gestures towards the science education texts that it subverts. Many of Prosser's 'annotations', such as those dealing with the structure, function, social organisation and communication processes of ants, would not be out of place in a standard science textbook or in the synoptic or encyclopaedic resource materials (whether they be in a library or on the internet) to which school students often refer when they are 'doing ants' as a topic. But *Cyberantics* does much more than these conventional texts. For example, the Afterword, a spoof biography of Mayakovsky (in which we learn, for example, of his disastrous dabblings in VAI – Viral Artificial Intelligence), raises many questions about the conduct of scientific research, the nature of human, animal and artificial intelligence, the social organisation of scientific labour and the reconstruction of scientific knowledge for public consumption. Also, by being cast within the conventions of a children's talking animal story, *Cyberantics* invites the reader to bring the wide range of cultural meanings associated with this literary mode to bear on the text, such as mocking and subverting the modern scientific practice of maintaining clear distinctions between humans and other beings.[15]

Cyberantics also reminds us that the 'cybernetic' operations of many insect societies are among the phenomena that provided scientists like Ilya Prigogine (1980; see also Prigogine & Stengers, 1984) with evidence of the biosphere's non-linear dynamics, including the amplification of fluctuations, the emergence of bifurcations, and the immense consequences of small, low-energy effects (the 'butterfly effect'). As David Porush (1991) notes, these phenomena also were described in literary works (and not only in science fiction) long before Prigogine and others provided mathematical explanations for them. The evolution of open, non-linear dynamic systems of communication and resource management – involving both chance and determinism – enables ant hill societies to resolve problems of a complexity which far outstrips the information-processing capabilities of an individual ant with the very limited data provided by their communications media (semiochemicals and pheromones). The association of ants with cybernetics has a long history in science fiction, notable examples including Philip K. Dick's (1991/1969) 'The electric ant'.

Some cyberpunk science fiction imaginatively rehearses the synergistic links between Prigogine's theories of self-organisation out of chaos and the cybernetic project to build intelligent artefacts. For example, Bruce Sterling's (1985, 1990) cosmos is explicitly 'Prigoginic': mind is a dissipative structure (itself a product of biological evolution – another dissipative structure) generating further dissipative structures such as literature and technology. More provocatively, in Gibson and Sterling's (1991) novel, *The Difference Engine*, an intelligent artificiality elucidates a moment in its own past when a chance event (a minor fluctuation) enables its own future evolution into an intelligence that can tell its own story. Gibson and Sterling use non-linear dynamics to explain how a machine in a far-from-equilibrium system might spring into autonomous life, and thus provide a plausible portrayal of being-and-becoming that transcends any attempt to essentialise such concepts in human terms. Another example is Rudy Rucker's (1994) novel, *The Hacker and the Ants*, which explores some possibilities (and difficulties) that might arise when cybernetics intersects with the biotechnologies and evolutionary mechanisms of a hive mind and offers a rationale for building a very different type of cybernetic ant from Mayakovsky's Ari. Rucker's protagonist describes his work as a hacker for GoMotion Incorporated as follows:

GoMotion had hired me a year earlier to help develop a new product: a kit and software for a customized personal robot called the Veep. The preliminary design work was all being done in virtual reality; instead of building lots of expensive prototype machines, GoMotion liked to put together computer models of machines that could be tested out inside cyberspace.

My contribution to the Veep project was to use artificial life techniques as a means of evolving better algorithms for the Veep. The idea behind artificial life was to create a lot of different versions of a program, and to let the versions compete, mutate, and reproduce until eventually a winner emerged. In certain situations – like figuring out the best way to set a thousand nonlinearly coupled numerical parameters – a-life was the best way to go, although not everyone in the business believed this. I owed my job at GoMotion to the fact that Roger Coolidge, the superhacker founder of the company, was a vigorous a-life enthusiast, actively engaged in a series of experiments with electronic ant farms (p. 5).

For my purposes, one of the most significant attributes of Prosser's (1992) *Cyberantics* is that it is a metafiction, a type of story that, in Patricia Waugh's (1984) words, 'draws attention to its status as an artefact in order to pose questions about the relationship between fiction and reality' (p. 2). As a metafiction *Cyberantics* functions as a complex system generating multiple interpretations – in other words, it displays the properties of what contemporary science calls chaos and complexity theory.[16] Thus, it explores and illustrates, in a form accessible to children and adults alike, an important correspondence between postmodern science and literature. As Peter Stoicheff (1991) writes, 'metafiction and scientific chaos are embraced by a larger revolution in contemporary thought that examines the similar roles of narrative, and of investigative procedure, in our "reading" or knowledge of the world' (p. 85). *Cyberantics* can be understood therefore as an alternative representation of what a postmodern science education text could possibly be. It embeds stories of modern science, a delightful children's story and a satire suitable for both children and adults within a complex and complicating metafiction that inhabits a conceptual space shared alike by much postmodernist science and poststructuralist textual criticism – a space in which 'the world is a text that is read, and our interpretation of our world is a function of our reading of texts' (Stoicheff, 1991, p. 95).

I do not think it is an overstatement to suggest that, for science educators, *Cyberantics* can work as a Deleuzian figuration. Certainly it embodies the art, paradox and humour that characterises much of Deleuze's (1994) theorising and writing.[17] As Braidotti (2000) writes:

Deleuze, not unlike Haraway or, for that matter, the performance artist Laurie Anderson, thinks by inventing unconventional and even disturbing conceptual personae. These mark different steps in the process of 'becoming-minoritarian', that is of undoing power relations in the very structures of one's subject position. Figurations of these multiple becomings are: the rhizome, the nomad, the bodies-without-organs, the cyborg, the onco-mouse and acoustic masks of all electronic kinds (p. 170).

In my view, that is precisely what *Cyberantics* does – or *can* do if the reader is open to its many implications for teaching and learning. The particular virtues of *Cyberantics* as a Deleuzian fabulation for becoming-cyborg in science education can be appreciated by comparing it with a different approach to cyborg pedagogy performed as an application of ANT.

CYBORG PEDAGOGY AND ANT

Tim Angus, Ian Cook and James Evans (2001) present a 'manifesto for cyborg pedagogy' that is explicitly grounded in ANT. Their article begins with a photograph (see Figure 4) and an explanation of its significance under a subheading, 'It's just a cuppa!':

Geoff was making a point when he included this annotated Polaroid in his journal for our 'Geographies of material culture' course. He was stirring together some instant coffee granules from that Nescafe jar, with water from a nearby tap connected to a reservoir by miles of piping and who knows what else, which he had poured into that plastic kettle to boil with the help of a heating element which was connected to the national grid, its wires, pylons, transformers, power stations and their fuels, via that plastic covered wire, plug, fuse and socket, attached by screws and maybe rawlplugs to a brick wall through those delightfully patterned ceramic tiles, with some milk from that plastic container, in that white ceramic 'Match of the Day' mug, resting on that beige formica kitchen top, using that stainless steel spoon with the blue plastic handle held in that hand, attached to that arm, which will lift the cup to pour its contents into a mouth which had recently been the site of important dental work, into a body which needed a hot caffeine hit to keep awake in order to finish that journal entry, and kept warm by that sweat shirt, and that central heating, in that kitchen, in that house, in that part of Birmingham, that day (pp. 195-6).

Angus, Cook and Evans (2001) elaborate on this opening paragraph by spelling out in exhaustive detail the multitude of connections that had to be made in order that Geoff could perform this simple everyday task: connections 'between heres and theres, between humans, between humans and non-humans, between non-humans and non-humans' (p. 195). After listing many of these connections (and pointing to both the durability and fragility of the networks they constitute), they suggest that the point of all this is Geoff's realisation that he is a 'cybernetic organism', 'a cyborg, a node in a network' (p. 196):

He's writing a journal about the connections you have to make when you wear your 'cyborg spectacles'. These are thoroughly grounded, fleshy connections; connections which illustrate the kinds of things that have to continually happen for him to be who he is today... connections which blur boundaries between internal bodily networks (organs, tracts, vessels, veins, synapses, etc) and external bodily networks which reach into fields, factories, tankers, commodity trading floors, mines, oil wells, bodies etc all over the place (pp. 196-7).

I AM A CYBERNETIC ORGANISM

Figure 4: Photograph from 'A manifesto for cyborg pedagogy' (Angus, Cook & Evans, 2001, p. 198)

Angus, Cook and Evans (2001) call what they do 'cyborg pedagogy':

Our 'Geographies of material culture' course attempts to encourage students to sink their teeth into these thorny but fundamental issues through insisting that they (a) adopt a cyborg ontology when considering their relations with commodities; (b) think through their connections with others in terms of 'commodity chains', 'circuits of culture' and/or 'actor networks'; (c) develop these understandings through reading and discussing in class detailed empirical studies of consumption, production, and flows; (d) work on group present-ations which further develop key issues arising from these discussions; (e) continually situate this knowledge in the mundane circumstances of their everyday lives; and (e) keep a journal which represents how this understanding can be grounded in these circumstances and how it develops throughout the course. We don't teach this course. It's not didactic. We deliver only one lecture, right at the start. After that, we orchestrate the course: prepare detailed handouts, make sure the right readings are easily available, orchestrate the class discussions, arrange extra course office hours for smaller discussions; assess the journals according to clearly set-out criteria; and decentre ourselves as much as possible (p. 197).

According to Angus, Cook and Evans (2001), the 'cornerstones of this cyborg pedagogy' are 'situated knowledge', 'cyborg ontology' (both of which they source to Haraway, 1991b)[18] and 'border pedagogy' (their formulation of which draws chiefly from Giroux & McLaren, 1994, and hooks, 1994).

There is much to admire and to be inspired by in Angus, Cook and Evans's (2001) version of cyborg pedagogy and my use of it for comparative purposes is not intended to diminish it in any way. Rather, I want to draw attention to some differences between a pedagogy located in the theoretical space of ANT and pedagogy configured by the 'movement' of rhizomANTically becoming-cyborg. When I look at Geoff's Polaroid photograph and at what Angus, Cook and Evans (2001) claim that it represents, what seems to be missing are Deleuze and Guattari's hallucinatory 'columns of tiny ants', the imagined and invented maps of connections that experiment with the real rather than provide only tracings of it. Angus, Cook and Evans's (2001) manifesto for cyborg pedagogy is *cyber* without the *antics* – without the art, paradox and humour that *Cyberantics* displays in abundance.

Cyberantics makes a rhizome.

ACKNOWLEDGMENTS

I am very grateful to Rick Geary for his permission to reproduce the artwork from *Cyberantics* in Figures 1, 2 and 3, and to Ian Cook for permission to reproduce the photograph in Figure 4. I also acknowledge prior publication of an earlier version of this chapter in a special issue of *Educational Philosophy and Theory* on Deleuze and education (Gough 2004).

NOTES

[1] I use the terms 'popular' and 'academic' to register my perceptions of difference across sites of cultural production, not to inscribe a binary distinction.

[2] Braidotti (2000) argues that 'the notion of "figurations" – in contrast to the representational function of "metaphors" – emerges as crucial to Deleuze's notion of a conceptually charged use of the imagination' (p. 170). Similarly, Haraway (1997) asserts that 'figurations are performative images that can be inhabited,... condensed maps of contestable worlds... {and] bumps that make us swerve from literal-mindedness' (p. 11).

[3] Drawing attention to the ANT in semantics is gratuitous, but if I don't someone else will.

[4] See The Actor Network Resource: Alphabetical List of Publications Version 2.2. Retrieved 17 November 2006 from http://www.comp.lancs.ac.uk/sociology/antres.html

[5] In Latour's keynote address at the 'Actor Network and After' Workshop, Keele University, July 1997, he also asserted that he 'never used the word actor-network'; see Latour, 'On Recalling ANT', published by the Department of Sociology, Lancaster University, Lancaster, UK. Retrieved 17 November 2006 from http://www.comp.lancs.ac.uk/sociology/papers/Latour-Recalling-ANT.pdf

[6] I emphasise this point because I share the suspicions of some feminist colleagues (e.g. Zoë Sofoulis 2001) that ANT conceptualises non-human actors in terms that perpetuate a humanist notion of an essential subject.

[7] See Bruce Sterling's (1986) anthology for a representative sample of other authors who constituted the first wave of cyberpunk science fiction.

[8] As Haraway (1991a) explains, cyborgs also disrupt many other binary oppositions and rigid categorisations of Enlightenment thought including 'self/other, mind/body, culture/nature, male/female, civilised/primitive, reality/appearance, whole/part, agent/resource, maker/made, active/passive, right/ wrong, truth/illusion, total/partial, God/man' (p. 177).

[9] The 'scare' quotes here signify that I read terms such as 'natural' and 'nature' *sous rature* (under erasure), following Jacques Derrida's approach to reading deconstructed signifiers as if their meanings were clear and undeconstructable, but with the understanding that this is only a strategy (see, for example, Derrida, 1985).

[10] Braidotti cites Marlene Barr (1993) as the source of 'fabulation'. However, Barr (1992) describes 'feminist fabulation' as a 'specifically feminist corollary to... structural fabulation' (p. 11) and sources her understandings of 'fabulation' and 'structural fabulation' to Robert Scholes (1976).

[11] *Ari* is the Japanese word for 'ant'.

[12] Like the cyborgs in Ridley Scott's (1984) movie, *Blade Runner*, A7 was a replic*ant*.

[13] *Cyberantics* is a temporally ambiguous text. Prosser's annotated edition is clearly dated 1992 but his bibliography cites the first edition as being published (by Jiffy Books, New York) in 2172 (p. 54). Prosser (1992) also refers to events that took place as late as the year 2197 (p. 53). However, as Ursula Le Guin (1986) points out, the difficulties of translating (and, by implication, publishing) a text that has not yet been written may have been exaggerated: 'The fact that it hasn't yet been written, the mere absence of a text to translate, doesn't make all that much difference... All we ever have is here, now' (p. xi).

[14] 'When asked why an ant needs to be equipped with a miniaturised cold plasma laser, Mayakovsky answered: "I'd want one"' (Prosser 1992, p. 30).

[15] See Gough (1990) and Le Guin (1987) for a more detailed discussion of children's talking animal stories and their significance.

[16] A further layer of metafictional complexity in *Cyberantics* is provided by its intertextual relationship to the *Aliens: Hive* comic series (Prosser & Jones, 1993) in which both Mayakovsky and Ari are main characters.

[17] For example, Deleuze (1994) asserts that 'Paradox is... the passion of philosophy' (p. 227) and that 'the art of the aesthetic is humour' (p. 245).

[18] Note, however, that Haraway (1991b) refers to 'situated *knowledges*' (plural); the construction of knowledges as multiple rather than singular might be a significant point of difference between her approach and Angus, Cook and Evans's (2001) adaptation of it for their purposes.

REFERENCES

Angus, T., Cook, I., & Evans, J. (2001). A manifesto for cyborg pedagogy? *International Research in Geographical and Environmental Education, 10*(2), 195–201.

Barr, M. S. (1992). *Feminist fabulation: Space/Postmodern fiction.* Iowa City: University of Iowa Press.

Barr, M. S. (1993). *Lost in space: Probing feminist science fiction and beyond.* Chapel Hill, NC: The University of North Carolina Press.

Braidotti, R. (2000). Teratologies. In I. Buchanan & C. Colebrook (Eds.), *Deleuze and feminist theory* (pp. 156–172). Edinburgh: Edinburgh University Press.

Deleuze, G. (1994). *Difference and repetition* (P. Patton, Trans.). New York: Columbia University Press.

Deleuze, G., & Guattari, F. (1987). *A thousand plateaus: Capitalism and schizophrenia* (B. Massumi, Trans.). Minneapolis, MN: University of Minnesota Press.

Derrida, J. (1985). Letter to a Japanese friend. In D. Wood & R. Bernasconi (Eds.), *Derrida and différance* (pp. 1–5). Warwick: Parousia Press.

Dick, P. K. (1991/1969). The electric ant. In P. K. Dick (Ed.), *We can remember it for you wholesale: Collected stories* (Vol. 5, pp. 290–308). London: Grafton.

Gibson, W., & Sterling, B. (1991). *The difference engine.* New York: Bantam.

Giroux, H. A., & McLaren, P. (Eds.). (1994). *Between borders: Pedagogy and the politics of cultural studies.* London and New York: Routledge.

Gough, N. (1990). Renewing our mythic links with nature: Some arts of becoming ecopolitical in curriculum work. *Curriculum Perspectives, 10*(2), 66–69.

Gough, N. (1993a). Environmental education, narrative complexity and postmodern science/fiction. *International Journal of Science Education, 15*(5), 607–625.

Gough, N. (1993b). *Laboratories in fiction: Science education and popular media.* Geelong: Deakin University.

Gough, N. (1993c). Laboratories in schools: Material spaces, mythic places. *Australian Science Teachers Journal, 38*(2), 29–33.

Gough, N. (1993d). Neuromancing the stones: Experience, intertextuality, and cyberpunk science fiction. *Journal of Experiential Education, 16*(3), 9–17.

Gough, N. (1994). Will cyberpunks save the nation? In J. Kenway & J. Collier (Eds.), *Schooling what future? Balancing the education agenda* (pp. 67–70). Geelong: Deakin Centre for Education and Change.

Gough, N. (1995). Manifesting cyborgs in curriculum inquiry. *Melbourne Studies in Education, 36*(1), 71–83.

Gough, N. (1998). If this were played upon a stage: School laboratory work as a theatre of representation. In J. Wellington (Ed.), *Practical work in school science: Which way now?* (pp. 69–89). London: Routledge.

Gough, N. (2004). RhizomANTically becoming-cyborg: Performing posthuman pedagogies. *Educational Philosophy and Theory, 36*(3), 253–265.

Grumet, M. R. (1981). Restitution and reconstruction of educational experience: An autobiographical method for curriculum theory. In M. Lawn & L. Barton (Eds.), *Rethinking curriculum studies: A radical approach* (pp. 115–130). London: Croom Helm.

Haraway, D. J. (1985). A manifesto for cyborgs: Science, technology and socialist feminism in the 1980s. *Socialist Review, 15*(2), 65–107.

Haraway, D. J. (1991a). A cyborg manifesto: Science, technology, and socialist-feminism in the late twentieth century. In *Simians, cyborgs, and women: The reinvention of nature* (pp. 149–181). New York: Routledge.

Haraway, D. J. (1991b). *Simians, cyborgs, and women: The reinvention of nature.* New York: Routledge.

Haraway, D. J. (1994). A game of cat's cradle: Science studies, feminist theory, cultural studies. *Configurations, 2*(1), 59–71.

Haraway, D. J. (1997). *Modest_Witness@Second_Millennium.Femaleman©_Meets_Oncomouse™: Feminism and technoscience* (with paintings by L. M. Randolph). New York and London: Routledge.

Haraway, D. J. (2000). *How like a leaf: An interview with Thyrza Nichols Goodeve.* New York and London: Routledge.

Hooks, B. (1994). *Teaching to transgress: Education and the practice of freedom.* London and New York: Routledge.

Latour, B. (1987). *Science in action: How to follow scientists and engineers through society* (C. Porter, Trans.). Milton Keynes: Open University Press.

Latour, B. (1988a). Mixing humans and nonhumans together: The sociology of a door-closer. *Social Problems, 35*(3), 298–310.

Latour, B. (1988b). *The pasteurization of France* (A. Sheridan & J. Law, Trans.). Cambridge, MA: Harvard University Press.

Latour, B. (1996). *Aramis, or the love of technology* (C. Porter, Trans.). Cambridge, MA: Harvard University Press.

Law, J. (1999). After ANT: Topology, naming and complexity. In J. Law & J. Hassard (Eds.), *Actor network theory and after* (pp. 1–14). Oxford: Blackwell.

Law, J. (2003). *Networks, relations, cyborgs: On the social study of technology*. Lancaster, UK: Centre for Science Studies, Lancaster University. Retrieved November 17, 2006, from http://www.comp.lancs.ac.uk/sociology/papers/Law-Networks-Relations-Cyborgs.pdf

Le Guin, U. K. (1986). *Always coming home*. London: Victor Gollancz.

Le Guin, U. K. (1987). *Buffalo gals and other animal presences*. Santa Barbara: Capra.

O'Riley, P. A. (2003). *Technology, culture, and socioeconomics: A rhizoanalysis of educational discourses*. New York: Peter Lang.

Porush, D. (1991). Prigogine, chaos and contemporary sf. *Science-Fiction Studies, 18*(3), 367–386.

Prigogine, I. (1980). *From being to becoming*. San Francisco: W. W. Freeman.

Prigogine, I., & Stengers, I. (1984). *Order out of chaos: Man's new dialogue with nature*. New York: Bantam.

Prosser, J. (Ed.). (1992). *Cyberantics* (Annotated Edition; Original work ostensibly written by S. Mayakovsky and illustrated by R. Geary). New York: Dark Horse Comics.

Prosser, J., & Jones, K. (1993). *Aliens: Hive*. New York: Dark Horse Comics.

Rucker, R. (1994). *The hacker and the ants*. New York: Avon Books.

Scholes, R. (1976). The roots of science fiction. In M. Rose (Ed.), *Science fiction: A collection of critical essays* (pp. 46–56). Englewood Cliffs, NJ: Prentice-Hall.

Sterling, B. (1985). *Schismatrix*. New York: Ace.

Sterling, B. (Ed.). (1986). *Mirrorshades: The cyberpunk anthology*. New York: Ace.

Sterling, B. (1990). *Crystal express*. New York: Ace.

Stoicheff, P. (1991). The chaos of metafiction. In N. K. Hayles (Ed.), *Chaos and order: Complex dynamics in literature and science* (pp. 85–99). Chicago: University of Chicago Press.

Waugh, P. (1984). *Metafiction: The theory and practice of self-conscious fiction*. London: Methuen.

Noel Gough
Faculty of Education
La Trobe University
Australia

ZELIA GREGORIOU

7. COMMENCING THE RHIZOME

Towards a minor philosophy of education

INTRODUCTION

In *The Postmodern Explained*, a pedagogical sequel to *The Postmodern Condition*, Jean François Lyotard reports on the domination of thought by the principle of realism: 'We are in a tenor of relaxation—I am speaking of the tenor of the times. Everywhere we are being urged to give up experimentation, in the arts and elsewhere' (Lyotard, 1993, p. 1). In postmodern discourse, the terms 'pedagogy' and 'pedagogical' are often used figuratively in order to connote didacticism, delivery of communiqués and the parceling and packaging of meaning into digestible (i.e., marketable) forms. The reader might find erroneous the characterization of Lyotard's book as pedagogical. But the explanation of the postmodern—a task set forth as a promise by the title of the book—entails a certain minoritarianism of answers.

Instead of delivering final answers and well-rounded, denotative statements about the meaning of postmodernism, Lyotard cites a series of letters written in the context of exchanges between him and friends; that is, encounters between 'children'. Sustaining the double sense of intimacy and fragmentation that emanates from letter writing, these philosophical explications do not claim any meta-discursive generalizability. Marked by the pragmatic context of their enunciation, they never claim to be anything more than what they are: a series of singular explications, each one evoked in a singular occasion. Their pedagogical quality lies in hailing the reader to join in, to pick up (or to be picked up by) an explication (which might also mean a concern, a question) at any point of the book and turn this into the starting point for another singular reading. Such minoritarian writing reports on the 'the demand' while denying to subscribe to its logic.

Lyotard speaks of a demand that threatens to totalize experience, to reduce language to Newspeak, to rob thinking of its childhood and pedagogy of its philosophical moment. It is the 'demand' for reality (for unity, simplicity, communicability) and remedy: remedy for the parceling and virtualization of culture, for the fragmentation of the life world and its derealisation into idioms, *petits récits* and language games. The demand is voiced most ardently by Habermas and his disciples in calling us to keep awaiting for modernity's still-incomplete project, believing in it, deriving our visions for transformative action from it and dedicating its achievements to it. It is this demand that marks the reception of Deleuze and Guattari's *Thousand Plateaus* as a non philosophical text, if philosophy is still understood as the discourse of reasonable argument, clarification and teaching of thought's history and future. 'I have read in a French weekly,' writes Lyotard while

I. Semetsky (ed.), Nomadic Education: Variations on a Theme by Deleuze and Guattari, 91–109.

reviewing kaleidoscopically instantiations of the 'demand', 'that people are unhappy with *A Thousand Plateaus* [by Deleuze and Guattari] because, especially in a book of philosophy, they expect to be rewarded with a bit of sense.' Lyotard's *Postmodern Explained* comes to rupture the readers' unhappy quest for a pedagogical apologia. He does take up the issue of postmodernity and he does explicate terms such as *récits*, incredulity and language games. Yet this response is not to be confused with his personal philosophical apology, intertwined with a pedagogical effort to clear himself of accusations of irrationalism. Lyotard's 'letters', composed in a minor style and arranged in a paratactic syntax that defies climactic moments, come to inaugurate a pedagogical experimenting with the postmodern.

Today the specter of this demand returns again to haunt philosophy of education. This time it is phrased not so much as a quest for combating postmodern incredulity and talking across difference in our classrooms but as the reclaiming of philosophy of education from its 'illicit' nuptials with the social sciences. While mounting it again in the home of philosophy and establishing it as the latter's envoy, philosophers of education still want to be mediators and translators of philosophy to the cosmic world of education. This essay attempts to engage Deleuze in this conversation and investigate the possibilities of doing philosophy of education in a non-foundational way. Philosophy of education is understood as 'continuing to read philosophers *in a certain way*' (Derrida, 1978, p. 288). But the encounter with Deleuze disentangles philosophy of education from this devotion to sense, communicability, and the latter's corollary for an ideal speech situation (i.e., a mutual interest between philosophers and educators about what each other has to say). In its Deleuzian moments this reading resists the temptation to apply a pedagogical speculum to *A Thousand Plateaus* (i.e., picking up the concept of the rhizome as a metaphor and searching for correspondences between that and organizations of knowledge in learning communities). Letting philosophy of education drift to a minoritarian study of *philosophy's moment in education* will be, hopefully, the effect of this text. This encounter with Deleuze and Guattari implicates a certain chance and experimentation, both of which are needed for the production of a *minor philosophy of education*: a philosophy that is not haunted by the big figures of philosophy's fathers, picks up ideas from social sciences without anxiety about risking its identity, and reconnects these ideas towards new encounters.

THE PREDICAMENTS OF PHILOSOPHY OF EDUCATION
(OR, WHY PHILOSOPHERS OF EDUCATION MOURN)

Since the late eighties the demand for reality has been permeating a broad range of reactions to the philosophers of the postmodern, some of them 'negative' and some of them 'positive'. 'Negative' reactions range from frantic allegations of neo-conservativism to mild concerns about the aestheticization of philosophy and the collapse of normative criteria. 'Positive' reactions usually produce a new meta-discourse, a didactics of postmodernism, and a pedagogically friendly translation of postmodern philosophers. But these, apparently disparate reactions coincide to the degree they attempt to freeze postmodern philosophical writing into meaningful statements and bulleted lists of key points: 'incredulity', 'petit narratives', 'différance', 'rhizomes'. The delivery mode of these ideas has not been neutral to what they have become. Language, says Deleuze, is not made to be believed but to be obeyed: 'When the schoolteacher explains an operation to the children, or when she teaches them grammar, she does not, strictly speaking, give them information, she communicates orders to them, she transmits "order words" to them, necessarily conforming to dominant meanings' (Deleuze & Parnet, 1987, p. 22). When a philosopher of education explains 'Deleuze', for example, she communicates the command to make some sense of him, to recognize in his writing concepts that facilitate our understanding of the educational experience or even command the understanding of ourselves as educators or philosophers. Teachers and students agonize to find whether an idea (e.g., 'rhizome', 'minoritarianism', 'event', to cite some of the ideas we will encounter later) is just or correct. If philosophy in its relation to the pure state has historically served as a grand narrative, as Lyotard maintains, history of philosophy has also served pedagogically as a discourse of intimidation in producing the pedagogical subject of education. How can you think without having read Plato, Descartes, Kant and Heidegger, and so-and-so's book about them, asks Deleuze, recapping with sarcasm philosophy's pedagogical genealogy in playing the 'repressor's role':

A formidable school of intimidation which manufactures specialists in thought—but which also makes those who stay outside conform all the more to this specialism which they despise. An image of thought called philosophy has been formed historically and it effectively stops people from thinking (Deleuze & Parnett, 1987, p. 13).

I just don't get it why you call Philosophy of Education a 'Foundations Course' when all you do in that course is anti-foundational, a colleague confided to me some years ago. Some years later, in another department, in another university, the Education Program Committee sent out a memorandum inviting faculty to submit 'good' reasons why the course 'Theory of Education' should not be removed from the list of courses set as requirements for the teacher education program. The committee's opinion was that the course lacked identity—it was just a 'composite of bits and pieces' from disciplines such as Philosophy, Sociology, History, 'even' Women's Studies—and, of course, took up valuable space which could have been allocated for other, more relevant, teaching methods courses. The committee's invitation elicited various kinds of response. The legitimization of pedagogical practice depends on its theoretical foundations, was one kind of response. The interdisciplinarity of the course needs to be defined and justified, was another kind of response. In the end, the course was 'saved' through a tactical rearticulation of its name, from 'Theory of Education' to 'Introduction to the Sciences of Education'. This renaming helped protect both the course's place among the requirements and the program's foundational philosophy. But it was also a dubious tactic, taking into consideration that it consented to evading the ambiguous and non-practical name of 'Theory.' And though it 'saved' the course and defended its interdisciplinarity, this tactical renaming was enacted (and at the same time disciplined) along the rules of what Deleuze calls philosophy's 'repressor's role.' The principle that was reinstated was that education cannot legitimize its goals or methods unless it has a philosophical grounding which connects it to the history of philosophical ideas.

On several occasions Deleuze pays tribute to Foucault for refusing to analyze power in terms of the emanations of a pre-existing State apparatus (in the aforementioned case, departmental apparatus). Segmentation as a device of discipline and disciplinarity does not function simply through the rigidity of its concrete assemblages, cells regulated through individuation and heterogeneity. It has at its disposal a supplementary dimension of overcoding (the taken for granted answers to the questions what is philosophy, what is education) recuperated by children of the disciplines when they cannot but defend post-foundational thinking in a foundational manner:

> The education of the subject and the harmonization of the form have constantly haunted our culture, inspired the segmentations, the planifications, the binary machines which cut them and the abstract machines which cut them again. As Pierre Fleutiaux says, when an outline begins to tremble, when a segment wavers, we call the terrible Lunette to cut things up, the laser which puts forms in order and subjects in their place (Deleuze, 1993, p. 229).[1]

How can a philosopher of education negotiate the disciplinary identity of her/his field with the epoch of flows, deterritorializations with the quest for meaning? How can Philosophy of Education renew its ties with what Lyotard calls 'the season of childhood, the season of the mind's possibilities' and resist its self-identification as a foundations course when caught into the forces of interpellation exercised by the 'terrible Lunette'?

In a symposium hosted in a recent issue of the journal *Theory of Education* ten philosophers of education consider how the becoming educationally relevant of philosophical thinking would compromise neither its philosophical quality nor its educational communicability. Prompted by Rene Arcilla's earlier article, 'Why Aren't Philosophers and Educators Speaking to Each Other?', some of these philosophers mourn the end of the discipline and others celebrate what can become its 'inbetweenness'. In an attempt to make their discourse more relevant to the real problems of education—a *telos* toward which the philosophical tradition of sceptical questioning does not seem to be viable, from an educational perspective— philosophers of education are unbecoming-philosophers by following the rest of the social sciences 'out' of philosophy and becoming, say, 'feminist anthropological theorists, or liberal political-science theorists, or postmodernist sociological theorists' (Arcilla, 2002, p. 10).

Though dispensing with modernity's quest for pure identity (Stengel, 2002) and disciplinarity (Abowitz, 2002), the conversation about the state and future of philosophy of education is haunted by an anxiety that draws its energies from modernity's investment in the idea of a public. The person who recognizes himself or herself as someone at stake in philosophy of education, Arcilla's syllogism goes, is to hear and respond to 'what is uncanny about the current silence parting philosophy and education' (Arcilla, 2002, p. 11). Identifying one's self as a philosopher of education means to experience one's identity as an insecure one because, among other reasons, what philosophers and educators have to say does not seem to interest each other. A common audience for philosophers and educators is yet to be found. Yet finding that public and writing for that addressee is what legitimizes the claim for that genitive 'of' that bridges philosophy and education in the proper name Philosophy *of* Education. The legitimacy of Philosophy of Education depends on reaching that philosophically concerned audience of educators in the same way the credibility of grand narratives of legitimization is grounded on the claim to speak for the people, in the name of the people. Finding that public[2] *and* preserving philosophical rigor,[3] going out but still searching for depth, becoming of practical use and yet keeping on asking the normative question 'How we should educate?' (Bredo, 2002) are some of the conversation's major tenets. If 'philosophers *of* education' are philosophers *and* educators who are mutually hearkening to the 'uncanny' parting of philosophy and education, as the reading Arcilla's paper performatively suggests, then another question seems to arise: isn't the remedy envisioned for this parting equally uncanny as it threatens to clothe the flights of newness in the shroud of a common language?

As we join together moments of this disjointed[4] conversation, we notice that several postmodern rhetorical figures from the social sciences—hybridity, mediators, heteroglossia—are used with credulity in order to delineate and defend the disciplinary locality (or, trans-locality) of philosophy of education. Yet, beyond its rhetorical supplementarity, postmodern discourse is not called on to examine the *philosophical* singularity of philosophy of education. Not a word about Derrida's reading of translation and living on borders; not a moment of restless agonizing with Foucauld's microphysics of disciplinarity; not a link to Deleuze and Guattari's post-innocent, post-Greek analysis of philosophy's double movement as '*amorous love*' that unites lovers and '*rivalry*' that prevents the engulfment of the one by the other through either an amorous conquest or a consensus (i.e., of a public);[5] not an *aporia* on how Lyotard's philosophical moment in pedagogy commands respect for the event. The epochality of Deleuzian thought (Surin, 1997) has instigated in philosophy of education an amorous love for passages but also a rivalry for both the social sciences and anti-foundational idioms. Is it because in appreciating a philosopher's pedagogical relevance by measuring the suitability of his thought for highlighting normative criteria and establishing shared interests, liquidating the legacy of the avant-gardes appears urgent once more? As this demand for realism and communicability becomes dominant, Deleuzian approaches to translation, multiplicity and creativity either become frozen into untranslatable idioms, cut out as skepticism's proper names, or they become all too translatable, user-friendly metaphors for explicating the old principles of critical pedagogy to the young generations of scholars.

THE LIMITS OF THE RHIZOME: RHIZOMATIC MICROFASCISMS

When I presented a paper on Deleuze in a recent conference, defending the position that in philosophy of education we should not teach, codify represent and deliver postmodernism but also become postmodern in our pedagogies, a colleague presented me with the following scenario:

> I have a student who has been trying to formulate the thematic universe for a paper for almost a semester now. She comes early in the semester to my office with a very tidy and 'tight' proposal. Her heart is tight too, bound by stress and confusion. We discuss different options, different ways to go on, various connections and inquiries to attempt. She starts to map various directions. She sounds exhilarated ... She comes back the next week with a completely different theme. She talks about ways to expand, settles down at a new thematic web. I suggest a preliminary bibliography. She comes back, again, excited to discover this new author ... She drifts again. Is this what following 'a line of flight' means? Is this rhizomatics? Is this growth? Am I going to grade this mapping of disparate things?

A variation of this scenario also illustrates the student's uncertainty when troubled by the lack of a linear format in what she perceives as the delivery of a lesson. Some students would consider inter-textual flows as the desacralization of pedagogy, others would find this entertaining, others entertaining in its unique style: 'My God, it is impossible to take neat notes in this class, I need a one-byone-meter notepad.' Assemblages initiated by the teacher can always be subsumed by the student's faith in representation as the image of thought (and *vice versa*).

The ideal for a book, writes Deleuze, 'would be to lay everything out on a plane of exteriority of this kind, on a single page, the same sheet: lived events, historical determinations, concepts, individuals, groups, social formations' (Deleuze & Guattari, 1987, p. 32). However, few students would be able to invent new interdisciplinary links in the readings and writings they produce. Usually, they feel that they lag behind, behind the 'master'. They often feel frustrated and disoriented as they try to map the flight of his/her thought in a comprehensible and reproducible manner. Scarcely do they convey or ride their own lines of flight. Applied in theory of education as a detour in interdisciplinary inquiry, the rhizome comes to signify for students a sense of loss. 'I'm confused, how does this fit in now, how is this going to be useful in my teaching, how do all these fit together ... why do we keep shifting from subject to subject ... why do we keep criticizing things ... ?' Whose book is this rhizome of anxious quests? Is it less authoritative than any other textbook? Such student comments might not sound unfamiliar to teachers of foundations courses. Students do not impugn foundations and meta-narratives. Student incredulity is more likely to erupt against modes of teaching that evade traditional modes of delivery, imprinting and organization, and defiant comments are more likely to erupt while questioning a course's utility. How can they invest in encounters with ideas where novelty escapes codification, ownership and repetition? The quest for legitimation does not take place at a tribunal of disciplines and incommensurable language games, as Lyotard invokes in *The Postmodern Condition*. It takes place in the post-graduate post-disciplinary world of marketable skills and anxious college graduates searching for that educational supplement that will bestow to them the benefits of a competitive advantage. This context flattens out the differences of idioms and the heterogeneity of assemblages as it over-codes learning with the criteria of operational and marketable knowledge. In a game where knowledge survives 'only when [it] changes and becomes operational', and in an economy of higher education where learning is 'circulating along the same lines as money' (Lyotard, 1984, pp. 4, 6), philosophy of education appears to be not hegemonic, 'root-like' or 'rhizomatic' but, rather, 'confusing'.

Trying to fabricate concepts of practical use with the rhetorical tools of postmodern discourse, postmodern philosophers of education might find in Deleuze a relatively positive philosophy of life. His philosophy of teaching is a philosophy of experimentation rather than a self-referential philosophy trapped in the agonistics of overcoming metaphysics. This questioning of metaphysics— deconstructing 'originals', 'killing' fathers, displacing philosophical thought from its purist state—the critics of postmodernism might argue, fails to overcome mourning and yields nothing but tired ironies and negative theologies. Deleuze, on the contrary, Rajchman argues, was 'from the start' a philosopher 'not of negation but of affirmation'. 'He tried to recast the problem of novelty and originality accordingly, not as transgression or mystical "interruption" but rather as a great art of connection and experimentation' (Rajchman, 2001, p. 13). Defending Nietzschean affirmation, both Derrida and Deleuze embrace 'play'. Derrida embraces the play of language made possible by the deconstruction of dominant signifiers and the displacement of any distinct borders between serious and non-serious kinds of speech (in his earlier response to Searle in *Limited Inc*), between categorical imperatives and the aporetic paralysis of certainty, the difficulty to adjudicate between singular and conflicting claims (*Aporias*):

> In the delineation of différance everything is strategic and adventurous. Strategic because no transcendent truth present outside the field of writing can govern theologically the totality of the field. Adventurous because this strategy is not a simple strategy in the sense that strategy orients tactics according to a final goal, a telos or theme of domination, a mastery and ultimate reappropriation of the development of the field. Finally, a strategy without finality, what might be called blind tactics, or *empirical wandering* (Derrida, 1982, p. 7; my italics).

Deleuze affirms play as the infinite connectability of multiplicities and repetition without a concept (the positive aspect of connectability recapitulates, as I will suggest later, the pedagogical nightmare of positivism, where riding every line of flight means not just bad pedagogy but the dissolution of pedagogy into chaos):

> We had no taste for abstractions, Unity, Totality, Reason, Subject. We set ourselves the task of analyzing mixed forms, arrangements, what Foucault called apparatuses ... to follow and disentangle lines rather than working back to points ... We weren't looking for origins, even lost or deleted ones,

but setting out to catch things where they were at work, in the middle (Deleuze, 1995, p. 86).

Besides these two philosophers' common fondness for play, concedes Bearn, the difference between them couldn't be greater: 'it is the difference between negation and affirmation, between Yes and No' (Bearn, 2000, p. 441). Despite its continuous critique of metaphysics, deconstruction's semantic play is still made possible by a lack.[6] Lack haunts the introduction of new concepts in the form of a negative theology, a theology that is always combating the nostalgia for presences (ibid.). In contrast to Derrida's admonitions, Deleuze's writing evokes an affirmation without reserve. Derrida often uses terms 'under erasure' (writing as ~~arche~~, that is, an-archic, without the presence of an authentic, original intention but still effective in commencing both poisonous and therapeutic effects, as the ambivalent semiotics of the Greek word '*pharmakon*' implies). This tactic allows him to use a language that belongs to metaphysics while reclaiming and restaging metaphysical terms and displacing their regression to empirical realities or to transcendental meanings. Deleuze and Guattari, on the other hand, do not hesitate to use new terms without reminding their readers with apologetic remarks of perpetual risk of a regress to metaphysics: 'the death of metaphysics or the overcoming of philosophy has never been a problem for us: it is just tiresome, idle chatter' (Deleuze & Guattari, 1994, p. 9). Speaking *about* or *for* the rhizome, they do not hesitate to pick up both organic and mechanic terms. They use metaphors for their shear connectability and yet deflate with laughter these metaphors' didactic (representational) optics. Starting from a naturalistic plantography and expanding it into an involuntary array of hybrid terms, they perform nuptials against nature. The goal is not to represent the rhizome but to implant it in theoretical thinking. The effect they are after is not the understanding of the rhizome but its functioning, the enabling of a whole apparatus that connects disparate, linguistic and non-linguistic things. The tragic paradox is that the rhizome finds a hospitable niche in pedagogical discourse only when used as a metaphor for de-centered and non-hierarchical systems of organization.

In their joint book *A Thousand Plateaus* Deleuze and Guattari use the names Root and Rhizome to map the levels of stratification and territorialization in books or thought. This mapping renders perceptible two models of thought, the 'arborescent model' (or 'root-book') and the 'rhizome'. Let us recap this mapping while also alerting ourselves to the possibility that the pedagogical (i.e., expositional) orientation of this repetition might territorialize as a separate and distinct entity a type whose name (Rhizome or Tree) is nothing more, as Deleuze and Guattari note, than 'the trace of an intensity'. The Root is dichotomous and hierarchical, operating on the law of reflection: 'The law of the book is the law of reflection, the One becomes two. ... Binary logic is the spiritual reality of the root-tree' (Deleuze & Guattari, 1987, p. 5). Trees are hierarchical structures and stratified totalities that function on binary logic and impose limited and regulated connections between their components. This kind of structure, according to Deleuze and Guattari, has dominated Western thought. Linnaean taxonomies and Chomsky's diagrams are often cited as paradigmatic trees, though we could also cite Freudian interpretations of the unconscious. The regulated field of psychoanalysis, for example, recuperates the tree through the over-cathexis of certain body parts and orifices of the Oedipal body. The tree resurfaces in interpretation of dreams as the certain signifiers become privileged entry points to the unconscious. The rhizome, in contrast, has no privileged point of entry, no intrinsic hierarchy of fragments (Bogue, 1989).

The rhizome is an uncentered growth, a multiplicity, characterized by connection and heterogeneity. It is constantly producing new shoots and rootlets. The rhizome as subterranean stem can be attributed to bulbs and tubers, but also to pack forms of animal life such as rats and burrows. Viruses are also rhizomes, in all of their functions of shelter, supply, movement, evasion, and breakout. The rhizome includes *the best and the worst*, as Deleuze and Guattari concede: 'potato and couchgrass, or the weed. Animal and plant, couchgrass is crabgrass' (Deleuze & Guattari, 1987, p. 7). But these botanical figurations of creative associationism do not signify corresponding stages of a teleological evolution. Behind the rhizome there is no foundation or essence. In fact, the excessive refrain of organic metaphors laughs at the anticipation of a deeper meaning. It juxtaposes paratactic syntax to the tropologies of surface and depth and the practice of survey to the logic of the example. It replaces desire for lack and the 'body without organs' for the ideological subject of enunciation that is enacted in its anticipation for what is awaiting behind, secret. In fact, there is no behind. The rhizome's relations to other territories, as well as the relations between its elements, defy any transcendental or phenomenological sense of 'behind' or 'depth'. They can be explicated only in terms of change and excessive exteriority:

> Rhizomes do not evolve from an original essence (model), by means of filiation or correspondence, that is, genetic representation. Instead, rhizomes are anomalous becomings produced by the formation of transversal alliances between different and coexisting terms within an open system (ibid., p. 10).

There is no unity to serve as a pivot, an anchoring multiplicity to the One, a subject or object: 'A multiplicity has neither subject nor object, only determinations, magnitudes, and dimensions that cannot increase in number without the multiplicity changing in nature (the laws of combination therefore increase in number as the multiplicity grows' (ibid., p. 8). But if the rhizome does not evolve from an original essence, if its attribution to a structure or mode of organization cannot be authenticated through correspondence and analogy, how can we be sure that it is indeed a Rhizome and not a Tree, or at least not a radicle system (a hierarchical and binary system from which the principal root has been aborted or its tip has been destroyed)? How can we follow multiplicities, which are rhizomatic to the nth degree and 'expose', as Deleuze and Guattari urge us, 'arborescent pseudo-multiplicities for what they are'? We cannot be sure. We cannot recap the Deleuzian affirmation of repetition into a normative educational vision. The rhizome does not distinguish the good from the evil, does not provide ground rules for adjudicating with justice between rivals, does not detect landmines and pitfalls. The urge to commence the rhizome, gay exploration and indeterminacy overcome the tragic sense of uncertainty but do not alleviate us from the task to expose microfascisms.

Having surveyed the tentative descriptions of these forms by Deleuze, we have to concede that tree and rhizome do not represent two separate entities, do not construe a typology of two distinct—one central and one decentralized—systems. The identity of each form is not definite or determinable. Rhizome and Tree do not signify repetition guided by some concept of an original. They are just moments in becoming. A book, *any book* (Root-like or Rhizome-like), is an assemblage and as such it is unattributable: 'It is a multiplicity—but we don't know yet what the multiple entails when it is no longer attributed, that is, after it has been elevated to the status of the substantive' (ibid., p. 4). It has a determinable side which 'faces the strata,' rendering it into an organism, a signifying totality. But it also has another side, a side 'facing a body without organs,' which is continuously dismantling the organism, causing asignifying ruptures and intensities. Rootlike and rhizomatic, sometime treated axiologically and other times attributed the status of a binary ontology, are nothing more than mappings of an assemblage's possibilities in connection with other assemblages. The *names* Rhizome and Tree are indexical signs, analytic concepts which can be put in the service of detecting correspondences, matching similarities and identifying entities. They are not signifying essences which guard their proper singularity and authenticate their repetitions in various contexts. The name is nothing more 'than the trace of an intensity' (ibid.). The survey of the book, tree and rhizome, examines not what each signifies but what it does; not what lies in its core but what happens at its fringes. Thus,

> we will not look for anything to understand in it. We will ask what it functions with, in which other multiplicities its own are inserted and metamorphosed, and with what other bodies without organs it makes its own converge. A book exists only through the outside and on the outside (ibid.).

Despite the fact that no transcendental signifieds or signifiers can be put in the service of guarding the threshold between tree and rhizome, it often appears pedagogically tempting, at least from the viewpoint of philosophy of education, to name, codify and qualify the rhizome. Many educational theorists attuned to postmodernism, find it empowering to point out empirical concretizations of the rhizome among social and cultural formations and to suggest how a non-authoritative pedagogy and organization of knowledge could be built after such a design. In contrast to deconstruction's deferral of tangible meanings and the proliferation of readings, the rhizome inhabits visual codifications that serve as points of repose in the vertigo of abstractions, as conceptual posts around which to organize one's understanding of Deleuzian terms, as rhetorical figures that could be offered to inpatient readers searching desperately for anything that will help them escape the negativity of writing 'under erasure'. It is a relief to be able to teach didactically sometimes, to be able to use the copula again, without any postmodern guilt for having recovered the metaphysics of presence: 'The rhizome *is* ...' 'Deleuze's point is that ...'.

It feels empowering to launch one's pedagogy from some theoretical concepts which, without instituting a normative ethics, can be pragmatically useful in helping us make sense of how we live our lives and how we teach and use philosophy in a postmodern world. Thus the rhizome is often used as a concept exemplified by metaphors, i.e., ferns and rhododendrons (Morss, 2000), or, as a metaphor that figures the organization of the World Wide Web as a rhizomatic system (Burbules, 1997). The indexical is followed by the expositions (what does it do): 'a model of communication and proliferation' (Morss, 2000, p. 193); 'a system that is rhizomatic, spreading in all directions' (Burbules, 1997, p. 3).[7] What is wrong with such codifications of the rhizomatic, the reader might wonder. After all, don't they recap Deleuze and Guattari's iconography of thought, their 'bulbs', 'tubers' and the 'becoming wasp' of the orchid? Though Deleuze's paratactic syntax of rhizomorphic things evolves into an overwhelming ontology where everything can be connected to everything else, it never culminates into normative statements on resistance or pedagogy: 'we still don't know what the multiple implies when it ceases to be attributed, that is to say, when it is raised to the status of a substantive' (Deleuze, 1993, p. 2). The appreciation that such chains of attributions, which evade a theoretical climax and conclusions, leave us without any normative pedagogical ethics, impels theorists to deduce analogies between the ontology of rhizomes and the utopia of a system without any central root. This iconography invoked is structural enough to help organize things but also de-centered enough to dismantle authoritative structures. Some theorists entertain the possibility that the rhizome transcends binary logic and hierarchical structures without compromising the devotion to Enlightenment's unfinished project of liberation: 'with no governing set of rules for deciding which of many branching options to choose' (Burbules, 1997, p. 3); 'there is an explicitly emancipatory impulse at work' (Morss, 2000, p. 193).

Such an articulation of the rhizome might always backfire by legitimizing microfascisms. Rhizome and Tree are stratified and delineated as separate forms of organization in the explanatory, cut-and-paste, didactic reading of Deleuze. Yet their difference becomes less foundational/eidetic and more temporal when it is applied towards exploring a multiplicity's variations, its visible connections but also its potential recoiling to pivotal centers of control:

Every rhizome contains lines of segmentarity according to which it is stratified, territorialized, organized, signified, attributed, etc., as well as lines of deterritorialization down which it constantly flees [...] That is why one cannot posit a dualism or a dichotomy, even in the rudimentary form of the good and the bad. You may make a rupture, draw a line of flight, yet there is still a danger that you will reencounter organizations that restratify everything, formations that restore power to a signifier, attributions that reconstitute a subject—anything you like, from Oedipal resurgences to fascist connections. Groups and individuals contain microfascisms just waiting to crystallize. Yes, couchgrass is also a rhizome. Good and bad are only the products of an active and temporary selection, which must be renewed. (Deleuze & Guattari, 1987, pp. 9–10).

Against the interpretation that there are 'rhizomatic' books (*Thousand Plateaus* is often cited as paradigmatic of such a kind) and 'root-like' books, I would argue that any book, despite its linear narrative structure, could become part of a rhizome, which includes its readers, its distributions and consumptions, its osmotic contacts with popular culture. A root-like book can induce the hybridization of genres, create new desires and new audiences that cut across the borders of traditional audiences, upset hierarchies and orthodoxies in the lists of bestsellers. Indeed, it can cause such unprecedented bottlenecking of queues at bookstore counters that even buying rituals would also have to change. Take *Harry Potter* and its sequels, for example. Such a rhizome could also culminate in new hierarchies, paralyze local production, reterritorialize the body without organs of the young reader around a single root, a single orifice, a new lack: the translation from English of the last *Harry Potter* book. Languages are being reterritorialized as 'local languages' by means of the interval that separates them from the original, i.e., English text, and local publishers are deterritorialized as translators and mediators of the global. The rhizome does not have any innate subversive quality, though a widespread fantasy would like to think of it as a virus that grows on structures of power and 'eats up' its hardware. The rhizome has nothing to do with essence and normative ethics. It can grow in many places. It can also be dangerous. It has already been at work in corporate capitalism, in modulations of control in human resource management, in education's corporative modulations in order to be able to produce graduates with flexible market skills. It is not a matter of exposing the Root and announcing the Rhizome. There are knots of arborescence in rhizomes and rhizomatic offshoots in roots. The rhizome is perpetually in a process of becoming or collapsing, a process that is perpetually prolonging itself, breaking off and starting up again. The rhizomatic structure of lifelong training—the linear model of school-to-college education is presumably cut off from its central root, that is, graduation—is actually reterritorializing itself around the forces of market economy and its necessary supplement, the post-utopian need of employability. In his 'Postscript on the Societies of Control' Deleuze already anticipated the reterritorialization of learning in market economy. Incompleteness, often valorized in textual politics as the ambiguity which exposes the limits of the metaphysics of voice, in the discourse of corporate training (which in a way has colonized the discourse of education) becomes another tactics of control in human resource management: 'Man [*sic*] is no longer man enclosed, but man in debt,' writes Deleuze. Education mutates to an open system of 'thousand plateaus' of training where 'one is always in debt' in the sense that one is never finished with anything: 'the corporation, the education system, the armed services being metastable states coexisting in one and the same modulation', like a global micro-training of educational deformation:

> Many young people strangely boast of being 'motivated'; they re-request apprenticeships and permanent training. It's up to them to discover what they're being made to serve, just as their elders discovered, not without difficulty, the *telos* of the disciplines. The coils of a serpent are even more complex that the burrows of a molehill (Deleuze, 1992, pp. 3, 7).

TOWARDS A MINOR PHILOSOPHY OF EDUCATION

Philosophers differ from psychoanalysts in that they have many fathers, too many to accept just one paternity. Or alternatively, in that philosophising is first and foremost an autodidactic activity [...] That is the first thing I mean of course of philosophy. You cannot be a master and master this course. You cannot open up a question without leaving yourself open to it. You cannot scrutinize a 'subject' (training, for example) without being scrutinized by it. You cannot do any of these things without renewing ties with the season of childhood, the season of the mind's possibilities [...] You need to recommence [...] we know that commencing does not mean proceeding genealogically [...] it is not done by acquisition (Lyotard, 1997, pp. 100–101).

> What is missing/repressed in this informatics, but still lower there, underneath, the face-information, as always the minimum required for the comprehension of orders; and lower still, something which could be either the shout, or silence, or stuttering, and which would be like language's line of flight, speaking in one's own language as a foreigner, making a minority use of language (Deleuze & Parnet, 1987, pp. 22–23).

Minor literature is that which a minority constructs within a major language. Philosophy of education constructs both minor philosophies in philosophy and minor pedagogies in education. Its grandeur lies not in providing the transcendental heading of/for education or feeding arboreal philosophical roots by deriving inspiration from its engagement in practical issues. It lies in the new encounters of ideas which the narrowness (but also comfort in becoming, changing, shifting, connecting) of the minor facilitates, necessitates, allows. The risk lies in territorializing the minor as a personal genealogy, as the redeeming of 'voice' or 'lived experience', as a new regionalism, e.g., women's, Greeks', educators' way of doing philosophy.

What is this 'minor' that produces rather than divests, if the minor would be reclaimed from its alleged inferiority, unimportantness, immaturity? Deleuze and Guattari's Kafka appears to be the proper site where to locate and localize a semiotics, a method and even a cultural anthropology of the minor. Such a genealogy must be resisted, however, for it closes off a series of different encounters with the minor: Kafka's reflections on the Jewish literature of Warsaw in *The Diaries* (Κάφκα, 1998, pp. 156–159); Benjamin's study of 'the great rules of asceticism [that] operate in Kafka'; postcolonial authors' appropriation of the minor in contesting both the centers of national literatures and the native roots of identities (e.g., Chicano literature, Hong Kong cinema (Yau, 2001)); our re-writing of the philosophers. All these instances explicate the creative possibilities of a writing which, cut off from both its Mother tongue (immanence and sense of belongingness) and the Father (a double anxiety: to measure one's art by the standards of the big masters, and to escape the influence of a style once this has been mastered), operates experimentally, connecting the literary with the political, the personal with the social. The former term in each of these equations is not conceived as a metaphor, representation, imprinting (popular allusions for the role of philosophy of education as mediator). There are two ways to miss the point of Kafka's works, writes Benjamin (a cautionary remark obeyed by Deleuze and Guattari): 'One is to interpret them naturally, the other is the supernatural interpretation. Both the psychoanalytic and the theological interpretations equally miss the essential points' (Benjamin, 1992, p. 123). In a similar manner, Deleuze and Guattari insist against representation. For them difference is primary and resemblance, identity and analogy are its secondary effects (Hayden, 1998). Benjamin calls the linking of the disparate in Kafka's writing '*gestus*'. Deleuze and Guattari call this primary repetition the 'becoming minor' of the major.

The minor is not the theme of exile or oppression, the *modus operandi* of an autobiographic writing that redeems the exilic self, or the new subject of enunciation invoked in the telling of displacement. It has nothing to do with nostalgia (for return), mourning (for lost homes and severed cords), the quest for one's recognition (as Other), voice (the impossible voice of the subaltern, the autobiographical voice of the displaced other). Nomadism does not belong to the history and legacy of the marginalized other but to that use of language that makes the dormant bilingualism of the major language, of every language as a major language, reverberate again. Kafka, a Czechoslovakian Jew writing in German, is a minor writer not in his being a native speaker of a minor language (in the Austrian empire Czech is a minor language in relation to German) but in his minor use of German. His minor language is German, the German of Prague, which is minor in relation to the German of Vienna or Berlin. This German becomes minor in the multiple deterritorializations to which Kafka submits it. Kafka's 'paper language' is a language of both deterritorializations and intensities. He

> submits German to creative treatment as a minor language, constructing a continuum of variation, negotiating all the variables: make language stammer, or make it 'wail,' stretch tensors through all of language, even written language, and draw from it cries, shouts, pitches, durations, timbres, accents, intensities (Deleuze & Guattari, 1987, p. 104).

Two conjoined tendencies of so-called minor languages, which according to Deleuze and Guattari have often been both noted and stained, are: (a) an impoverishment (e.g., a 'shedding' of syntactical and lexical forms), and (b) a simultaneous, strange proliferation of shifting effects, 'a taste for overload and paraphrase.' The restriction of constants linked by overloading in a sweeping continuum of variations applies to the German of Prague, Black English and Quebecois. But with rare exceptions, Deleuze and Guattari note, the interpretation of linguistics has been rather 'malevolent', invoking a consubstantial poverty and preciosity (ibid.).

The creative force of the minor language could be paralleled to the form of the rhizome only if the rhizome were also minoritized, rescued from its literary overcoding in pedagogical discourse as a metaphor for excessive multiplicity and radical openness. The multiple *must be made*, Deleuze and Guattari tell us in the opening pages of *A Thousand Plateaus*, not by always adding a higher dimension, 'but rather in the simplest of ways, by dint of sobriety, with the number of dimensions one already has available—always $n - 1$ (the only way the one belongs to the multiple: always subtracted)'. In Kafka's short story 'A Report to the Academy' an ape tells his captive of his decision to become human. But escaping does not mean adding to his freedom by increasing his degree of humanity. ' "No", he says, "freedom was not what I wanted. Only a way out; right or left, or in any direction. I made no other demand" ' (Bogue, 1989, p. 100). Subtract the unique from the multiplicity to be constituted, Deleuze and Guattari prescribe in *A Thousand Plateaus*. Write at $n - 1$ dimensions: 'A system of this kind could be called a rhizome' (Deleuze & Guattari, 1987, p. 6).

In *Kafka: Toward a Minor Literature* (a work that precedes *A Thousand Plateaus)*, Deleuze and Guattari itemize three effects of minor writing, of writing at $n - 1$ dimensions: deterritorialization of language, political immediacy of the personal, and collective value of enunciation (or, surpassing the necessity of an ideal speech situation). The deterritorialization of language marks the creative process by the double impossibility to be native and to be major: 'the impossibility of not writing, the impossibility of writing in German, the impossibility of writing otherwise'. Philosophy of education, like Kafka's Prague German, is deterritorialized. Yet the impossibility of drifting into philosophical skepticism and the impossibility, also, of delivering normative statements for regulating educational practice, is experienced not as a problem or difficulty but as the shift to a new philosophical style, a new assemblage of enunciations. Like Prague Jews who write in a 'paper language' (a characteristic which Kafka attributes to Prague German), philosophers of education write in a *paper philosophy* (allegedly 'soft' or 'diluted' philosophy) and introduce a 'paper pedagogy' (allegedly 'nihilistic' or 'confusing' pedagogy). A style means exactly this: *managing* to stammer in one's own language but not by retreating or recovering the subject of *énoncé* (utterance) as a solid actor: 'Not being a stammerer in one's speech, but being a stammerer of language itself' (Deleuze & Parnet, 1987, p. 4).

Whereas the performativity of talking back, drag, pastiche, etc., implicate the risks of cultural reification in parody and the privatization of politics in dandyism, the 'vital stammering' which Deleuze and Guattari attribute to the becoming minor of the major implicates the connection of the individual to a political immediacy. Everything in a minor literature is political: 'its cramped space forces each individual intrigue to connect immediately to politics. The individual concern thus becomes all the more necessary, indispensable, magnified, because a whole other story is vibrating within it' (Deleuze & Guattari, 1986, p. 17). When Kafka writes that one of the aspects of a minor literature is the 'purification' of the conflict that opposes father and son and 'the possibility of discussing that conflict,' Deleuze and Guattari comment, 'this isn't a question of an Oedipal phantasm but of a political program' (ibid.). The personal is not the drama played against the background of the sociopolitical milieu, but the two become connected in an enlarged political sphere. When philosophers of education reflect on student teachers' stagnation in the logic of performativity and the inertia this habit of learning that such habit normalizes, this isn't a question about identity anxiety regarding their own disciplinary position but a political question regarding the future of philosophical thinking. When women educators turn to philosophy of education to write about caring and the severing of intimate links and milky flows by institutionalized schooling, their writing isn't a sedimentation of cut off desires, or a remuneration for their own 'bitter milk', an illegitimate harbouring of 'gender issues' in philosophy, a *petit recit* playing the role of philosophy's 'other'. It is not the feminine philosophical way toward the foundation of a new method of teaching, i.e., a caring or feminine pedagogy. It is philosophy at the $n-1$ *dimension*: breaking from the 'referential genre' and commencing philosophical thinking again, acting new allusions to what is conceivable.

One does not inaugurate philosophizing by theorizing incredulity toward grand narratives. Autodidactic practice does not mean anti-philosophy. Reflecting on life as immanence (a process of creative power),[8] Deleuze concedes that the life of the individual has given way to a life that is impersonal but singular nevertheless, and which releases a pure event freed from the accident of inner and outer life: 'Very young children, for example, all resemble each other and have barely any individuality; but they have singularities, a smile, a gesture, a grimace—events which are not subjective characteristics' (Deleuze, 1997, pp. 4–5). If there is something in education to be preserved alive by philosophy of education, something which for the social sciences is neither conceivable nor presentable, this is not 'the Foundations' but the respect for the singular. By becoming a bridge between philosophy and education and by facilitating the dialogue among these disciplines, philosophy of education becomes another meta-discourse, another techno-science. Philosophizing in education recommences by minoritizing the language of philosophy in such a way that that singularities in the classroom—a lesson, an encounter, a face, a face-to-face—can be re-assembled into new multiplicities instead of reproducing the binaries teacher–student, child–adult, passive–active, right–wrong. Deleuze and Guattari's style of description minoritizes philosophical discourse. Narrative statements prevail over argument and intervals of indirect discourse open up in the heart of every statement: sidestepping a constant instead of tackling it head on, approaching it from above or below instead of positioning oneself within it. Such a style of philosophizing, Millet writes, is allied with the indefinite article to the point of collapsing 'the power to say I' (Millet, 1997, p. 59). Erasing the subject of enunciation, facilitating the erosion of universals and allowing anonymous assemblages of voices, acts, affects and bodily habits to invoke a new sensibility, philosophers of education become bilingual or multilingual in speaking their own philosophical idiom.

The third effect of the minor that Deleuze and Guattari pick up in their reading of Kafka is the scarcity of talent or, more accurately, the collective value of enunciation:

> precisely because talent isn't abundant in a minor literature, there are no possibilities for an individuated enunciation that would belong to this or that 'master' and that could be separated from a collective enunciation. Indeed,

scarcity of talent is in fact beneficial and allows the conception of something other than a literature of masters (Deleuze & Guattari, 1986, p. 17).

Philosophy of education is yet to become deterritorialized by experimenting in fields of unformed expression, though the absence of 'masters' in the discipline creates such possibilities. 'Nuptials without conjugality' rather than 'mediation' between philosophers and educators is the sense of singularity Deleuze and Guattari present of philosophy of education with. But the philosophical moment in education is often contained through a remedial teaching of the history of philosophy. A didactic sobriety in everything one encounters would be Kafka's repetition in a minor pedagogy: finding instead of regulating, encountering instead of recognizing. Likewise, the philosophical moment in our writing also freezes in the regulation of conditions that would secure an ideal speech situation and a receptive audience. Tragically, we have become the ideal students for our didactic teaching of philosophy. We usually try to find whether an idea is just or correct. We forget how to pick up ideas, how to link them to other possibilities instead of treating them like speculums. You don't have to be learned, to know or to be familiar with a particular area, but to pick up this or that in areas which are very different, Deleuze tempts us to do. Those who were unfortunate enough to be born in a major language can also develop their own *patois*, their own bilingualism: 'This is better than the "cut-up". It is rather a "pick-me-up" or "pick-up"—in the dictionary = collecting up, chance, restarting of the motor, getting on to the wavelength; and then the sexual connotation of the word' (Deleuze & Parnet, 1987, p. 10).

'Metaphors are one of the many things that make me despair of writing,' Kafka proclaims with indignation in his *Diaries*, 1921 (Κάφκα, 1998, p. 421; my translation). This lack of autonomy in literary writing and the assignation of metaphors by means of a figurative sense synthesize elements into a narrative structure while effacing their heterogeneity and hindering their potential for future rearranging. Despite its genealogically ambivalent relationship with literariness, philosophy of education, as philosophy's proper translator in the field of education, becomes the conveyor of philosophical metaphors to be used an analytic tools by educators. While dreaming of its hybrid, middle ground, it continues to recuperate the referential language of a meta-discourse. To the contrary, the minor use of language which Deleuze and Guattari pick up from Kafka, 'deliberately kills all metaphor, all symbolism, all signification, no less than all designation' (Deleuze & Guattari, 1986, p. 22). If philosophers of education are bilingual, it is not by mixing, intermingling or bridging the languages of the disciplines into a comprehensible discourse which educators can understand and perhaps join; it is by creating an unformed philosophical expression which in pedagogy's encounter with philosophical ideas sustains a field of experimentation, a field that is non-translatable against the barren rationality of representationalism.

NOTES

[1] Deleuze's reference to 'the terrible Lunette' is from Pierrette Fleutiaux (1976), *Histoire du gouffre et de la lunette* (Paris, Julliard).

[2] In Arcilla's analysis, the contradiction that philosophy of education hosts in its own name cannot but be associated with the a mutual shunning of the two cultures, mostly due to the borders of institutional enclaves, formed and solidified by disciplinarity. For Stengel, however, these disciplinary borders do not necessarily produce 'straight' disciplinary subjects or exclude the creation of inbetween action zones. Philosophers of education, exactly because they are both philosophers and educators, can play a leading role in initiating these assemblages and making visible their shared concerns in concrete tasks. Figured as 'border crossers'—intermediaries, mediators and bilinguals—'fluent in the language of each inquiry', philosophers of education are summoned to start up and assist the conversation by ensuring that a common language is used, all participants are heard and every participant's contribution is recognized (Stengel, 2002, pp. 288–289)

[3] In an effort to build bridges of communication across the parting disciplines of philosophy and education, Abowitz embraces the heteroglossia of philosophy of education and the post-disciplinary hybridity of its subjects, i.e., their ability to converse in multiple languages in multiple contexts. Cornel West is cited as a paradigmatic performer of heteroglossia, one who, like philosophers of education, is speaking the language of philosophy from outside the walls of philosophy departments, and, like philosophers of education, is often addressing many diverse English languages. Like West, she points out, 'we in philosophy of education are "caught in a type of heteroglossia," inasmuch as we speak the languages of philosophy in and through the many contexts of educational theory and schooling' (Abowitz, 2002, p. 292). Nevertheless, reflecting more critically on West's Inside–Outside performance, she cautions us on the risk that adjusting philosophy to the practical may entail a certain compromising of philosophical quality, rigor and depth.

[4] Participants in the symposium were invited to write in response to what is identified as the 'malady' of philosophy of education: its decreased visibility and influence on the community of educators. No exchanges were contacted between writers in responding (see editor's notes in the opening essay of the special issue).

[5] Deleuze and Guattari warn against the didactics, pedagogical or political, of any form of cosmopolitanism that claims to restore the universal society of friends: 'A great deal of innocence or cunning is needed by a philosophy of communication that claims to restore the society of friends, or even of wise men, by forming a universal opinion as 'consensus' able to moralize nations, States, and the market' (Deleuze & Guattari, 1994, p. 107). Friendship, a vital constituent in both philosophy's love (*philia*) of wisdom (*sophia*) and an audience's shared sense of brotherhood, 'must reconcile the integrity of the essence and the rivalry of claimants' (ibid., p. 4).

[6] Boundas calls Deleuze's empiricism a minor deconstruction in that it 'detouches itself from language as such and rather attaches itself in what makes language possible and to the arrangement with the outside forces that sustain its possibility' (Boundas, 2000, p. 174).

[7] References are made to the Internet versions of Deleuze's 'Postscript' and Burbules's 'Aporia.'

[8] Immanence, a concept Deleuze uses to displace transcendence from its foundational position in Western thought, has no outside and nothing other than itself (Colebrook, 2002, p. xxiv).

REFERENCES

Abowitz, K. K. (2002). Heteroglossia and philosophers of education. *Theory of Education, 52*(3), 291–302.

Arcilla, R. (2002). Why aren't philosophers and educators speaking to each other? *Theory of Education, 52*(1), 1–11.

Bearn, G. C. F. (2000). Differentiating Derrida and Deleuze. *Continental Philosophy Review, 33*(4), 441–465.

Benjamin, W. (1992). Franz Kafka: On the tenth anniversary of his death. In H. Arendt (Ed.), *Illuminations*. London: Fontana Press.

Bogue, R. (1989). *Deleuze and Guattari*. London and New York: Routledge.

Boundas, C. V. (2000). On tendencies and signs: Major and minor deconstruction. *Angelaki: Journal of Theoretical Humanities, 5*(2), 163–176.

Bredo, E. (2002). How can philosophy of education be both viable and good? *Theory of Education, 52*(3), 263–271.

Burbules, N. (1997). Aporia: Webs, passages, getting lost, and learning to go on. In *Philosophy of education 1997* (pp. 33–43). Urbana: Philosophy of Education Society. Retrieved October 12, 2001, from http://www.ed.uiuc.edu/eps/pes-yearbook/97_docs/burbules.html fnB9.

Colebrook, C. (2002). *Understanding Deleuze*. Crows Nest: Allen & Unwin.

Deleuze, G. (1992, October). Postscript on the societies of control. *59*(1), 3–7. Retrieved October 30, 2000, from http://www.dds.nl/<n5m/texts/deleuze.htm

Deleuze G. (1993). On the line. In C. V. Boundas (Ed.), *The Deleuze reader*. New York: Columbia University Press.

Deleuze, G. (1995). *Negotiations*. New York, Columbia: University Press.

Deleuze G. (1997). Immanence: A life. *Theory, Culture, and Society, 14*(2), 3–7.

Deleuze G., & Guattari, F. (1987). *A thousand plateaus: Capitalism and schizophrenia*. Minneapolis, MN: University of Minnesota Press.

Deleuze G., & Guattari, F. (1994). *What is philosophy?* Great Britain: Verso.

Deleuze, G., & Parnet, C. (1987). *Dialogues*. New York: Columbia University Press.

Derrida, J. (1978). *Writing and difference*. London and New York: Routledge.

Derrida, J. (1982). Différance. In *Margins of philosophy*. Chicago: University of Chicago Press.

Derrida, J. (1993). *Aporias: Dying—awaiting (one another at) the 'limits of truth'*. Stanford: Stanford University Press.

Fleutiaux, P. (1976). *Histoire du gouffre et de la lunette*. Paris: Julliard.

Hayden, P. (1998). *Multiplicity and becoming: The pluralist empiricism of Gilles Deleuze*. New York: Peter Lang Publishing, Inc.

Κάφκα, Φ. (1998). *Τα ημερολόγια*. Αθήνα: Εκδόσεις Εξάντας.

Lyotard, J.-F. (1984). *The postmodern condition: A report on knowledge*. Minneapolis, MN: University of Minnesota Press.

Lyotard, J.-F. (1993). *The postmodern explained*. Minneapolis and London: University of Minnesota Press.

Millett, N. (1997). The trick of singularity. *Theory, Culture and Society, 14*(2), 51–66.

Morss, J. R. (2000). The passional pedagogy of Gilles Deleuze. *Educational Philosophy and Theory, 32*(2), 185–200.

Rajchman, J. (2001). *The Deleuze connections*. Cambridge: MIT Press.

Stengel, B. (2002). Cause for worry or agenda for action? *Theory of Education, 52*(3), 281–290.

Surin, K. (1997). The 'epochality' of Deleuzian thought. *Theory, Culture, and Society, 14*(2), 9–21.

Yau, K.-F. (2001). Cinema 3: Towards a 'minor Hong Kong cinema.' *Cultural Studies, 15*(3–4), 543–563.

Zelia Gregoriou
Department of Education
University of Cyprus

EILEEN HONAN AND MARG SELLERS

8. (E)MERGING METHODOLOGIES:
PUTTING RHIZOMES TO WORK

My intent, in short, is to extract from Deleuze's project an apparatus of social
critique built on a utopian impulse. Its insistent question is 'how does it
work?' (Buchanan, 2000, p.8).

INTRODUCING IDEAS

This chapter is a contribution to a growing body of work that applies the
philosophical work of Deleuze and Guattari (1987) to educational research (see for
example, Semetsky, 2004 and others in the special issue of Educational Philosophy
and Theory). We are interested in the application of rhizomatic thinking to
educational research and in performing rhizomatic methodologies with/in our own
research. The commonalities between our rhizomatic approaches to educational
research include:
- An approach to writing that is partial and tentative, that transgresses generic
  boundaries, and allows the inclusion of the researchers' voice(s).
- Understanding that discourses operate within a text in rhizomatic ways, that they
  are not linear, or separate; any text includes a myriad of discursive systems,
  which are connected to and across each other. A rhizomatic discourse analysis
  follows the lines of flight that connect these different systems in order to
  provide accounts of (e)merging (mis)readings.
- Data collected for educational research, while appearing to be disparate, can be
  analysed rhizomatically to find connections between writing, artworks, video,
  interview transcripts and textual artefacts, for example. This kind of analysis
  enables (e)merging~(im)plausible[1] readings of connections between, across and
  within various data.

While these commonalities are evident to us as Deleuzian researchers, in writing
this chapter it has become obvious that the disparate methods of approaching these
three issues are more important. In what follows, we attempt to present, in a
rhizomatic fashion, our different, yet common, thoughts on developing Deleuzian
methods for educational research. We begin this representation by following a line
of flight through the rhizome that explores some of the figurations used by Deleuze
and Guattari and by us in our writing.

RHIZOMATIC FIGURATIONS

In A Thousand Plateaus, Gilles Deleuze and Felix Guattari (1987) introduce the
figuration of a rhizome to explore multiplicities in thinking and in writing. While

I. Semetsky (ed.), Nomadic Education: Variations on a Theme by Deleuze and Guattari, 111–128.

they are careful not to engage in constructing the type of binary thinking they are attempting to disrupt, rhizomes are compared and contrasted (but not opposed to) the arboreal metaphors that are often taken up in linear and modernist expressions of thought. Rhizomatic thinking and writing involves making ceaseless and ongoing connections:

Any point of a rhizome can be connected to anything other, and must be...
A rhizome ceaselessly establishes connections between semiotic chains, organizations of power, and circumstances relative to the arts, social sciences, and social struggles (Deleuze & Guattari, 1987, p.7)

Mapping these connections can involve following 'lines of flight', another figuration used by Deleuze and Guattari. 'There are no points or positions in a rhizome, such as those found in a structure, tree, or root. There are only lines' (p. 9). In our own writing following lines of flight means being open to making connections between quite different thoughts, ideas, pieces of data, discursive moments. These connections assemble as 'plateaus' – 'we call a "plateau" any multiplicity connected to other multiplicities by superficial underground stems in such a way as to form or extend a rhizome' (p. 24). Without conventionally linear beginnings and/or endings, a network of interconnections forms – an amassing of middles amidst an array of multidirectional movement – as we travel nomadically in our thinking and in our writing (St.Pierre, 2000).

This kind of rhizomatic thinking and the forming of plateaus through following lines of flight through/across/within various assemblages of middles is very difficult to portray in a linear text such as this chapter. Indeed Deleuze and Guattari draw attention themselves to these difficulties in their introduction to A Thousand Plateaus (1987, p. 10). Thus, we begin our attempts to explore what rhizomatics mean for educational research methods through a reflexive 'plateau' on the acts of attempting to write rhizomatically – both in this chapter, and in our separate research work. One of the first decisions we had to make in our representations here was around the use of the first person, the 'I' that connotes individual authorship. We take our lead here from Deleuze and Guattari themselves who point out the 'we' of their writing partnership also indicates the multiplicity of subject positions taken up by each author at any one moment. So while each of us wrote different parts of this chapter, and while the data that we use here was collected by one or the other, we refer to 'we' in our thinking and writing.

WRITING A RHIZOMATIC TEXT – THIS TEXT

The logistics of bringing together a text that meets academic requirements and has the possibility of making sense to readers is forever 'steering' us in the 'direction' of producing a 'linear' text – an 'ordered' 'progression' of 'theoretical ideas' and 'practical applications' that 'leads' to a 'coherent' 'conclusion'. All of these concepts are potentially problematic to rhizomatic thinking as it works to overcome binary polarisations, to go beyond dichotomous thought and linear thinking, instead working towards/producing points of intersection, overlaps, convergences, twisting and weaving through infinite folds and surfaces (Deleuze, 1993).

Trying to work within sections, by default, bounds our thinking and writing – any kind of segmentation creates boundaries, albeit blurred – as asides are forever appearing and we want to create a horizontal text as we 'attempt a nomadic journey, to...travel in the thinking that writing produces...' (St.Pierre, 2000, p.258). A text that continuously appears in new spaces, is fragmented and does not have to explain how it got there. But, how to produce a text, particularly when two of us are working together – as each and every, separate and together – that is workable and readable when we are enmeshed, albeit unwillingly, in conventional linear ways of writing, that expect we will trace a straight path from beginning to end, and that inevitably permeate our thinking and understanding?

In this chapter, in the process of sighting/citing data from both research projects, we have worked rhizomatically, writing separately but at the same time, each adding contributions that enabled a smooth flow into/through the collaborative writing. As each of us worked with the other's words, any power(full)ness [2]that emerged, simultaneously belonged to, and was disrupted by us both. In places we are no longer sure (or have concern about) whose writing we are reading – rhizomatics-in-action enacting rhizome. This is especially important to us, as we embody positions of supervisor and student, positions that are usually re-presented dichotomously and that are notoriously difficult to re-negotiate (see for example, Davies et al, 2006, pp. 114-144)

WRITING A RHIZOMATIC TEXT – EDUCATIONAL RESEARCH TEXTS

These linear constrictions of sections, chapters, pages, headings and footnotes, impact on us as we attempt to write rhizomatically/nomadically for research purposes. We therefore follow various pathways through educational rhizomes in order to produce writing that is rhizomatic, in that it transgresses generic boundaries, is partial and tentative, but that will also be accepted within the educational community. We have used poetry, lyrical stories, unending sentences, drawn on the personal to explain the abstract, and other techniques in this production. So for example, in our writing about teachers and teachers' work, we cannot ever forget that we are teachers ourselves, and our memories of those teaching days hang like dark clouds over the lines of flight we take through sets of data we collect as researchers. The ambivalence we feel as we are positioned as teachers is expressed here in this memory-poem of one of our experiences as a teacher:

The boy has been labelled, ADD
Requiring special treatment, consideration
He sits sullen at his desk
Refusing to work, to write, to obey
You will do what I say
This is my classroom
You will stay there until you have finished

No play
No lunch
No football
This is my classroom
In here, you do what I say
I sit at my desk
While he cries, and sobs, and throws paper and pencils around the room,
Until finally he scrawls something on the page
Only five minutes left in the lunch hour
No time to eat, or play, or go to football
You can go now I say
And remember
In here you do what I say

These kinds of memories form part of our collections of data, become the focus for reflexive analysis of the positions taken up by teachers, just as much as the data collected through interviews or classroom observations. So is the teacher here a bad teacher? Or a disciplinarian? (and is a disciplinarian a good teacher or a bad teacher?) Is she a moral force, contributing to the moral regulation of the boy, teaching him how to be a good school boy, or is she a drill sergeant? Is she a professional or an abuser? Reading this as a representation of a bad teacher and drill sergeant, we could tell the story that follows this one, of parents at the school office, complaining to the principal about the treatment of their son. Reading this teacher as a professional, we could tell the story that ended that school year, when the boy has stopped taking the medication prescribed for his condition. The children in the classroom on one of those play days that mark out the end of the school year, saying, 'you know, he could do what ever he liked last year, he used to do that stuff and the teacher would let him go outside and play under the trees, he never did any work last year, not like now'.

It is not easy to tease out the complexity of these subject positions; to hold a moment where one is in the act of becoming teacher (Deleuze & Guattari, 1987). Deleuze and Guattari remind us not to dwell on fixing that moment of becoming, but instead to follow the lines of flight that connect these subject positions. Writing rhizomatically allows the following of these lines, mapping the pathways through and across different data by re-presenting these data in myriad forms.

Thinking rhizomatically also allows for a certain kind of discursive analysis of re-presented data. A rhizo-textual analysis (Honan, 2004) depends on under-standing that discourses operate within texts in rhizomatic ways – that is they are not linear, or separate. This also requires an understanding that what emerges from within such an analysis may be far removed from the intention(s) of the gathering of that data. We now discuss these forms of analysis.

RHIZOMATIC DISCOURSE ANALYSIS

A rhizomatic discourse analysis follows the lines of flight that always/already connect different systems in order to provide accounts of (e)merging~(im)plausible~

(mis)readings. Many accounts of discourse analysis (eg., Gee, 1990, Gill, 2000) lead researchers to believe that discursive systems operate alongside each other within any text. We believe that discourses operate within texts in a rhizomatic fashion, intersecting and parting, over and under lapping. None disappear completely, one does not render another invisible. Bronwyn Davies (1994) uses the concept of palimpsest to describe the complex layering of discourses within a text. This use of 'palimpsest' draws on the historical meaning, which refers to the resurfacing and reuse of a writing material, to signal the potential embeddedness of many layers of meaning within the superficial 'surface'. Understanding texts as rhizomatic helps make sense of this layering – each discourse interweaves and interconnects with each other forming a discursive web.

A rhizo-textual analysis involves mapping these discursive lines, following pathways, identifying the intersections and connections, finding the moments where the assemblages of discourses merge to make plausible and reason(able) sense to the reader. Any one discursive pathway does not render another (im)plausible. St.Pierre (2000) explains this Deleuzian approach as going beyond the layering of a palimpsest that relentlessly overwrites (p. 261), rather lines of flight are always in the middle, in flux, 'disrupt[ing] dualisms with complementarity' (p. 279). Each discourse interweaves and interconnects with others forming a discursive web or map.

As well, and following Deleuze and Guattari, each text's complex web~map connects with other texts, so that forms of discourse taken up within one text can be mapped across and into other texts. This kind of analysis reveals that there are particular lines of flight that connect discourses to each other through linkages that are commonalities and taken-for-granted assumptions that seem reasonable and unquestionable. These discursive linkages are like the lumpy nodes that can appear within a rhizomatic root system, or like the couplings that connect varied systems of pipes in some underground water systems. These linkages provide connections between quite different sets of data that we have collected. In what follows, the linkage explored is that of the world of childhood, in that we trace what it means to be a child in two quite different contexts – a policy text from Queensland, Australia, that constructs a version of the ideal literate child, and a videorecording of children at play in an early childhood setting in Aotearoa New Zealand.

The individual child

In the Queensland P-10 English Syllabus (D. E. Q, 1994), the construction of the individual child is one of the rationalities that makes the power of literacy seem to be sensible. This individual child forms one of the provisional linkages that assemble the meanings of the different discourses on teaching of literacy that are present in the syllabus. The individual, rational, child is central to the discourses surrounding progressivist pedagogies (Walkerdine, 1984). But, even when the syllabus is using the discourses of systemic linguistics, or of functional skills, the subject that is being constructed is always, still, the individual child of progressivism.

A dichotomy present in discourses about the individual child is that she is at one and the same time, unique, but also representative of common humanity. The presence of this dichotomy in the syllabus texts allows the child to be spoken about in terms of her individual characteristics, while at the same time statements are made that generalise, universalise the learning of language. While the child is unique, she makes generalisable choices about language, and these choices are controlled by establishing limits to the availability of 'correct' choices.

The syllabus makes various statements about the universality of the ways in which people learn language:

> People learn a language by using it often with others and by reflecting on its use;

> Children learn language in the same way that they learn many other things – they learn by doing (D. E. Q, 1994, pp. 13-14).

The point here is not that language is essential to humans, which is a truism, but, rather, the implication of a universalised view that all children learn language by doing so in the same way. This is potentially problematic and in opposition to what the syllabus says about the influences of social and cultural contexts on the types of language used: "Language varies according to factors in the cultural and social context" (D. E. Q, 1994, p. 9). It would seem that the syllabus texts are saying that while the social and cultural contexts influence the *uses* of language, they do not influence the *learning* of language. There is a generalising move here that constructs the individual child as representative of all humanity. But then what follows is a contradiction, in that attention is paid to individuals' 'intrinsic' characteristics:

> Each child's individuality can be described as a unique combination of these cultural circumstances and intrinsic characteristics;

> The intrinsic characteristics of each child are, therefore, a unique combination of their functioning in sensory, intellectual, physical, neurological, and social areas;

> Each child is a complex being whose experiences of life and language use are constantly changing (D. E. Q, 1994, pp. 15-16).

This call to the individual's 'intrinsic' characteristics is a feature of psychological approaches to child development. In these terms, the individual child is born with particular innate ways of being ('sensory, intellectual, physical', etc), and these characteristics are the determining factors in distinguishing one individual from another. What the syllabus does here, is makes language learning one of these innate ways of being, so that the possibilities for changing or adapting the discourses a subject uses are limited. Importantly though, even while describing unique and complex characteristics of social beings, the generality and universality of these characteristics remain static and fixed.

The simultaneous mastery/subjection (Butler, 1997) of the individual child is made visible through the texts' emphasis on the rationality of correct choices made by individuals about the language they use:

Cultural diversity in English-speaking communities is reflected in the language choices made;

New genres evolve as people exercise the choices available to them in using the many systems that comprise any language (D. E. Q, 1994, p. 6);

Through the language resources available to us, individuals and communities make choices about which textual features will best communicate our personal purposes. These choices take account of conventional social and cultural patterns of language use (D. E. Q, 1994, p. 11).

While individuals make choices about language use, these choices are determined by 'social and cultural patterns'. Individuals are therefore bound and tied to the social and cultural circumstances in which they find themselves. They are also bound to make 'correct' choices in order to be constructed as a successful subject. The paradox of the master/submitted subject is made clear here: mastery of language is achieved through making choices, yet the subject must submit to the regulation of the choices made. What is not made visible, is how to judge, or who makes the judgements, about the correctness of these choices, or in Butler's terms, who makes the decisions about the successful mastery of language use.

One of the ways in which the syllabus texts attempts to answer these questions is to draw attention to methods of controlling choices. In the syllabus, control of these choices is achieved through an explanation of the innate humanist need to belong to society:

The need to communicate with others impels most children to develop effective language skills

The human need to communicate drives children to attend to the meanings associated with particular language structures

Through their need for affection and companionship, most children are anxious to develop communication skills

To enhance their acceptance with family and friends, and to promote self-esteem, children often reflect on the language they use with others (D. E. Q, 1994, p. 21).

Control of language choices thus becomes a form of governmentality, where "to govern is to act upon action" (Rose, 1999, p. 4). The child is driven or impelled to make the correct language choices, through some inner need, and this inner need is controlled through the necessity to be correct in others' eyes.

The child of the syllabus is thus constructed as a rational humanist identity; the stable humanist individual, of course, makes rational choices about language based on her innate need to communicate. The essentialism of this humanist individual is so fundamental to all educational discourses that it becomes a feature of discourses that, on the surface, appear to be attempting to construct some other view of a different kind of subject. In what follows here, we attempt to portray a different version of children, as (a) rhizomatic subject(s), whose discursive and embodied play reveals power(full) agentic work done to negotiate curriculum spaces.

Entering the world of childhood

Before beginning this rhizo-textual analysis, there are issues to raise from within a middle of a/the plateau. A rhizo-textual analysis not only draws out and makes visible discourses operating within and across various texts, but it also focuses our attention on the discourses, with which we ourselves as researchers engage, in talking, reading, writing and re-presenting our data. This is especially important in our research with young children. We are aware not only of the inclusion of our voice, but of enabling the voices of the children involved in the research to become audible. However, ensuring this happens is not straightforward. Because of the discourses at play, entering the children's world as (co)researcher is problematic. While discursive plateaus of children, childhood(s) and curriculum emerge as open and connectable maps, they are inevitably affected by various hierarchical tracings of power(full-ness). Thus, plugging such (arboreal) tracings of power back into the (rhizomatic) map of children, their childhoods and curriculum is significant to growing the rhizome (Deleuze & Guattari, 1987; Deleuze, 1988).

We need to signal the discursive pathways that we use, around childhood, children and curriculum, remembering each informs and works alongside the others, that each is a plateau to be moved across horizontally. The discourses of childhood, children and curriculum (as analysed from data produced in one early childhood setting in Aotearoa New Zealand) inform and work alongside (not above/over) others so that each is a plateau to be moved across horizontally.

Childhood is a part of society as well as a period in which children live their lives. While it is a temporary period for children, it remains a form in society. Also, while childhood is exposed to the same societal forces as adulthood, children themselves create their childhoods (Corsaro, 1997). Children are thus inseparable from their childhoods as they grow through[3] them. As becoming-children their childhoods evolve around them and they (can) become power-full players in their childhoods and 'influential actors' (Corsaro, 1997, p. 54) in adult society.

Working within early childhood education in Aotearoa New Zealand, we are cognisant of Te Whāriki's [NZ early childhood curriculum] view of curriculum as:

the sum total of the experiences, activities and events, whether direct or indirect, which occur within an environment designed to foster children's learning and development. (Ministry of Education, 1996, p. 10)

In children's everyday experience, curriculum may be understood as, 'investigation and exploration, walks and puddles and cuddles, books and blankets and anything that is part of the child's day, play and routines' (Rouse, 1990, cited in Anning, Cullen, & Fleer, 2004, p. 59). Rhizomatically, curriculum becomes every situation, event, person, artefact happened upon during children's learning journeys as well as the journeying itself and the territory negotiated.

By working rhizomatically we are attempting to de/re/territorialize (Deleuze & Guattari, 1987, p. 381) various aspects of power-full relationships and interactions towards enhancing young children's learning. This means paying critical attention to what voices we hear and how we hear them. We are aware of the limiting affect of the (hand-held) video camera's lens used during the data collection. While it enables a focus on a particular activity and this illuminates the intensity of the activity and the interactions in/at play, inevitably there are frustrating moments of (invisible) happenings off the screen.

The technique of panning in order to capture images of all the children working in a particular space can mean that significant exchanges among some children are not captured on the actual videotape. For example, while recording conversational contributions, which seem to have meaning to the (rhizo)analysis, without seeing who was speaking, who was there but not speaking, what they were doing, where their attention was directed, limits the meaningfulness of that particular fragment of data. The video camera thus enables and frustrates the task of a power-full re-presentation of children's voiced understandings.

In responding to the question, 'how does it work?', we are aware that in the process of problematising methodology, curriculum also becomes problematic as we explore young children's understandings of the importance of the what, how and why of their learning experiences. We are mindful of not speaking for the children who, in various moments, participated as co-producers of the data. Rather, what we provide below is just one (e)merging reading of moments in these children's learning experiences.

This is indeed a messy process (Hargreaves, 1996; Law, 2003). Also, even in theorising about power relationships, we presume to speak *for* children, despite wanting to learn *from* and *with* them and despite promoting them as becoming-articulators of their own expert understandings. The voices of children are integral to this research, not only for producing and analysing data, but also as a plateau which speaks of their understandings of curriculum and what that means for their learning. However, de/re/territorialising children's understandings and introducing the becoming-child, is a struggle. This becomes even more of a struggle when we begin to produce readings of the data collected, as we attempt to deterritorialise children's understandings through our interpretations of their actions, words, and drawings. Along the next line of flight of this chapter we explore these (e)merging~(im)plausible readings of data.

RHIZOMATIC CHILDREN

In response to the universalised, individual child discussed above, we offer an explanation of children as rhizomatic, as uniquely~individual when working~playing together as one (one group and one individual). Even though the(ir) co-operation may be (mis)read – through adult interpretations – as a universalised notion, when viewed rhizomatically, the uniqueness of individual children and their actions with/in the collective (of their) play(ing) goes beyond developmentalist under-standings of 'the' 'individual', 'rational' child.

Children themselves are like rhizomes within early childhood settings that provide smooth spaces (Deleuze & Guattari, 1987, pp. 474-500) for them to work and play in, uninterrupted and unhurried – where they have the space within the setting, and time within the programme, to go about their learning in their own way supported by adults who believe in children's powerfull-ness to enact optimal learning situations. Within the Kindergarten in which this data was co-produced (i.e. produced with the children), the children performed rhizomatically as they flowed through the spaces of the setting, through the programme and with/in relationships they encountered. As they flow through the territory of the physical environment, they follow lines of flight conversationally and within their game[4] they explore various folds and surfaces (physical and imaginative) that they happen upon, they slip in and out of discursive spaces. In this attempt to re-present this play, we focus on one particular aspect of the rhizomatic space: three girls engaging in mapping, both in the figurative sense in relation to the learning spaces they are territorialising as well as in the literal sense as they make maps and then use them to negotiate the territory of the game and the play space.

These girls flowed nomadically through smooth spaces, re/de/territorialising spaces that they needed to occupy for their game to work. It was like Deleuze and Guattari's (1987, p. 23) description: there was 'a flow of children; a flow of walking with pauses, straggling and forward rushes... a collective assemblage...one inside the other...plugged into an immense outside that is a multiplicity'. This multiplicity or plateau involved forty other children, several adults, the physical surroundings, resources at hand, the uninterrupted space of the programme. We see these three children 'space themselves out and disperse...jostle together and coexist... begin to dance' as the game grows (Deleuze & Guattari, 1987, pp. 23-24). There was continuous ebbing and flowing of ideas and energy, as the tracing was continually plugged into the map.

Libby proclaims, "We better be strong girls."
Lee objects strongly, "No!" Alice says nothing.
Libby shouts, "We can be strong girls now...and...WE...CAN...DO...IT!" punching her arms in the air. Then, "We have to have maps to see where to go."
Despite Lee's earlier objection, they all run inside to the drawing table.

Their use of mapping is intriguing and demonstrates a tacit understanding of rhizome. Emerging here, and continuing throughout their game, there is continuous moving through virtual/possible, actualising/realising (Deleuze, 1993) mapped spaces, through the map of the imaginary game; through deciding they needed to create a real map; through mapping the next part of their game; through consulting their drawn maps; and so on...they flow rhizomatically through a Deleuzian middle, negotiating virtual and possible spaces of the game and of their childhoods. Mapping becomes a way of affirming the roles they each play and exploring their their relationships with each other, of confirming the next movement through the informally improvised script of their game, of working out which part of the playground they will flow into next, of exploring their understandings of the physical and social context(s) they are playing with/in and how this might relate to the outside world. (Re)turning to the game:

They draw similar maps – Libby selects yellow paper for them all, and the others eventually follow her choice of a felt pen. Alice iss the last to choose and while Alice is choosing the colour to write her name, Lee says, "[...]you have to do it in girlish colours."

The power relations enacted within this rhizome of (the) play interact in rhizomatic forms, in that the forces of power cannot be ascribed to any one person, or set in any essentialised form. As Deleuze reminds us:

> Power has no essence; it is simply operational. It is not an attribute but a relation: the power-relation is the set of possible relations between forces which pass through the dominated forces no less than the dominating (1988, p. 27)

We map here the moments in which power is enacted in the process of mapping and playing. At one moment, Libby is in charge, as she takes up a leadership position. Lee had earlier objected strongly to becoming strong girls, but other than a loud "No!' in response to Libby's idea, there is no lasting indication of challenging the leadership. Within the rhizomatic flowing that eases contributions from everyone, Lee seems happy to accept Libby's decision. While Libby exhibits her powerfull-ness as leader; Lee claims powerfull-ness in that moment by choosing not to resist, instead following the line of flight – creating a map – which Libby declared as their next action. Lee's powerfull-ness comes to the fore again as she gives instructions, explicitly to Alice, implicitly to Libby, as to the colours to use. Lee also brings the powerfull-ness of becoming-girl into (the) play. Now, more about (the) mapping...

Libby: "Now we can draw a map." As she begins drawing she says, "Ok! Now!" which seems to be a signal for Lee and Alice to watch, which they do. Libby draws a stick figure in the centre bottom of her page. Lee then makes a partially inaudible comment, inquiring of Libby about "[...] what you did." Libby indicates the legs first. Without further instruction, Lee replicates Libby's figure in the bottom corner of her page. Alice has watched as well and by now is drawing a more detailed figure that takes up most of her page (positioned as portrait whereas Libby and Lee's is landscape).

Libby continues as leader with Lee her ardent follower. Alice, the quietest of the three now enacts her powerfull-ness. The orientation of her paper suggests she was less intent on doing things exactly as Libby dictated, while her drawing – a large person, with round body, detailed facial expression and hair – is considerably different from the stick figures that Libby and Lee are drawing. She demonstrates powerfull-ness in both not following Libby's lead exactly and in not being overt about doing it her own way. Although she does not claim a leadership role in this moment, she is also not operating as conventional follower, thus destratifying (adult?) understandings of leadership. In the process of using their powerfull-ness in ways that are not destructive to the others or to the game, all three are mapping (as Deleuzian figuration and within their actual drawings) their understandings of being children within childhoods.

Libby meanwhile is drawing a line, leading from her person, a line which wiggles and zig-zags and loosely follows the edge of her page. As she draws, she explains, "You need to do [...] in here so we know where to go...we go through the prickly grass...by the tree..." She joins another line to the first, indicating the prickly grass with zigzags along the top of her page and the tree by a thinner zigzag in the top right corner. The line then loops back onto the initial line around the page. Lee draws a line surrounding her person, a 'pathway' with less detail and without explanation. Alice meanwhile has discarded her first drawing and is drawing another figure in black, again large and detailed. The lines around the edge of her person are a series of disjointed squiggles.

Their maps now indicate the pathway they intend to negotiate as strong girls. Libby explains her pathway as she draws it, communicating verbally to the others how she is thinking their exploration will proceed. She creates a pathway with no beginning or ending, indicating they will process through a middle. Just as this game did not 'begin' as being one about strong girls (the strong girl theme emerged through playing mums and dads) it appears there is no explicitly planned terminus either. Lee's simpler pathway is similarly positioned on her paper while Alice's is again (power-fully) different. The map Alice has created is dominated by the large, carefully detailed figure, surrounded by several unconnected wiggles. That her pathway does not form a complete circle around the page and the figure is of no concern to any of them. What seems important is the indication of various spaces that they will pass through. Perhaps lines of flight to be followed. More experiences of powerfull-ness come to the fore, as well as further understandings of mapping (within) their childhoods and how these relate to their playing out their discursive understandings of becoming child/ren.

They each write their name on their map, then spend several minutes conversing about the similarities and differences in the spelling of their names. They have each folded their maps by now and because of the different paper orientations, Libby and Lee make a lengthwise fold while Alice folds hers crosswise. Lee notices the difference and points this out: "She did a long one." Libby responds, "That's ok. She's fine...C'mon, let's go...to save the world outside."

At this point, the discursive understandings of curriculum, in conventional terms, become visible as they share their understandings about literacy, both reading and writing. This also involves affirmation of each other's abilities to form the various letters and affirmation of each other as children with/in childhoods, foregrounding their social learning experiences (of curriculum). Some maths learning appears also as Lee notices the different shapes created by the different folds. While they enjoy the interchange about their literacy and mathematical skills and knowledge, Libby is mindful of ensuring all are included as successful performers of their understandings – she is ensuring they are each affirmed as individuals and using her leadership skills to make their rhizomatic game work.

Once outside Libby pauses, pointing to her map, "Start there and y' go all the way round...We need to go to the playground...it said playground." They twist and weave through the playground, pausing to play on various pieces of equipment, to interact with other children and with me, to seat themselves on a large log. Libby does the map-reading: "Our map says to go to um to go to..."; "Treasure...the treasure is here...see the little x here"; "Hey...hey, wanna go to the pool? If you want to go to the pool, that's OK." They continue to negotiate the outdoor equipment – over, under, through, across, balancing, jumping...

And so they continue mapping their play(ing), flowing through the middle space of their game, a flow of walking~running~skipping~jumping, pausing~rushing, together~an assemblage, with/in a multiplicity. As they danced through their game, they played out the discourses of child/ren, their childhoods and curriculum with power-full affects appearing in various folds and surfaces, twisting and weaving through all...

When perceived as performing rhizomatically, these children were far from rational. In modernistic rational terms, and on the surface, there may have seemed no reason for what they were doing, yet their game was rhizomatically reasonably reasonable. They were acting individually and collectively without (beyond?) adult control in that the choices made were theirs. Yet while there were no controls as such imposed from outside, neither were the controls entirely intrinsic. Throughout the rhizomatic performance, played out through their game, they were self-involving – their honour of the collective mediated any un/intentional attempted individual control. There were moments when any of them could have walked away from the game, but Libby's style of leadership worked to ensure all remained included, for example, her lack of response to Lee's power-full objection to the idea of being strong girls, her acknowledgement that Alice's folding was 'ok'. Alongside that, Lee's desire to belong apparently overrode any desire to continue with her objection; also, Alice's quiet insistence that she did not have to conform to belong, as in her different approach to making the map despite Libby's expectation that the others would follow her lead (literally and figuratively). However, while each of them can be viewed as individuals within the game, each of them as individuals was not always distinguishable within their game, this being neither desirable nor necessary to their mapping exploration. They flowed together through/out the physical and discursive territories of their game.

Also, there was nothing static or fixed about the children, the game, the geographical or discursive territories to be negotiated, the way they communicated (orally through language; pictorally through their maps), the time 'frame' – when did it begin and/or end? It did neither, rather the strong girls game and associated mapping emerged from within another middle/plateau of their play (mums and dads) and eventually merged with/on yet another plateau, as they followed (chose) various lines of flight...in the middle of the plateau, along the way, the game and the children followed other lines of flight, as they paused to play on the bars and log, to interact with other children, with a teacher, with me...

CONCLUDING THOUGHTS

In this chapter we have presented some of our re-presentations of Deleuzian methodologies used in our educational research as we worked with/in rhizomatic ways. When entering this nomadic space, we presented some commonalities in these methodologies, at the same time alerting the reader to the differences we have encountered during our writing(s). We think that these differences are important, in that they remind us of the impossibility and undesirability of prescribing a set of methods to be used in following Deleuze and Guattari's work. Like St. Pierre, we are "not much interested in any search for originary and correct meanings of their work, an impossible task (trying to fix meaning in language), but rather in the multiplicity of the effects of their work" (2001, p. 150). We have illustrated these multiple effects throughout this chapter as we have re-presented our (rhizo)analyses of diverse educational data, drawn from diverse research experiences.

We have mapped a path through a policy text that produces an account of an individual and rational child, who develops the ability to make considered decisions and choices in ways that are familiar to adults, indeed in ways that are provided by adults. At the same time we have negotiated rhizomatic(ally) territories of children's play – discursively, and following their actual (mapped) lines of flight. In particular, mapping (in a Deleuzian sense) has been foregrounded by bringing together 'disparate' scholarly discourses with the children's mapping – as they mapped their play and played out their map(s) – and with enactments of collective and individual powerfull-ness intertwined. These enactments reveal particularly agentic positions taken up the children during their play, positions not controlled by adults or by any requirements of curriculum or policy.

While we are careful not to engage with/in any kind of methodolatory or concretising, we do believe that there are signposts along any pathway through a research rhizome, pathways that may be useful for educationists interested in using Deleuze and Guattari's work.

One of these signposts is that associated with the writing of a rhizomatic text. In the writing of this chapter, and in our writing in other forums, we work reflexively to avoid linear or structuralist metaphors or figurations. Each word or phrase is thoughtfully produced as it is our contention that thinking rhizomatically and writing rhizomatically are inextricably entwined. Our use throughout this chapter of ellipses, unending sentences, broken and re-constructed words are some examples of this kind of writing. Our use of the pronoun 'we' as we move across and within different discursive spaces is another. As the children flow through, across, with/in physical and imaginary spaces of their game and their learning and as the memory poem flows from/with/in/through our reflexivity, so we allow our writing to flow as we record the negotiation of students' living territory and our discursive one(s). The 'we' of our writing, the collaborative map-making become plateaus of/for negotiation. It is important, we believe, to continually and reflexively focus on the minutiae of the written text when producing rhizomatic writing.

Another signpost along our journey through an exploration of rhizomatic research indicates different understandings of the interactions among discursive systems within any rhizome. Discourses do not operate as straight lines through a text: rather, they (e)merge (im)plausibly, connect, and cross over each other. Libby, Lee and Alice depicted various aspects of the game they were playing out, simultaneously planned and (e)merging as in tracing and mapping – they were putting the tracing back on the map. Unperturbed by the evolving complexity, through their map-making and their enacted mapping, they (simply) showed pathways and spaces that were/to be negotiated in the course of their game; they also described characters as they were evolving, talking them(selves) into be(com)ing. Their powerfull-ness became apparent through and with/in the uninterrupted and unhurried nature of their spaces, as they planned and negotiated their game/play/work/learning/curriculum development, as they loudly announced their strong girl status to the world, as they supported each other while claiming individual spaces of powerfull-ness. These negotiations are very different to the 'correct' choices that are made by the rational individual child of the English Syllabus: the planning, talking, playing are constantly in process, providing powerful illustrations of the "and, and, and" of the becoming subject.

As (rhizo)analysts, we can map discursive journeys through texts, and such mapping can illuminate the moments of convergence, when connections allow reason(able) readings of contradictory and conflicting discourses. On the surface, the prospect of linking in any meaningful way children's drawings or play with philosophical understandings seems unlikely. Even more unlikely is the linkages we have explored between the construction of the individual child in a syllabus text devoted to the teaching of English, and the construction of the rhizomatic child within moments of informal playing in an early childhood setting. However, the lines of flight that we have followed do provide (im)plausible readings of these linkages. What appeared in the making of the video and in the subsequent transcript, is that young children unaware of Deleuzian figurations or rhizomatic methodologies, enact complex understandings of these concepts. The depth of this complexity is unexpected when put alongside taken-for-granted versions of childhood as presented in policy texts.

The children created maps as a way of collectively planning how their game was to proceed and identifying the territory to be negotiated. In drawing the maps, and as the maps evolved, the children followed lines of flight in their thinking, making personal connections with the territory they would negotiate and with each other's maps and ideas expressed through/with/in them. And other lines of flight appeared later as they followed the pathways of their mapping, as they enacted their powerfull-ness – collaboratively, collectively, individually – as new ideas (e)merged, such as a mark on the chapter, an 'x' that suddenly became 'treasure' and a 'pool' that had not been mentioned before. As they flowed through their mapping, they paused literally (to rest on the log and to swing from the bars) and figuratively on plateaus to contemplate the progress/process of their learning. This is not static and fixed learning that takes place as children make rational choices about language use, but rather (e)merging learning, constantly in process and moving onwards and backwards, across and through their geographical and cognitive spaces.

For us, working rhizomatically provides a generative and transformative approach to discourse analysis, perhaps replacing that kind of analysis that has previously focused on the deconstruction rather than the transformative possibilities that are produced through a re-generative approach . For example, a re-generative reading of teachers' understandings of policy texts focuses on the plausibility of their disparate and contradictory readings. While some policy makers and curriculum writers decry how teachers' use policy (in common terms, they just don't use the curriculum in the way it was intended), a rhizo-textual analysis provides researchers with the possibility of describing much more productive and agentic relations between teachers' work and policy documents. Similarly, engaging with transformative possibilities with/in children's map/ping(s) enables linkages between adult understandings of children's learning experiences and young children's expressed understandings of their curriculum, played out through their games. In the video-recorded moments described here, this involves understandings about how to decide what spaces of learning they are going to de/re/territorialise and how they enact powerfull-ness. The children's (e)merging readings of what is important to their learning in any particular moment (can) become ours through reading re-generatively.

Still another part of our rhizomatic journey is a multiplicity of signs that suggest a variety of paths that can be taken in the interpretation of data. Reading, analysing, interpreting particular fragments of data is a highly personal and individual task. Even in deciding which fragments to read alongside others, such as children's maps alongside Deleuzian mapping, or the selection of certain sentences within a policy text, we become aware that the intent of the analysis remains open to responding to (e)merging connections. We have described the complexity of attempting to interpret data that involves young children's voices, voices that we want to make audible while at the same time acknowledging our part in silencing them. These rhizomatic interpretations of data can only produce (e)merging readings, following poststructuralist understandings of the impossibility of forming generalisable findings, not only from any particular educational context, but also from any particular reading of that context.

While these signposts indicate various directions, and allow educational researchers to follow a myriad of paths through Deleuze and Guattari's work, they may also provide some guidance to those who are interested in exploring what it means to work in rhizomatic ways within educational research. We offer these signposts as guiding possibilities for negotiating rhizomatic spaces. We hope that others will join us in our journeying as we continue to explore what it means to attempt to answer the question, "how does it work?"

NOTES

[1] We use the tilde to indicate an interchangeability of the words concepts linked in this way.

[2] We use 'powerfull-ness' as a way of problematising conventional notions of 'powerfulness' and 'empowerment'.

[3] We use 'through' in the sense of 'by means of' and as 'passage'.

[4] In this text, to ease our conversation, 'games' mean situations of imaginative play, dramatic play and informal, improvised, enacted storytelling that flow from the collective imagination of the children.

REFERENCES

Alvermann, D. (2000). Researching libraries, literacies, and lives: A rhizoanalysis. In E. A. St. Pierre & W. S. Pillow (Eds.), *Working the ruins: Feminist poststructural theory and methods in education* (pp. 114–129). New York: Routledge.

Anning, A., Cullen, J., & Fleer, M. (Eds.). (2004). *Early childhood education: Society and culture*. London: SAGE Publications Ltd.

Buchanan, I. (2000). *Deleuzism: A metacommentary*. Edinburgh: Edinburgh University Press.

Butler, J. (1997). *The psychic life of power. Theories in subjection*. Stanford, CA: Stanford University Press.

Corsaro, W. (1997). *The sociology of childhood*. USA: Pine Forge Press.

Davies, B. (1994). *Poststructuralist theory and classroom practice*. Geelong, Vic: Deakin University.

Davies, B., & Gannon, S. (2006). A conversation about the struggles of collaborative writing. In B. Davies & S. Gannon (Eds.), *Doing collective biography* (pp. 114–144). Maidenhead, Berkshire: Open University Press.

Deleuze, G. (1988). *Foucault*. Minneapolis, MN: University of Minnesota Press.

Deleuze, G. (1993). *The fold: Leibniz and the baroque* (T. Conley, Trans.). Minneapolis, MN: University of Minnesota Press.

Deleuze, G., & Guattari, F. (1987). *A thousand plateaus: Capitalism and schizophrenia* (B. Massumi, Trans.). Minneapolis, MN: University of Minnesota Press.

Department of Education Queensland. (1994). *English in Years 1 to 10 Queensland syllabus materials. English syllabus for Years 1 to 10*. Brisbane, Qld, State of Queensland.

Gee, J. P. (1990). *Social linguistics and literacies: ideology in discourses*. New York: Falmer Press.

Gill, R. (2000). Discourse analysis. In M. W. Bauer & G. Gaskell (Eds.), *Qualitative researching with text, image and sound. A practical handbook*. London: Sage.

Harding, S. (1987). Is there a feminist method? *Hypatia, 2*(3), 17–32.

Hargreaves, A. (1996). Revisiting voice. *Educational Researcher, 25*(1), 12–19.

Honan, E. (2004). (Im)plausibilities: A rhizo-textual analysis of policy texts and teacher's work. *Educational Philosophy and Theory, 36*(3), 267–281.

Law, J. (2003, December 20). *Making a mess with method*. Retrieved May 13, 2005, from http://www.lancs.ac.uk/fss/sociology/papers/law-making-a-mess-with-method.pdf

Ministry of Education. (1996). *Te whāriki: He whāriki mātauranga mö ngā mokopuna o aotearoa: Early childhood curriculum*. Wellington: Learning Media.

Rose, N. S. (1999). *Powers of freedom: Reframing political thought*. Cambridge: Cambridge University Press.

Semetsky, I. (2004). Experiencing Deleuze. *Educational Philosophy and Theory, 36*(3), 227–231.

St. Pierre, E. A. (2000). Nomadic inquiry in smooth spaces. In E. A. St. Pierre & W. S. Pillow (Eds.), *Working the ruins: Feminist poststructural theory and methods in education* (pp. 258–283). New York and London: Routledge.

St. Pierre, E. A. (2001). Coming to theory: Finding Foucault and Deleuze. In K. Weiler (Ed.), *Feminist engagements: Reading, resisting and revisioning male theorists in education and cultural studies*. New York: Routledge.

Walkerdine, V. (1984). Developmental psychology and the child-centred pedagogy: The insertion of Piaget into early education. In J. Henriques, W. Hollway, C. Urwin, C. Venn, & V. Walkerdine (Eds.), *Changing the subject: Psychology, social regulation and subjectivity*. London: Methuen.

Dr Eileen Honan
The University of Queensland
Australia

Marg Sellers
Whitireia Community Polytechnic
New Zealand

DAVID LINES

9. DELEUZE, EDUCATION AND THE CREATIVE ECONOMY

INTRODUCTION

In the preface to the English edition of *Difference and Repetition* Gilles Deleuze observes that "art, science and philosophy seem to be caught up in mobile relations in which each is obliged to respond to the other, but by its own means" (Deleuze, 1994, p. xvi). The inter-relationships between different planes of thought are an interesting thread of discussion and insight in Deleuze's written works, including those he wrote with Felix Guattari. In *A Thousand Plateaus,* for instance, Deleuze and Guattari juxtapose different representations and images of thought and culture giving a vivid impression of interdisciplinarity by using surprisingly creative and unusual linguistic tools and artistic analogies (Deleuze & Guattari, 1987). Many of these analogical thinking tools are process orientated such as in his notion of the rhizome—the natural line of flight or process of deterritorialisation that occurs, for example, in the territorial shifts and changes that emerge in association with bird song (see Bogue, 1997). Deleuze goes on to explain that he intentionally set out to invoke a new image of thought: "a rhizome in opposition to the tree" that provoked prevailing hierarchical and rational forms of 'arborescent' thought (Deleuze, 1994, p. xvii). The example of art as a rhizome or deterritorialising impulse is used frequently by Deleuze to describe a changing and often untimely line of thought that is strategically different in quality to representational or 'captured' expressions of thinking.

As a 'diagnostician' and 'scathing critic' (Osborne, 2003, p. 510) of ways of thinking in philosophy and culture, Deleuze provides philosophy of education scholarship with a challenging style that opens up insight into educational theory and practice. This is reinforced in his philosophy by a critical exploration of the way different forces work their way through planes of thought and regimes of practice. Stimulated by a Nietzschean conception of force and power Deleuze's work rethinks culture as the interplay of different emphases and alliances of force (Deleuze, 1983). Nietzsche's 'will to power' thesis projected a notion of existence as a moving dynamic flux of directional energy where shifts and pressures of forces both act and re-act. Deleuze uses this idea as a "plane of immanence" (Deleuze & Guattari, 1994, p. 65) to investigate predominant forces in contemporary culture such as capitalism and other systems of 'machinic' practice, which include the sphere of education.

As a site of thought-development and a place where artistic, economic and national forces intersect, education is a pertinent site for the application of Deleuzian thinking, critique and analysis. As such, this chapter draws on Deleuze's

I. Semetsky (ed.), Nomadic Education: Variations on a Theme by Deleuze and Guattari, 129–141.

ideas to examine more closely forces in two competing fields of thought in education. One plane of thought is orientated around contemporary notions of culture and creativity (and additional terms) in relation to economy. This thought plane is relatively new to education but has far reaching implications for future curriculum development in line with the recent neoliberal endorsement of life long education. The other plane is the 'arts'—the collection of creative and performance based thought fields of music, dance, visual arts, drama, poetry, literature and other related domains that contribute to the holistic education of children and adults.

Like Nietzsche, Deleuze thinks art is a stimulant for creativity and becomes an important image of thought in much of his writing. Drawing from Nietzsche's edited collection 'The Will to Power' (Nietzsche, 1968) Deleuze finds that art is a "stimulant of the will to power", and "something that excites willing" (Deleuze, 1983, p. 102). Further, artists are "inventors of new possibilities of life" (ibid.)—the act of art making brings forth new possibilities and opportunities of thought, expression and change. Art provides an opportunity to 'go outside' the norm and create a perspective that challenges or even resists common perception, affect, thinking and representation. Deleuze refuses to regard philosophy as a stagnant search for the underlying 'truth' of things for this sort of inquiry is seen by him as 'reactive', a style of thinking that imposes limits on ideas and restricts insight. Philosophy is 'active'—it is the art of inventing or creating concepts and new knowledge. Juxtaposed in this way, art and philosophy are interlinking processes in mobile relations—a force or impulse from one system of thought potentially stimulates or energises another and sets it free from the inevitable prospect of debilitating or restrictive repetition. Good philosophy releases art from excessive performativity. It helps us consider art's relation to its constitutive environment and enables us to critique art that is subsumed by controlling or restrictive cultural forces. Similarly art helps us see philosophical concepts as active and changing forces, which bring with them percepts and affects—intensities that are able to pierce and break away from prevailing determinations of meaning. As Deleuze says "the affect, the percept and concept are three inseparable powers; they go from art to philosophy and from philosophy to art" (Deleuze, 1995, cited in Bogue, 2004, p. 2) Concepts, in this sense, are affirmed as changing formations of knowledge rather than as signifiers containing specific contents of 'set' information.

Deleuze's artistic, innovative and challenging approach to thinking is distinctly different from present day manifestations of the term 'creativity' and the associated notion of the 'creative subject'. Commonly associated with art making, creativity has increasingly become a kind of catch phrase in contemporary business and educational discourse. New notions of the 'creative industries', the 'creative economy' and the new 'creative class' highlight the meeting place of creative and economic concerns in contemporary urban life. A new economic discourse of creativity now saturates both business and educational interests to the degree that creativity is now described as "a resource in the personal psychology of everyday life" (Osborne, 2003, p. 508). Commentators such as Osborne (2003) and Jeanes (2006) note concern about this new notion of creativity because of its reductive and limited philosophical depth, its intrusion into both business and educative milieus and its close and rather subservient affiliation with commercial production.

This essay considers the notion of creativity and the new 'creative economy' with particular attention to its resonance in contemporary arts education. I consider the use of creativity in its various guises—as a new concept aligned with the broader notion of the creative economy—and as an artistic process that constitutes our very existence as creative beings in the present day. I consider how in a contemporary context, the term 'creativity' plays a performative role in a fixed and limiting field of knowledge in the various pretexts of the creative economy. Following Deleuze's example I suggest a 'musical' image of thought for arts education pedagogy and practice—the 'music improvisation'. Arts inspired 'anti-normal' images of thought allow us to rethink and respond to movements of thought immersed in economic rationalism. With this in mind, I explore what 'artistic creativity' can mean for learning and how education can become more attuned to the affects, freedoms, uncertainties and departures that are experienced in artistic processes.

THE CREATIVE ECONOMY

The notion of 'creative economy' has emerged alongside a family of related concepts (see Hartley, 2005, p. 36). These include labels such as 'knowledge economy', 'knowledge society', 'cultural economy' and 'creative industries'. Taken together, the family of concepts (and others) identifies a growing discourse of economic innovation and knowledge considered to be important for contemporary business and trade. The appropriation of *new* knowledge is now an essential part of business life, in particular, the ability to design new digital applications and quickly respond to new and changing commercial markets, shifts in market need and changing attitudes about products.

Within the knowledge economy, creativity is considered essential to maintain a constant need for innovation in the competitive global marketplace. This is linked with the endorsement of the values of individuation, innovation, performativity, productiveness and the valorization of the 'new' in the global market. In this context, creativity is seen as essential for our survival, both economically and socially (Jeanes, 2006, p. 128). The pursuit of knowledge has become a substantial economic practice, especially with regard to the production, distribution and use of information drawn from intertextual databases. New knowledge is intrinsically aligned with "clusters of innovation based on new technologies and new business models" (De Long, cited in Peters & Besley, 2006b, p. 2). As such, innovation is a key aspect of the formation of new business enterprises and is closely associated with recent advances in digital technology driving virtual digital software and multimedia developments now referred to as the "weightless economy" (Peters & Besley, 2006b, p. 3). Moreover, the need for innovation goes hand in hand with recent acceleration of software improvements and improved accessibility and immediacy through Broadband Internet, which also plays an important part in linking global business interests.

The knowledge economy also appropriates ideas from the arts. Jeanes (2006, p. 127) observes how notions of creativity and the arts now dominate management discourse. Pick up any management text, says Jeanes, and you will find examples of the importance of creativity, innovation and artistic approaches. Creativity has become a means of self-actualisation in management discourse, focussing on the performing managerial self. The creative self, here, is constructed as a mode of existence—encapsulated as 'living the life' of successful management. The practice of management is said to be like performance art (Vaill, 1989)—a practice not unlike the theatre where aesthetic judgement and sensitivity is critical to good performance. This is associated with an increasing emphasis on the aestheticization of business culture, the quality of the social environment and the value of communication style in the multicultural/multinational corporate world. Artistic and creative analogies are frequently employed in both popular psychology books on business and in business and management academic articles. Along with these trends is the emergence of a new 'cultural class', a large and significant demographic located in distinctive urban centres around the globe (eg. the San Francisco Bay area) (Florida, 2002). The cultural class is said to have particular cultural needs that require ready attention—including of course artistic and educative needs that necessitate a flourishing culture of innovation and creativity.

On the face of it, the recent creative and cultural 'turn' in business seems positive. After all, what can be problematic with a focus on creativity, innovation and new knowledge? The difficulty lies in creativity's complete subservience with capital as it functions within the discourse. In the context of these recent developments the notion of creativity becomes subject to what Deleuze and Guattari call "machinic enslavement" or, to use another phrase, an "apparatus of capture" (Deleuze & Guattari, 1987, pp. 424-473). "Capitalism arises as a worldwide enterprise of subjectification by constituting an axiomatic of decoded flows" (ibid, p. 457). Part of this machinic process has been the turning of the idea of creativity into a unidirectional and limited creative enterprise focussing primarily on production—that is economic outputs. The subjection of creativity to capital involves the "reinvention of a machine in which human beings are constituent parts" (ibid, p. 458). Within the weightless economy, metal machines of industrialisation are reinvented as virtual machines of human capture. The knowledge economy is fed by a new kind of human capital where the mode of creativity becomes a dominant force of subjectification, orientated around the notion of 'competencies' (human capital). The new mentality of rule calls for creativity and innovation to be a normative, everyday way in which humans perceive their own "Thought-Being" (Deleuze & Guattari, 1994, p. 65), an image of thought of themselves as creative capital, as innovators of new ideas that, in turn, produce economic gain.

The subtle deployment of language oils a virtual machine of creative capital. The family of connected concepts—knowledge economy, creative economy, cultural economy etc.—form a delicate yet pliable collective of discursive force. As performative concepts, these notions freely penetrate different business, cultural and educational interests, working as forces of control and realignment, reterritorialising diverse components into a captured scheme of creative capital. This kind of virtual machinic operation continues to silence minoritarian or potentially disruptive resistance (for instance from arts or education communities) by means of a flexible language base; the family of concepts work collectively towards a normative base of ultimate value—capital gain. 'Knowledge economy' as a label, for instance, functions more effectively than the more arts-associated 'creative economy' in discursive contexts where creative arts are looked upon as 'unproductive' or perceived as being outside normal business interests. In such circumstances terms like 'innovation' come into play more effectively than 'creativity' because of the latter's close association with the creative arts (see Santagata, 2004, p. 82). The family of concepts are more noted for their performative power than their philosophical depth or clarity. In fact, the event making power of a 'slippery' or 'surface' concept is, in a sense, an advantage. The impact of the 'slippery' concept lies in its force as a controlling association rather than as a well-defined philosophical concept—and as such it reinforces a limited ontology of the subject by means of its normative presence.

Life long education is seen as a key aspect of the production, reproduction and transmission of knowledge and is valued as a training ground for the 'weightless economy' where students gain skills in accessing information through information technology. A student's ability to find information at speed via online databases is a key concern of educational programmes across a range of curricula, especially those based on individual research. Further, in arts and media education the rapid selection, manipulation and arranging of multimedia materials using digital software has become a growing point of focus with students combining modes of text, sound, vision and movement in their projects of work. Peters and Besley (2005a, pp. 95-112) theorise the new requirement for immediacy in the knowledge economy as the "theatre of fast knowledge". In education, fast knowledge is collected, packaged, collated, and assigned value in accordance with teaching and learning timetables and assessment criteria. The speed, efficiency and effectiveness in which students access and process knowledge into acceptable assessment structures becomes an increasing concern in schools seeking to comply with curriculum demands and successfully implement qualification training requirements. It also gives students an opportunity to demonstrate the required 'competencies' in speedy fashion in order to perform instructional tasks.

While educational programmes place increasing value on digital technology skills it is in the area of curriculum and assessment policy where the apparatus of capture is perhaps most apparent. Curriculum policies that accentuate ideas such as entrepreneurship, innovation, creativity and 'competencies' point to a merging of educational policy makers' intentions with broader objectives of the knowledge and creative economies. The capture of curriculum language as concepts of knowledge capitalism performs a limiting function on different kinds of 'non-conforming' knowledge that can emerge in the creative processes of daily learning. Active forces become "decomposed" by reactive forces: "they separate active force from what it can do" (Deleuze, 1983, p. 57). The process of decomposition is more likely to be observed in assessment and evaluation processes where curriculum language that initially informs teacher planning once again returns to frame learning for the intention of reporting to authorities and parents. As such, the language of curriculum and assessment decodes and normalises difference. Well intentioned teachers help students produce 'creative' or 'artistic' work that push boundaries of innovation only to find normalising forces of assessment nullify the qualitative differences that emerge—differences, as it were, become subsumed by the standardised criteria of assessment value. Schools in the present day are interesting sites of transition and tension between forces of knowledge capital and demands of accountability on the one hand and traditional/historical disciplinary structures on the other, within which familiar 'subjects' are maintained. These complex issues and points of tension raise important questions for philosophers of education as they seek to theorise cultural change in learning institutions.

DELEUZE, ART AND MUSIC

We lack creation. *We lack resistance to the present.* The creation of concepts in itself calls for a future form, for a new earth and people that do not yet exist. Europeanisation does not constitute a becoming but merely the history of capitalism, which prevents the becoming of subjected peoples. Art and philosophy converge at this point: the constitution of an earth and a people that are lacking as the correlate of creation. (Deleuze & Guattari, 1994, p. 108, italics in original)

Like Nietzsche, Deleuze finds art to be a prospect of hope for a new kind of liberation and becoming in the face of Western/European capitalism and its diverse functions in present day culture. Art's relationship with thought (philosophy) is a critical feature in this liberation because of its potential to excite creativity (creation) and trigger new concepts, new forces, and new forms of subjectification. Art brings a possibility of resistance to the present, and offers an alternative image of thought that has the capacity to labour outside the dominant and normative styles of thinking common in Western capitalism. Art—and here I am referring to a Deleuzian kind of becoming-art—stimulates new images of thought that enable us to rethink the limited and curious philosophically mundane concept of creativity advocated in the creative/knowledge economy alluded to in the previous section. As stimulants of thought the creative arts are the "machineries of creativity" (Osborne, 2003, p. 515), that is they are active and functional forces of cultural change affecting our bodies and environments.

In his writing Deleuze strives to describe the function of art rather than its meaning. The book, *Francis Bacon: The Logic of Sensation* (Deleuze, 2005), for example, uses artistic, musical and literature based concepts and sensations to explore and create new philosophical ideas that interact and engage with each other in the course of the book's dialogue. Deleuze is interested in both what art can become—as new sensations and expressions—and in what function art can play in the stimulation of a philosophical (and scientific) style that works to create new beings, new thoughts, and new territories. He thinks that philosophy, art and science, as planes of thought, are never very far from one another and indeed their co-engagement is a necessary condition of becoming.

The idea of 'force', as articulated in Deleuze's exegesis of Nietzsche (see Deleuze, 1983; 1987), has a close association with art and the functions of art, understood as 'affects' and 'percepts'. Deleuze thinks that change and becoming emerges as a function of both active and reactive forces and that this is linked with the process of engagement with art. As Colman (2005, p. 11) explains: "Affect is the change, or variation, that occurs when bodies collide, or come into contact." Deleuze uses the term 'affect' to refer to "the additive processes, forces, powers and expressions of change" (ibid., p. 11) that one experiences when encountering art, or when some kind of 'collision' occurs between bodies. Colman thinks that the alteration of bodies (things, beings) through affects "describes the forces behind all forms of social production in the contemporary world" including these "forces' ethical, ontological, cognitive and physiological powers" (ibid, p. 12). While affects are viewed here as part of the function of art they simultaneously connect us with a diverse array of cultural forces. Along with affect, Deleuze creates the notion of 'percept' to express the changing individual sensations, nuances or 'perceptions' that occur frequently in art experiences. Percepts allude to the fringe or movement of sensation that takes place prior to any act of representation or meaning. As such, the percept is a kind of "membrane that is both in contact with, and is actually part of, the external world" (Marks, 2005, p. 200). Deleuze and Guattari see percepts as belonging to nature—the membranes of sensation in forms of nature become the figure of change or fold between the inside and outside world.

Deleuze goes to some length to ensure that his descriptions of the function of art exceed any kind of lived human experience or human construct.

> Percepts are no longer perceptions; they are independent of a state of those who experience them. Affects are no longer feelings or affections; they go beyond the strength of those who undergo them. Sensations, percepts and affects are *beings* whose validity lies in themselves and exceeds any lived (Deleuze and Guattari, 1994, p. 164).

The artist then is a kind of actor who projects art works into a given milieu. At this point art works, as sensations, percepts and affects take on a life of their own, they exist in themselves (ibid, p. 164) and become free to engage as it were with audiences, art makers and environments alike. Following composition, art works become 'rhizomatic', creating connections and alliances and forming impressions and affects with the environment. As art works enter a given milieu creative opportunities emerge in a moment's 'shimmering', that is, in the stimulation of forces on an occasion of percepts and affects. These qualities and moments of art stimulation are not necessarily aligned with commercial or other dominant forces in culture but take on a life of their own as singularities. They can be taken up, in turn, as new opportunities for artists to work with, question or critique as the case may be. The Deleuzian function of art is thus a repeating and profoundly educative process.

This exegesis of the artistic process may at first seem idealistic in theory, as if art privileges some kind of romantic experience of 'wonderment' in the moment of creativity not found in other kinds of experiences. Deleuze however expels any prospect of romanticism by emphasising the damaging or even destructive possibility of creativity. Art can stimulate and align with disturbing and destructive functions in addition to those that are more ethically palpable. Deleuze and Guattari note that affirming all possibilities in a musical transformation also means the prospect of dangers, music gone bad, "a note that pursues you" (Deleuze & Guattari, 1987, p. 350). Art thus may be unsettling, it may form configurations and affects that may cause disgust or disagreement to some. This is commonly experienced in music reception when music artists actively seek to push the boundaries of normal expectations or commercial pop-fashions and sound clichés. In such circumstances audiences will cringe when they hear unsavoury sounds that challenge their normative expectations of musical sensation and value. Affects that unsettle normal expectations and representations (ie. music that is difficult to categorise) work 'outside' normalising forces. As such, artistic affects carry the potential to resist reterritorialisation.

Such resistance and unsettling can be found even in the commercially saturated field of popular music. Working against the tide of normative sound styles some music artists continue to support processes of deterritorialisation in their work often producing musically powerful results. As Hainge (2004, p. 48) describes, the commercially successful Icelandic popular musician Björk manages to do just that:

> Björk deterritorialises the English language with her every utterance ripping its signifiers from their syntactic chain with her Icelandic inflections whilst the idiosyncrasies and singularity of her musical vocalisations deterritorialise her songs' refrains by rendering them unrepeatable.

Creativity in the artistic and Deleuzian sense retains a sense of openness to the possibilities of new affects and percepts and to the exploration of new territories that emerge as a result of the functions of art. This openness contrasts with the limiting and reductive image of creativity appropriated through alliances with capital and the reterritorialising forces of the creative economy. Deleuze explains:

> The difference between music and sound is definitely not a basis for a definition of music, or even for the distinction between musician birds and non-musician birds. Rather it is the *labour of the refrain*: Does it remain territorial and territorialising, or is it carried away in a moving block that draws a transversal across all coordinates – and all of the intermediaries between the two? Music is precisely the adventure of the refrain…the way it lays hold of the refrain, makes it more and more sober, reduced to a few notes, then takes it down a creative line that is so much richer, no origin or end which is in sight… (Deleuze & Guattari, 1987, p. 302, italics in original)

Deleuze's concept of music as a deterritorialising refrain provides us with an artistic analogical tool to stimulate our understanding of creativity through art. This creativity is not linked to an 'essence' or the notion of a genius composer. Rather creativity in this sense is linked to the music event and what becomes of music once it is performed or disseminated; to the differences and affects that emerge in the labour of the refrain. The emergent territories of the refrain can lead down an active and more richer creative line, or conversely be carried away by what Deleuze calls a 'moving block' that captures and transverses all coordinates. In terms of our understanding of the concept of creativity and its function, 'artistic' creativity can be understood as the active creative line of affect, to which there is no end in sight—a line that retains a sense of openness to possibility and style from which future compositions and changes may materialize. The danger of the notion of creative-capital alluded to previously, is that the 'moving block', as a recoding force of economic production, renders creativity inactive—or becomes 'reactive' as Deleuze would say; it no longer becomes a stimulating affect open to possibility and instead becomes a predetermined construct of innovation that is judged according to its merits as a contribution to capital production.

Following Deleuze we can say that artistic creativity takes on a new image of thought: the *music improvisation*. This image of thought emphasises the qualitative territory of collective impulses that form an emerging synchrony of music sound, technology (instrument), nuance, mood and difference. The act of music improvisation can be seen as a 'voice' (melody) that emerges out of a broader community of 'voices' (harmonies); a singularity that comes out of a historical community of styles and affects. In the course of the improvisation, a soloist forges a distinct pathway of meaningful expressive action in relation to unified and dispersed forms of music expression. The solo comes out of the accompanying ensemble and plays with it, savouring the new musical relationships that open up. The improvised melody is like a returning refrain, each new melodic nuance carves a new qualitative relationship or territory in the course of performance. Moving outside the musician, the melody draws in a life of its own through the different musical relationships that unfold beyond the musicians' projections and intentions. Similarly, we (listeners, performers, learners, thinkers, teachers) engage in 'musical dialogues' with historical memories of expression that distinctively re-emerge in the play of our own events. These dialogues consist of particular configurations of dynamic (political, forceful, powerful) and expressive (qualitative, nuanced, affective) returning 'refrains' of events. Our aim, as artists, is to keep the refrain *open* to a range of artistic possibilities—to keep the improvisation alive and meaningful. The open refrain is what Readings (1991) speaks of 'poetic work', a type of work (labour) that, unlike paid human capital, reaches beyond the power relations of identities because it manages to retain a free relation with its own variations.

IMPLICATIONS FOR EDUCATION

Deleuze defines the concept in a very educational way. He says " the concept speaks the event, not the essence or thing" (Deleuze & Guattari, 1994, p. 21). Like the musical refrain, each unfolding event is articulated by the concept as it takes on a new set of relational configurations.

A concept (also) has a becoming that involves its relationship with concepts situated on the same plane. Here concepts link up with each other, support one another, coordinate their contours, articulate their respective problems, and belong to the same philosophy, even if they have different histories (Deleuze & Guattari, 1994, p. 18).

Deleuze emphasises the event as a relational configuration of a community of concepts that come together in a shared space, despite their respective histories. The idea here is to recognise the becoming of concepts as a moment of singular relations. This is a practice familiar to educators. Teachers consider different concepts in their planning as they deliberate over their learning purposes and goals for their prospective classes. However, experienced teachers also know that it is in the dynamics of classroom practice where the engagement with a concept fully takes hold, as that concept plays with the relational environment of the class and the other concepts of the moment, forming its own resonance with the unique learning situation at hand. In addition, the concept's refrain brings forth sensations, affects and percepts that stimulate and artistically invigorate the learning situation with their presence. Teachers sometimes call the blend of concept/sensation the 'aha' moment. This is a time when teachers and students resonate with the learning moment and intuitively concur with the particular configuration of the learning experience at hand.

Returning to Deleuze's quote in the first sentence of this chapter, it seems that there is some rich ground to explore in education between the practices of arts education and concept formation (philosophy) utilising the triad of concept, percept and affect as a tool to stimulate and enhance an educational practice. We need then to find space and time to explore ideas through artistic means and strategies. Taking this point seriously means giving arts education a more interdisciplinary function in the curriculum and in the classroom. Art (music, dance, drama, painting, literature etc.) can be infused into the curriculum in addition to the usual specialist 'art-production' classes. This would involve new artistic strategies to inform knowledge making such as: reflections on new perspectives of thinking, artistic questioning and exploration, descriptions of percepts and affects, strategic artistic images of thought and a retaining a sense of openness in the creative engagement of classroom work.

As an academic field, the philosophy of education needs to begin to articulate and research the nature and value of arts education, and develop more articulate expressions and understandings of how the arts can stimulate learning in the general curriculum. This means looking beyond specialist, disciplinary arts teaching (which have their own value) and developing theoretical insights that will inform this type of interdisciplinarity through the arts in the classroom. We need to begin to better understand what it means to have an 'artistic philosophy' that informs educational theory and practice. This means developing artistic images of thought about education, imagining them in classroom or studio practice, and then trialing and articulating them in schools, noting the changes and differences that emerge under particular circumstances. In addition, we need to build a stronger sense of a philosophical art, that is, art that responds to critical reflections of (local, national, global) cultures—art that is more linked to the resonance of daily life in communities. One major issue in arts education is a lack of (creative and critical) theorising about its own condition in broader education. A deeper theoretical and interdisciplinary exploration of the arts in learning would help address, to some degree, concerns about the marginalisation of the arts in education (see Mansfield, 2002). Art educators need to look beyond specialist, disciplinary teaching as the only vision of education in their domain.

To conclude we now return to our discussion of the 'cultural economy' and its impact on education. As discussed there are problems and issues with a limited and restrictive concept of creativity (and its close relation, 'innovation') that has emerged alongside the language of the creative and knowledge economy. Our discussion of 'artistic creativity' has alluded to an alternative, more resonant view of creativity in education, a view that could be further enhanced through artistic interdisciplinary strategies and images of thought. The open orientation of artistic creativity contrasts with the rather more limited ends-orientated creative-capital and fast knowledge that has infiltrated both educational policy and practice to some degree. Educators need to be able to theorise the forces, language and performative practices informed by creative and knowledge economy discourses and observe how these are being played out in classroom practice. This calls for a close analysis of policy and practice and the employment of analytical thinking tools that can assist the understanding of fluid concepts such as 'creativity' and 'competencies' such as those produced by Deleuze.

Neoliberal notions of the creative economy tend to become abstracted in education; removed as it were from their origin as key concerns of corporate business. The abstraction is not so much a theoretical shift but more a collection of compliance practices, normative values and curriculum choices that implicitly support the creative economy. These are centered on the key concerns of fast knowledge, innovation (ie. new ideas for different markets), flexible citizenship (eg. communication and cultural skills) and competencies (skills that produce results). In the classroom these concerns become part of everyday teacher decision-making (planning, lesson structure), compliance (eg. intense focus on assessment tasks), curriculum examples and assessment (value judgments and criteria).

What kind of creativity is possible then in education? One notable feature of arts education is the opportunities for the stimulation of the imagination. Arts classes trigger the potential for students to form new links and connections (often through juxtapositions) rather than concur with pre-set imaginative responses. This is a key value to be nurtured. In turn, arts tasks do not necessarily proceed as performative ends-driven events, but rather tend to accentuate the unfolding meanings that develop in the process of task-action. Further, critical approaches to arts learning promote new forms of subjectivity and new possibilities of life. They allow students to stand outside common preconceptions and perceive of themselves in different ways.

A dualistic or dialectical approach however may not be sufficient—by this I mean the suggestion that one merely 'advocates' one particular philosophy of creativity over another. It is not sufficient to say that artistic creativity is superior to production creativity for that merely provides the opportunity for artistic creativity to be ignored or reterritorialised (recoded), put to the side as a separate, non essential discipline by a moving block of sustainable forces that continue to force education to comply with the need to develop human capital. Rather than merely propose a contrary argument, change needs to take place through the engagement of the arts directly in the sites where undemocratic practices are being realised in daily common practice. The practice of art has always been connected to economic concerns and will remain in that zone.

Art educators can apply resistance through affirmative and active means. This could include challenging normative educational values and discourse through artistic performances and displays, building philosophical critiques of creativity in education, developing new artistic images of thought in education, and redesigning assessment procedures that retain creativity from a qualitative perspective. The most potent strategy to affirm artistic creativity in education could perhaps be the development of interdisciplinary practices and strategies in the wider curriculum that employ Deleuzian artistic methodologies. Art can be a stimulant for a rich education and a creative line for learning if we open up opportunities for artistic creativity in all spheres of learning.

REFERENCES

Bogue, R. (2004). *Deleuze's wake: Tributes and tributaries*. New York: State University of New York Press.
Bogue, R. (1997). Art and territory. *The South Atlantic Quarterly, 96*(3), 465–482.
Colman, F. (2005). Affect. In A. Parr (Ed.), *The Deleuze dictionary*. Edinburgh: Edinburgh University Press, 11–12.
Deleuze, G. (2005). *Francis Bacon: The logic of sensation* (D. Smith, Trans.). Minneapolis, MN: University of Minnesota Press.
Deleuze, G. (1995). *Negotiations 1972–1990* (M. Joughin, Trans.). Columbia: Columbia University Press.
Deleuze, G. (1994). *Difference and repetition* (P. Patton, Trans.). New York: Columbia University Press.
Deleuze, G. (1987). *Foucault* (S. Hand, Trans.). Minneapolis: University of Minnesota Press.
Deleuze, G. (1983). *Nietzsche and philosophy* (H. Tomlinson, Trans.). New York: Columbia University Press.
Deleuze, G., & Guattari, F. (1994). *What is philosophy?* (G. Burchell & H. Tomlinson, Trans.). London: Verso.
Deleuze, G., & Guattari, F. (1987). *A thousand plateaus: Capitalism and schizophrenia* (B. Massumi, Trans.). London: University of Minnesota Press.
Florida, R. (2002). *The rise of the creative class: And how it's transforming work, leisure, community and everyday life*. New York: Basic Books.
Hainge, G. (2004). Is pop music? In I. Buchanan & M. Swiboda (Eds.), *Deleuze and music*. Edinburgh: Edinburgh University Press.
Hartley, J. (2005). Creative industries (introduction). In J. Hartley (Ed.), *Creative industries* (pp. 1–40). Oxford: Blackwell.
Jeanes, E. (2006). Resisting creativity, creating the new: A Deleuzian perspective on creativity. *Creativity and Innovation Management, 15*(2), 127–134.
Mansfield, J. (2002). Differencing music education. *British Journal of Music Education, 19*(2), 189–202.
Marks, J. (2005). Percept and literature. In A. Parr (Ed.), *The Deleuze dictionary* (pp. 199–200). Edinburgh: Edinburgh University Press.

Nietzsche, F. (1968). *The will to power*. New York: Random House.

Osborne, T. (2003). Against 'Creativity: A philistine rant. *Economy and Society, 34*(4), 507–525.

Peters, M., & Besley, A. (2006a). *Building knowledge cultures: Education and development in the age of knowledge capitalism*. New York: Rowman & Littlefield.

Peters, M., & Besley, A. (2006b, November). *Public knowledge cultures*. Paper presented at the Philosophy of Education of Australasia annual conference, Sydney.

Readings, B. (1991). *Introducing Lyotard: Art and politics*. London: Routledge.

Santagata, W. (2004). Creativity, fashion and market behaviour. In *Cultural industries and the production of culture*. London: Routledge.

Vaill, P. (1989). *Managing as a performing art*. London: Jossey-Bass.

David Lines
University Of Auckland
New Zealand

TODD MAY AND INNA SEMETSKY

10. DELEUZE, ETHICAL EDUCATION, AND THE UNCONSCIOUS

While teaching values is an important part of education, contemporary moral education, however, presents a set of pre-established values to be inculcated rather than comprising a critical inquiry into their possible rightness and wrongness. This essay proposes a somewhat different direction by saying that education, rather than concerning itself with the moral, should concern itself with the *ethical*. Although morals and ethics are usually equated, we use *ethical* here as posited by Gilles Deleuze's question of who we might be, based on the recognition that we have no real idea of who we might be because we do not yet know what a body (which for Deleuze, after Spinoza, is both physical and mental, corporeal and incorporeal) is capable of.

This essay addresses the *ethical* dimension of Deleuze's philosophy in the context of education and pedagogy as based on several important conceptual shifts. First, it proposes a broader inquiry into who we *might* be. Second, it proposes that it is what we do *not* know, rather than what we do, that is of educational significance. Third, it asserts that much of our world, as well as our learning, are unconscious rather than conscious. This postulate accords with Deleuze's larger ontology, in which there is more to this world than appears to common sense in immediate experience. And fourth, it proposes education as committed to experimentation rather than the transmission of facts or inculcation of values.

There is a lot of talk these days about the teaching of values in education. The idea is that students need to learn to be more moral, and that it is the job of education to contribute to that task. Rather than simply teaching facts, the kinds of facts that Dickens decried in *Hard Times*, what needs to be learned are values that will make students better citizens and better people. Customarily, when the idea of moral values in education arises, however, it is usually from quarters where the issue is not so much that of a critical inquiry into rightness and wrongness but rather of compliance with an unquestioned set of pre-established values. To teach values in education becomes equivalent to the practice of religious education, that is, teaching people how to be good Christians, in a particular and particularly narrow view of what a good Christian is.

How might one advocate for an ethically oriented education without embracing a parochial return to instilling outdated values? One way, of course, would be to argue for a critical relation to a society's values. On this model, values would be brought forward for reflective inquiry, assessed as to their nature and adequacy, and then adopted or not as a result of that assessment. There is surely room for such an undertaking. However, another counter would move in a very different

I. Semetsky (ed.), Nomadic Education: Variations on a Theme by Deleuze and Guattari, 143–157.

direction. We want to signal this direction by saying that education, rather than concerning itself with the moral, should concern itself with the *ethical*, and specifically the ethical as the philosopher Gilles Deleuze articulates it. Deleuze's concept of the ethical contrasts sharply with that of moral values. If moral values are pre-given and ratified by common sense, the ethical pushes in the opposite direction. The ethical, for Deleuze, asks the question of who we might be. And it does so on the basis of recognizing, with Spinoza, that we have no real idea of who we might be, that, as Deleuze and Spinoza put the matter, we do not yet know what a body is capable of. What this essay will do is to investigate a Deleuzian approach to an ethical education, and to ask what this approach might accomplish.

In order to do this, we will have to start with ontology, even if it is quite unusual to begin with ontology in order to write an educational theory. However, Deleuze's ethics makes sense only against the background of his ontology, and therefore our attempt to utilize that ethics for educational purposes must start from an understanding of that background. Although Deleuze's ontology is notoriously elusive, we can lay out the elements of it necessary for our purposes fairly straightforwardly. In the Anglo-American tradition of philosophy, ontology concerns what there is. It seeks to account for the stuff of which universe is composed, what it often calls "the furniture of the universe." Is there nothing more than physical matter? Is Descartes right in thinking that there are two types of substance-mental and physical? What can we say about the substance or substances or types of substance that make up the universe? These are the questions addressed by Anglo-American ontological thought. In the Continental tradition of philosophy, particularly since the writings of Martin Heidegger, it is not the question of what there is but rather the question of Being (with a capital B) that is the ontologist's concern. Heidegger distinguishes sharply between beings, which the Anglo-American philosopher asks about, and Being. He wants to understand the Being of beings, what he sometimes calls the meaning of Being or the question of Being. Heidegger recognizes that the question of Being cannot be answered in any way analogous to that of beings. There is no adequate philosophical account of Being that would start with the phrase, "Being is ..." To think about Being requires more of a meditative thought rather than an analytical approach. As his work evolves, it becomes more meditative, and even, some would say, mystical.

Deleuze's ontology can be seen in dialogue with both the Anglo-American tradition and Heidegger's particular inflection. Like the latter, it is a thinking of Being. Deleuze, however, in contrast to Heidegger, does not hold to a purely meditative approach to Being. He believes there are certain things we can say about it, that Being has a certain character that can be, if not analytically unfolded, at least conceptually approached. Being can be, to appeal to a term one author (May) has used elsewhere in considering Deleuze's thought, *palpated*. In approaching Deleuze's ontology, however, the better contrast is probably with Anglo-American ontology. For the Anglo-American ontologist, whatever is to be said about what there is, about the matter or matters that compose the universe, can be said by means of what Deleuze would call *identities*. Identities have the quality of being what they are and not being what they are not. Identities can be brought under our conceptual sway, because they can be recognized as falling under particular groupings. Atoms, quarks, forces, or, if you like, souls and minds: all of these are identities. When one asks, in Anglo-American fashion, what there is in the universe, the expected answer is going to go along the lines of "There is ..." where the blank is filled in with a concept or set of concepts that refer to identities, in virtue of the verb "to be" serving as logical copula.

For Deleuze, what there is, ultimately, are not identities. There is difference. "Being," he writes, "is said in a single and same sense of everything of which it is said, but that of which it is said differs it is said of difference itself." (Deleuze, 1994, p. 36). We must understand what Deleuze means when he says that Being is difference itself. The first step in this understanding is to recognize what Being is *not*. It is not an identity or a set of identities. Deleuze's ontology does not give us what Anglo-American ontologists seek as an answer to the question of what there is that can be rendered by means of recognizable conceptual unities or totalities. In Deleuze's view, what there is not amenable to conceptual identification in this sense. He marks this when he says that Being is difference.

This is only a negative characterization, however. Can we give a more positive view of what the claim that Being is difference might mean, one that tells us something without falling into conceptual identification? In order to do so, we have to introduce two other Deleuzian terms: the virtual and the actual. For Deleuze, the actual is what we experience directly. The actual is composed of identities with which we interact. However, the actual is not *all* there is. Behind, beneath, and within the actual is the virtual. The virtual gives rise to the actual, and yet remains a part of it. To grasp this, consider Japanese origami. A piece of paper is folded, refolded, and unfolded in different ways to yield a particular figure. We can think of the particular figure as the actual and the paper as the virtual. The virtual is that out of which the actual comes, but it remains within the actual. The next step is to realize that while the actual is composed of identities, the virtual is not. The virtual isn't some kind of mirror of the actual that exists only in potentiality, so that the actual would be the virtual with the extra characteristic of its being real. "The possible is opposed to the real; the process undergone by the possible is therefore a 'realisation.' By contrast, the virtual is not opposed to the real; it possesses a full reality by itself. The process it undergoes is that of actualisation." (Deleuze, 1994, p. 211). The virtual does not resemble the actual; instead, it is a wellspring out of which the actual arises. The virtual can give rise to a particular actuality, but it can also give rise to others. The fact that *this* actual exists now, that the virtual folded, unfolded, refolded itself into *this*, is contingent. It could have been otherwise, and could perhaps be otherwise in the future. Contingency, we should bear in mind, is not the same thing as arbitrariness. The virtual can unfold into many things, but it cannot unfold into anything at all.

But if the virtual is distinct from the identities of the actual, and if it is itself real, then what is it? It is difference, the ground of difference, out of which the actual emerges and which the actual carries with it. Think here of genetics. A gene does not resemble the living creature it becomes. But it unfolds itself—or, to use a Deleuzian term—differen*c*iates itself—into a particular living being. In this unfolding or differenciating, the genetic material remains the actual of the living being and unfolding of the virtual of its genetic material. The virtual is both distinct from and inherent in the actual. Moreover, to continue the example, given a particular genetic makeup, a living being does not have to become the particular living being it does in fact become. Various environmental conditions could both alter its genetic structure or affect how the particular unfolding of this being is to occur. So the virtual can become many things, even if not anything at all. Being, then, is this virtual/actual nexus of difference. Difference as what Deleuze calls differen*t*iation (with a "t") in the virtual; difference as differen*c*iation (with a "c") in the actual.

For Deleuze, the objects that take the form of ideas *subsist* in the preconscious, out of awareness, state of virtual potentialities or tendencies. The realm of the virtual is reminiscent of, as Deleuze put it, the shadow around the words. Still, it can be actualized, or brought into consciousness as a thought-form, that is, *reterritorialized* during the process of becoming-other. There are affects that "traverse [one's universe] like arrows or ... like the beam of light that draws a hidden universe out of the shadow" (Deleuze & Guattari, 1994, p. 66); the affects are immanent, and immanence is understood by Deleuze as being immanent to nothing else than itself. The transversal connection is the unique feature of Deleuze's transcendental empiricism. This philosophical method is empirical by virtue of the object of inquiry regarded as real, albeit sub-representative, experience. Yet, it is transcendental, rather than transcendent, because the very foundations for the empirical principles are left outside the common faculties of perception.

While not all virtualities may become actualized in the present, they are nevertheless real. The process of actualization of objects/events subsisting in the virtual field depends on information being active and producing a difference. Deleuze's concept of difference is not only an index of diverse and conflicting experiences in the phenomenal world. For Deleuze, difference "is the noumenon closest to phenomenon" (Deleuze, 1994, p. 222), that is, by virtue of its own ontological status it is difference that can *make a difference* in the world of human experiences. "Being as fold" (Deleuze, 1988a, p. 110) is more than a simple projection of the interior. Its meaning cannot be reduced to terms of local, even if nuanced, representation, but "is an internalization of the outside. It is not a reproduction of the Same, but a repetition of the Different. It is not the emanation of an 'I' but something that places in immanence the always other" (Deleuze, 1988a, p. 98). The complex conceptualization of the repetition of the different might seem to be a contradiction in terms if not for the epistemic role of the unconscious that exists *outside* the intentional, phenomenological consciousness or the ego-consciousness of psychoanalysis. Philosophy, for Deleuze, needs an intense non-philosophical understanding. This happens when thought enters "an echo chamber, a feedback loop" (Deleuze, 1995, p. 139) that filters it, and filters it again and again in a process of subtle reflexive am-pli-fications (*le pli* in French means the fold). During each of the iterations something different is being repeated, until a rational thought forms an assemblage with a non-thought and thus "guides the creation of concepts" (Deleuze, 1995, p. 148).

The folding of thought brings forth an element of novelty and presents "life as a work of art" (Deleuze, 1995, p. 94). There is no return to the subject, to the old self, but invention and creation of new possibilities of life by means of going beyond the play of forces. The world is folded and, as such,

> we can endure it, so that everything doesn't confront us at once. ... It's not enough for force to be exerted on other forces or to suffer the effects of other forces, it has to be exerted upon itself too. ... There's no subject, but a production of subjectivity: subjectivity has to be produced, when its time arrives. ... The time comes once we've worked through knowledge and power; it's that work that forces us to frame a new question, it couldn't have been framed before (Deleuze, 1995, pp. 112-114).

Deleuzian "critical and clinical" (Deleuze, 1997) thought presents values as future-oriented vs. pre-given, that is, plural values that are as yet to (be)come. It is not a set of identities that can be conceptually circumscribed, but rather a multiplicity that can actualize itself in a number of different ways. One way Deleuze speaks of this is in terms of problems. "We call the determination of the virtual content of an Idea differen*t*iation; we call the actualisation of that virtuality into species and distinguished parts differen*c*iation. It is always in relation to a differen*t*iated problem or to the differen*t*iated conditions of a problem that a differen*c*iation of species and parts is carried out, as thought it corresponded to the cases of solution of the problem" (Deleuze, 1994, p. 207). Deleuze's reference to problems and solutions is a helpful one, if we think of it in the right way. When Deleuze refers to problems, he is not referring to problems with determined solutions, like two plus two equals four. Rather, he is thinking of problems as creating an open field in which a variety of solutions can occur. To come back to the biological metaphor, the emergence of a particular species can be seen as a solution to the problem an environment sets: terrain, climate, food sources, etc. There may be other species that could arise that would answer that problem, but this particular actualization arose and was a solution to the problem.

It is with this view of ontology that we can begin to approach the question of an ethical education. We should begin this task by saying what an ethical education is *not*, since that will cover most of what passes for education in pedagogical institutions around the world. What an ethical education is not is a learning of a set of identities, for instance a stable set of traditional values. It is not the passing of identities from one person who knows them to another who does not. In a traditional classroom setting, there are three things: the teacher, the students, and the subject matter, that is, material to be learned. (There are also the various media, but in a traditional orientation these are nothing more than technological extensions of the teacher.) Each of these is a pre-constituted identity. The teacher is the one who knows. The student is the one who does not know. The material is what is to be known. Everybody recognizes this pedagogical approach in one way or another. It seems to be the inescapable horizon of institutional education. What else could there be? This is precisely the picture that many people who are in favor of reintroducing values into the classroom have. The problem with students is that they have not learned the values they need to learn. They are not being taught these values at home, because their parents are those permissive folks from the 1960's. They are not being taught them at school, because those same parents are on the Parent-Teacher Associations and bring their permissiveness to their dealings with school. If some of the Christian fundamentalists are to be believed, there is a threat of the imminent collapse of civilization if traditional moral values are not re-introduced into the classroom setting.

Now we may snicker at these folks, and perhaps we should. But we should also recognize that, for most of us, if we differ on the kinds of values that should be taught to students, we often operate within the same broad framework. "Everyone knows," we might say, "what kinds of values ought to be taught to students, except those people." In saying that, we remain within the orbit of the traditional pedagogy we have just described and which is based (even if implicitly) on the traditional ontology and the logic of identities. If the world is composed of identities, then it is possible, in principle at least, to know them. And if we know them, then we can pass them on. Traditional pedagogy is of a piece with traditional ontology. But what if the world is not composed of identities? Or, more precisely, what if the world's identities are themselves moments of a larger virtual field whose ways of folding, unfolding, and refolding itself we do not and cannot know in advance? What if the world we experience and recognize rests on a virtuality that outruns experience and recognition on all sides? Then, in teaching actualities as though that were all there is, we would be missing entirely the difference out of which these actualities arise. Pedagogy like this would be an exercise in impoverishment rather than enrichment. In order to overturn such a pedagogy, we have to rid ourselves of all three elements of the traditional model: the teacher who knows, the student who doesn't, and the material to be known. Instead, we might substitute the following tripartite structure: the teacher who learns, the student who investigates, and the material that appears.

When Deleuze discusses the activity of philosophy, he says the following: "it is a question of someone—if only one—with the necessary modesty not managing to know what everybody knows, and modestly denying what everybody is supposed to recognise." (Deleuze, 1994, p. 130). That, it might be argued, is the starting point not only for a Deleuzian philosophy but also for a Deleuzian inspired pedagogy. If philosophy exists in an "essential and positive relation to non-philosophy" (Deleuze, 1995, p. 140), then rational thought alone would not suffice. New means of philosophical/pedagogical expression rather than merely a language of propositions become imperative. Citing Proust "who said that 'masterpieces are written in a kind of foreign language'" (Deleuze & Guattari, 1987, p. 98), Deleuze and Guattari emphasize the potential of such, as if foreign, language to be truly creative. Its mode of expression may be any regime of signs, such as poetry or images, writing or film, music or painting. A new language of expression must be created: a language within language, which may take either linguistic or extra-linguistic forms, or hybrids like legible images, exemplified in what Deleuze called a performative, or modulating, aspect of language. Language, as any other philosophical concept for Deleuze, is an intensive multiplicity, that is, language as a system possessing a certain structure. Deleuze would have agreed with Lacan that the unconscious too is structured like a language, but he reconceptualizes language to posit it as an assemblage or a system of signs (both verbal and non-verbal) embedded in structures that are "unconscious, [and] necessarily overlaid by their products or effects" (Deleuze, 1968 in Stivale, 1998, p. 270). The subtle language of the unconscious is nevertheless to be perceived. Deleuze wants to achieve the means so as to be able "to show the imperceptible" (Deleuze, 1995, p. 45), that is, become capable of bridging the eternal gap, haunting us since antiquity, between the sensible and the intelligible. Respectively, one may become able to "to show ... the possibility of the impossible" (Deleuze & Guattari, 1994, p. 60).

The task of what Deleuze and Guattari specified as *transversal communication* is "to bring [the] assemblage of the unconscious to the light of the day, to select the whispering voices, to gather ... secret idioms from which I extract something I call my Self (*Moi*)" (Deleuze & Guattari, 1987, p. 84). Deleuze affirms that language, in its multiple forms, is the only thing that can properly be said to have structure, "be it an esoteric or even a nonverbal language" (Deleuze, 1968 in Stivale, 1998, p. 259), such as pictorial, imaginary, or the language of dreams. The diverse means of expression enable one

> "to bring something to life, to free life from where it's trapped, to trace lines of flight. The language for doing so [is] something unstable, always heterogeneous, in which style carves differences of potential between which ... a spark can flash and break out of language itself, to make us see and think what was lying in the shadow around the words, things we were hardly aware existed" (Deleuze, 1995, p. 141).

One is not consciously passing through the line of flight; just the opposite, Deleuze insists that "something [is] passing through you" (Deleuze, 1995, p. 141). Becoming-other is established via "diversity, multiplicity [and] the destruction of identity" (Deleuze, 1995, p. 44); it presupposes breaking out of old habits and into new territories so as "to bring into being that which does not yet exist" (Deleuze, 1994, p. 147).

How might the ethics of pedagogical process look in practice? Let us make four suggestions that can stand as elements of a Deleuzian pedagogy. There are certainly more, and these can only be made suggestively. The hope is that they would contribute toward opening other, non-traditional approaches to pedagogical activity. We would like to orient these changes in an ethical direction, to contrast the ethics embedded in a Deleuzian pedagogy with traditional morality. First, a Deleuzian pedagogy would require jettisoning the question of who should be in favor of a broader inquiry into who we might be. The question of who we should be, or, if we are to take it in the direction of modern moral philosophy, what we should do, is grounded in the view that there are pre-given values that can be discovered and articulated. Values exist as identities, even if we don't yet know them. These identities, when discovered, are to be passed on to those who don't know them in order that they may come to know them. However, if we abandon the idea of values as identities, then the field is opened up for a different kind of investigation. Instead of asking who it is that we should be, we can ask instead who it is that we *might* be. This shift is not simply one from the morality of should to the possibility of might. As we have seen, the idea of possibility assumes that the virtual is a potential mirror of the actual. To ask what we might be, then, is not to ask what possibilities there are for us out there in the virtual. It is to ask what we might be able to make of ourselves, how we might touch the virtual in such a way as to draw out new arenas for living. Moreover, these new arenas don't have to be individualistic in the way our society often promotes. The question need not be solely one of who *I* might be. It can also be a question of who *we* might be, and in many different senses and combinations of that *we*.

This leads to the second aspect of a Deleuzian pedagogy: it would ask of education that it be committed to experimentation rather than inculcation. If what is of educational interest is the question of who we might be, and if we do not yet know who we might be, and if who we might be is not a set of pre-given identities there to be discovered, then in order to learn this, we must experiment with that question rather than assume it to be already answered. This, perhaps, would be the deepest change suggested by the embrace of ontology of difference. Traditional pedagogy assumes that, in the end, the student will arrive at what the teacher already knows. But if we follow Deleuze's ontological steps, virtual wellspring of Being cannot be known—at least in the sense of being captured by conceptual identities. Even a Deweyan pedagogy, whose orientation is so far advanced over most of our own practices, would set up experimentation where the teacher already knows what the student is supposed to discover through his or her experiments. For Deleuze, education would begin, not when the student arrives at a grasp of the material already known by the teacher, but when the teacher and student together begin to *experiment* in practice with what they might make of themselves and the world. This may seem abstract and far removed from the world we live in. However, there is nothing Deleuze is saying here that would be foreign to most artists and to many scientists. An artist of real creativity is not one who manipulates the formulas of the past, but rather one who stakes out a journey into unknown areas. It almost always helps to have some knowledge of what has gone on before one, both so that one gets a sense of what paths have been taken and what they have to offer and so that one doesn't run the risk of simply repeating what others have done. In the end, though, a Virginia Woolf or a Francis Bacon or a John Coltrane become who they might be through a willingness to experiment with their arts, to go off in directions whose destinations are not guaranteed. What takes place is an experiment on ourselves: the mode of nomadic thinking and living. Nomad is always in-between, always in the process of becoming, "the life of nomad is the intermezzo" (Deleuze & Guattari, 1987, p. 380), distributed at once between here and there, between now and then, "always the day before and the day after" (Deleuze, 1995, p. 77). What, Deleuze might ask, is a real education if it does not teach us to take the risks of those who have gone beyond themselves, and in many cases beyond the rest of us?

In order to engage in experimentation, we have to abandon the idea that common sense ought to be our guide. This is the third element of a Deleuzian pedagogy. Deleuze uses the term *common sense* in a technical fashion, to refer to the identity that arises when the faculties (in the Kantian sense) agree with one another. We might extend this idea outward from faculties to individuals. Common sense is what everyone knows. It is what is obviously true, so obviously true that it would be a sign of ignorance to deny it. But that is precisely what needs to be jettisoned in an ethical education. It is, as Deleuze has told us, what one manages not to know that opens the doors to the virtual. It is what we do not know, rather than what we do, that is of educational interest. We must disrupt our common sense with problems that do not yield its answers as our solutions. "What is a thought," Deleuze asks, "which harms no one, neither thinkers nor anyone else?" (Deleuze, 1994, pp. 135-136). If an ethical education is to commence, then we must abandon the answers that common sense has ready and waiting for us and allow ourselves to be harmed by a thought that defies it. It is inherent in experimentation, if it is to be something other than a pretense, that one makes oneself vulnerable, no longer resting assured in the comfort of common sense. The fourth element of a Deleuzian pedagogy would start from the recognition that much of our world, as well as our learning, are unconscious rather than conscious. This follows, not directly from the last three elements, but instead from Deleuze's larger ontology, in which there is more to this world than appears—or can appear—to us in our immediate experience. If the virtual is coiled within the actual and is immanent rather than transcendent, and if our conscious experience is bound to the actual, then much of who we are is outside our conscious awareness and, by implication, exceeds also what we can represent in thought and articulate in the language of propositions.

The Deleuzian unconscious is reconceptualized - it is a multiplicity that does not belong to the scope of traditional psychoanalytic thought. It cannot be reduced to psychoanalytic drives or instincts as well as "playing around all the time with mummy and daddy" (Deleuze, 1995, p. 144). Over and above the personal unconscious, it always deals with some collective frame and is "a productive machine, ... at once social and desiring" (Deleuze, 1995, p. 144). Unconscious formations are to be brought into play because an individual is a desiring, rather than solely cognitive, being for whom the "family drama depends ... on the unconscious social investments" (Deleuze, 1995, p. 20). The unconscious as collective entails the insufficiency for understanding ourselves in terms of a single identity of an intentional speaking subject. The unconscious, as yet a-conceptual part of the plane of immanence is always productive and constructive, making "self" and "subjectivity" transient and unstable notions. According to Deleuze, the conscious and rational "intentionality of being is surpassed by the fold of Being, Being as fold" (1988a, p. 110). In this respect, the unconscious perceptions are implicated as minute-, or micro-perceptions (Deleuze, 1993); as such, they become part of the cartographic microanalysis of establishing "an unconscious psychic mechanism that engenders the perceived in consciousness" (Deleuze, 1993, p. 95). We are made up of much more than we can say. This has at least two implications for an ethical education. First, it deepens the first element we discussed - abandoning the question of who we should be for who we might be. If we are composed not only of the actual but also of a virtual difference, then who we might be is not divorced from who we are. To become who we might be is not to become something other than ourselves; rather, it is to become something other than our actual selves in the process called by Deleuze *becoming-other*. "The other in me" (Deleuze, 1988a, p. 98) is ultimately implicated because of the twisted and folded relationship between a rational thought and a non-thought. The latter is unconscious: as inherent in one's relation to oneself, it belongs not to a preexistent *Ego*, but to "the fractured I of a dissolved Cogito" (Deleuze, 1994, p. 194). The reason the *otherness* is not foreign to us, is because we are *of* it, it is immanent. The fractured pieces of a dissolved Cogito are to be put together, however, not in virtue of identity, but within a dynamic process of becoming-other, which is always already collective or "populated" (Deleuze, 1987, p. 9). Deleuze introduces his notion of *rhizomatics* as a process of drawing multiple connective lines between conflicting experiences thereby constituting what he calls the plane of immanent consistency. The plane of immanence "does not immediately take effects with concepts" (Deleuze & Guattari, 1994, p. 41): it is pre-rational and a-conceptual, ultimately enabling "the conquest of the unconscious" (Deleuze, 1988b, p. 29) during its own immanent and constructive process. The Deleuzian level of analysis is not solely "a question of intellectual understanding ... but of intensity, resonance, musical harmony" (Deleuze, 1995, p. 86). It is guided by the "logic of affects" (Guattari, 1995, p. 9) and as such is different from a merely rational consensus based on cognitive reasoning.

Hence follows the second implication: we must recognize that learning is not simply cognitive; it is also corporeal. Our bodies learn outside our conscious awareness, and it is often these bodies that can engage in an experimentation to which our consciousness, because of its anchoring in identities, resists. The corporeal affects and percepts are complementary to intellectual concepts and they make *un-thought,* that is, the unconscious of thought, *immanent* to rational thinking. The paradoxical "thinking" of this sort constitutes "the supreme act of philosophy: not so much to think *the* plane of immanence as to show that it is there, unthought in every plane, and to think it in this way as the outside and inside of thought, as the non-external outside and the non-internal inside – that which cannot be thought and yet must be thought" (Deleuze & Guattari, 1994, pp. 59-60). The immanent becomings function in a mode of nomadic—movable and moving—distributions that break down "the sedentary structures of representation" (Deleuze, 1994, p. 37), and a thought encounters crisis, a shock, similar to a novice athlete who is thrown into water. For an athlete who finds herself in a novel situation, there is no solid foundation under her feet, and the world that she has to face loses its reassuring power of familiar representations. Deleuze reconstructs a powerful story of an athlete who learns to swim through a *becoming*—herself in the water, indeed among and not over or above the "intensities [that] rise and fall" (Deleuze, 1995, p. 147)—that carries the problem as the unknown along with it. The swimmer struggles against the waves because she is facing the unknown that includes her not-yet-knowing-how to swim, and the swimmer's movement does not resemble the movement of the wave. Nor does it imitate the instructor's movements given while not in the water but on the shore. The swimmer is learning "by grasping [the movement of the wave] in practice as signs" (Deleuze, 1994, p. 23). Going beyond recognition, the Deleuzian thought without image—an experimental thought that has its "origin" in practice necessarily becomes a model of learning. Thinking without recognition is oriented towards evaluation of one's current, here-and-now, mode of existence, and "beneath the generalities of habit in moral life we rediscover singular processes of learning" (Deleuze, 1994, p. 25), that is, transforming our old habits of thinking and acting. The problematic situation—that is, one that requires learning—is of the nature of real experience, which forms "an intrinsic genesis, not an extrinsic conditioning" (Deleuze, 1994, p. 154). Learning cannot take place by means of representation: this would be the reproduction of the same, denounced by Deleuze. For learning to occur, the meaningful relation between a sign and a response must be established, leading—through experiential and experimental *encounter* with the other—to what Deleuze identified as a repetition of the different. Deleuze emphasizes the corporeal dimension as "sensory-motivity" (Deleuze, 1994, p. 23) of the genuine learner who, exemplified in the image of the athlete, tries to co-ordinate her own sensor-motor activity—that is, at every moment evaluate her own mode of existence—with an intense, as if opposing, force of water. Such an evaluation is an effect of the encounter with the unknown, therefore as yet unthinkable. Deleuze is adamant that an ethical education cannot base itself on the instruction:

> 'Do as I do'. Our only teachers are those who tell us to 'do with me', and are able to emit signs to be developed in heterogeneity rather than propose gestures for us to reproduce .... When a body combines some of its own distinctive points with those of a wave, it espouses the principle of a repetition which is no longer that of the Same, but involves the Other— involves difference, from one wave and one gesture to another, and carries that difference through the repetitive space thereby constituted. To learn is indeed to constitute this space of an encounter with signs, in which the distinctive points renew themselves in each other, and repetition takes shape while disguising itself (Deleuze, 1994, p. 23).

The meaning of what Deleuze identified as spatio-temporal dynamisms becomes clear in their embodying the very idea of difference as a *process* before it may become a conceptual identity, a category: the identity of the athlete is "swallowed up in difference, each being no more than a difference between differences. Difference must be shown *differing*" (Deleuze, 1994, p. 56). What will there be left to learn if the difference refers back to some primary identity rather than moving forward to further differences? Deleuze writes, in a passage whose complexity we cannot entirely unpack here, "To learn is to enter into the universal of the relations which constitute the Idea, and into their corresponding singularities. The idea of the sea, for example, as Leibniz showed, is a system of liaisons or differential relations between particulars and singularities corresponding to the degrees of variation among these relations—the totality of the system being incarnated in the real movement of the waves. To learn to swim is to conjugate the distinctive points of our bodies with the singular points of the objective Idea in order to form a problematic field." (Deleuze, 1994, p. 165).

We see in this passage the elements we have been discussing. The sea is not a block of identity but a swarm of differences. These differences cannot be recognized by common sense. Swimming is an experiment that seeks to immerse itself in them rather than to comprehend them conceptually. In that immersion, the question becomes not one of who one should be but of who one might be, of what one might make of oneself in relation to the water, how one's own virtual difference intersects with that of the sea. Much of that making and intersecting is unconscious. It is a corporeal activity whose parameters cannot be reduced to conscious thought. What Deleuze calls thinking is "not just a theoretical matter. It [is] to do with vital problems. To do with life itself" (Deleuze, 1995, p. 105). For Deleuze, then, an ethical education is one that involves not simply our minds but our lives, taking it to places it has not gone and did not know were there. And, indeed, those places are not there until they are created from the virtual out of which we live. It is harder to imagine something more threatening to those who would teach us traditional moral values, or more vital to those of us who find those values stifling. An education defined as ethical, in Deleuze's sense of the word, is not to be reduced to learning given values, nor is it "looking for origins, even lost or deleted ones, but [is] setting out to catch things where they were at work, in the middle: breaking things open, breaking words open" (Deleuze, 1995, p. 86). An ethical education produces subjectivities that are capable of inventing new concepts and articulating new values contingent on the dynamics of experience. Acknowledging a particularly narrow approach to education, Deleuze described it as students' discovery of solutions to the problems posited by teachers. In this way pupils lack power to constitute problems themselves, and it is the construction of problems that constitutes an ethical dimension because, for Deleuze, it is paramount for one's sense of freedom. Only if and when "thought is free, hence vital, nothing is compromised. When it ceases being so, all other oppressions are also possible" (Deleuze, 1988b, p. 4).

A free thought is capable of realizing its creative potential, of actualising the virtual. The newly created concepts, or concepts the meanings of which have been altered, impose new sets of evaluation on the modes of existence, and – sure enough – for Deleuze, no thinking, no speaking, and no acting, are value-free. New values are to be created because life is not a straightforward affair but presents problems whose multiple solutions constitute an open field—it is how we might solve a particular problem, that would give a particular value to a certain experience: an experiment on ourselves. For Deleuze, "once one ventures outside what's familiar and reassuring, once one has to invent new concepts for unknown lands, then methods and moral systems break down" (Deleuze, 1995, p. 103). A given moral standard simply does not enter Deleuze's discourse because a concept always "speaks the event, [and] not the essence" (Deleuze & Guattari, 1994, p. 21). Event is always an element of becoming, and the becoming is unlimited. Deleuze is firm on the question of the impersonality of event: as a multiplicity, an event is profoundly social and collective therefore "irreducible to individual states of affairs, particular images, [or] personal beliefs" (Deleuze, 1990, p. 19). One – in whose body an event is localized – is to be worthy of this event. For this purpose, one has to attain an ethical responsibility or, as Deleuze says, "this will that the event creates in us" (Deleuze, 1990, p. 148) as if us ourselves subsequently becoming a quasi-cause of that what is being produced. The Deleuzian line of flight "effectively folds into a spiral" (Deleuze, 1993, p. 17), each fold – in its function as a repetition of the different – adding up to the totality of the whole process of becoming-other. It is a creative *becoming* indeed because it brings forth "the tenor of existence, the intensification of life" (Deleuze & Guattari, 1994, p. 74) and the previously unknown creative potential expressed by "the manner in which the existing being is filled with immanence" (Deleuze, 1997, p. 137). Learning presupposes an encounter with something as yet unknown, and one always "has to invent new concepts for unknown lands" (Deleuze, 1995, p. 103). For Deleuze, life itself is educative: it is a long experiential process requiring wisdom in a Spinozian sense, that is, wisdom as practical and ethical, and overcoming in this process the limitations of narrow subject-centered knowledge. If the centrality of subject-position is questioned, then all learning and teaching are to be reconceptualized: learning is enabled by means of the common engagement in transversal communications ensuring potential transformations of old habits at the teaching "end" as well. Without the relation in practice between "the sign and the corresponding apprenticeship" (Deleuze, 2000, p. 92) all signs would remain meaningless.

New meanings are capable of self-expression only as eventual outcomes of the total process to which they are immanent and not as externally given in a forceful and often destructive manner. There should not be any special educative aim imposed from without but an immanent desire only. We remember that Deleuze, describing difference, stressed that it must be inherently differing, that is, itself being capable of making a difference. Expression is impossible without construction, and the educational growth is a function of both as inscribed in experience. The absence of any transcendent aim in the immanent process of becoming also eliminates the hierarchical power structure specific to traditional schooling. The distribution of knowledge becomes a function of the shared experience rather than of a centrally administered curriculum. The body of knowledge is being held together not by some abstract "end" but by the immanent production of meanings, the latter including not only the sense and worth of chemistry, or literature, or history, or any other subject-matter, but first and foremost, the sense and worth of self. In this respect Deleuze's philosophy tends toward the ethical position of care theorists in education (see Noddings, 1984, 1998, 2002). The ethics of care emphasizes moral interdependence and "rejects the notion of a truly autonomous moral agent. ... As teachers, we are as dependent on our students as they are on us" (Noddings, 1998, p. 196). Deleuze's conceptualization of becoming asserts a self-*becoming*-autonomous, as if tending to its own ideal limit, as a continuous function – always already incorporating difference into itself – of the educative, always creative, process that does not provide a room for the old set of values, nor are eternal ones stored there.

The ethical question, for Deleuze, consists in evaluation of multiple modes of existence that would not be expressed solely in rational value judgments. Consistent with the intent of contemporary philosophy of education to stay in pursuit of "new vocabularies and new meanings for old vocabularies" (Noddings, 1993, p. 6), Deleuze prefers affective tones specified in terms of "'I love or I hate' instead of 'I judge'" (Deleuze, 1989, p. 141) that serve as a means for ethical evaluations blending therefore a fundamental critical aspect with an ethical (aka, clinical, as Deleuze would have said) conception. Ethical concerns are embedded in experience because the pluralism of values breaks down any *a priori* moral ideal as being the same for everyone and under any circumstances. As pertaining to education, ethics will be specified as a mode of existence rather than a pre-existing set of values, according to which human nature is supposed to be judged on the basis of how well it would fit into the hierarchy of values. It is evaluations, for Deleuze, and not prescribed values that characterize one's ways of being or modes of existence:

> The notion of value implies a *critical* reversal. ... The problem of critique is that of the value of values, of the evaluation from which their value arises, thus the problem of their *creation*. ... [W]e always have the beliefs, feelings and thoughts that we deserve given our way of being and our style of life. ... This is the crucial point; *high* and *low, noble* and *base,* are not values but represent the differential element from which the value of values themselves arise (Deleuze, 1983, pp. 1-2).

Instead of conforming to fixed moral criteria, Deleuze-Spinoza's system of affects replaces the strict and rigid moral code. Because ethics is sharply distinguished from morality, the latter tending to substitute transcendent values for the immanent ethical criteria that serve to evaluate various modes of existence, no mode of existence, or any newly created possibility of life, is to be judged so that in all possibility it might lead to a devaluation of real life for the sake of some abstract higher values. For Deleuze, any mode of life is organic and vital by definition, and therefore good in the sense of its potential power to transform itself and, as a result, "to open opportunities – never to close them" (Noddings, 1993, p. 13). Deleuze's ethical education is the ethics of an education whose direction and destination are pursued not by those who know what is good for us and ask only for our assent, but by those for whom the world still has mysteries left to offer (new opportunities to be opened, new meanings and values to be created in experience) and believe that education might still have something to do with those mysteries.

REFERENCES

Deleuze, G., & Parnet, C. (1987). *Dialogues* (H. Tomlinson & B. Habberjam, Trans.). New York: Columbia University Press.

Deleuze, G. (1988a). *Foucault* (S. Hand, Trans.). Minneapolis, MN: University of Minnesota Press.

Deleuze, G. (1988b). *Spinoza: Practical philosophy* (R. Hurly, Trans.). San Francisco: City Lights Books.

Deleuze, G. (1989). *Cinema 2: The time-image* (H. Tomlinson & R. Galeta, Trans.). Minneapolis, MN: University of Minnesota Press.

Deleuze, G. (1993). *The fold: Leibniz and the Baroque* (T. Conley, Trans.). Minneapolis, MN: University of Minnesota Press.

Deleuze, G. (1994). *Difference and repetition* (P. Patton, Trans.). New York: Columbia University Press.

Deleuze, G. (1995). *Negotiations 1972–1990* (M. Joughin, Trans.). New York: Columbia University Press.

Deleuze, G. (1997). *Essays critical and clinical* (D. W. Smith & M. Greco, Trans.). Minneapolis, MN: University of Minnesota Press.

Deleuze, G. (2001). *Pure immanence: Essays on a life* (A. Boyman, Trans.). New York: Zone Books.

Deleuze, G., & Guattari, F. (1987). *A thousand plateaus: Capitalism and schizophrenia* (B. Massumi, Trans.). Minneapolis, MN: University of Minnesota Press.

Deleuze, G., & Guattari, F. (1994). *What is philosophy?* (H. Tomlinson & G. Burchell, Trans.). New York: Columbia University Press.

Guattari, F. (1995). *Chaosmosis: An ethico-aesthetic paradigm* (P. Bains & J. Pefanis, Trans.). Bloomington & Indianapolis: Indiana University Press.

Noddings, N. (1984). *Caring: A feminine approach to ethics and moral education.* Berkeley: University of California Press.

Noddings, N. (1993). Excellence as a guide to educational conversation. In H. Alexander (Ed.), *Philosophy of education society* (pp. 5–16). Urbana, IL.

Noddings, N. (1998). *Philosophy of education.* Boulder, CO: Westview Press.

Noddings, N. (2002). *Educating moral people: A caring alternative to moral education.* New York & London: Teachers' College Press.

Todd May
Clemson University
USA

Inna Semetsky
The University of Newcastle
Australia

KAUSTUV ROY

11. DELEUZIAN MURMURS

Education and Communication

A CRITIQUE OF COMMUNICATION

Ever since the structuralist critique of meaning, Wittgenstein's (2001) notion of language games, and most notably, the poststructupal critique of the signifier (Foucault, 1972; Derrida, 1982), the notion of communication has shown itself to be a deeply troubled one. Despite Habermas' (1984) attempt to repossess the term and work out its conditions of possibility, the 'com' in communication is a source of embarrassment to many, who, having discovered the web of hegemonistic filigree spun throughout communicational practices, hesitate to engage the term. For, communication often seems to flow along established power grids or "State" lines with its voltage a determination of privilege, raising immediately the questions: what speaks or who is silenced in the process of exchange? What murmurs are glossed over? What knowledges are suppressed? Which meanings are inscribed within what dominant semantical order? These are by no means remote theoretical questions. Even a casual survey of the literature of oppressed groups such as women, Blacks, indigenous populations, and others will show that the question of loss of life-world and meaning is intricately linked to the hegemony of linguistic practices and the consequent loss of expression.

In general, the assumptions underlying the mainstream, techno-rational idea of communication, such as the conservation of intent, content as pure transmissible data, and the medium as non-interfering carrier of information, all of these have been shown to be problematic. For instance, Foucault (1972) showed that we do not speak or communicate transparently as the modernist vision holds, but instead, it is the movement of "discourse" that shapes and limits speech and what is possible to say. To put it differently, we can only say what we can say within the discourses that are prevalent at a certain historical moment. In addition, this also puts a question mark against the taken-for-granted subjectivities of the sender/ receiver model, because now, the issue, following Foucault, is not 'who speaks' but 'what speaks'.

Further, Gilles Deleuze's (1994) critique of representation casts serious doubts on yet another key assumption on which communication rests—the possibility of repetition without difference. Pure repetition masks processual change and therefore inescapable internal variation. In one extreme sense, the very presence of the observer introduces a degree of flux in any situation. Thus the fundamental ambiguities in the communicational model have been revealed by qhowing the difficulty of assuming a fixed, objective existence of content prior to the form of expression. Also, intent now is seen to be the function of discursive formations,

I. Semetsky (ed.), Nomadic Education: Variations on a Theme by Deleuze and Guattari, 159–170.
© *2008 Sense Publishers. All rights reserved.*

slogans, and idealized representations, and reception becomes a function of the web of ideas that is disturbed by an act of communication with its corresponding ambiguity and contingency.

But more work is necessary to grasp what all this might mean in terms of the performative pragmatics of communication. For it is precisely the possibility of unproblematic communication that is assumed within the 'apolitical' imaginary of mainstream education. In particular, the techno-rational approaches assert the possibility of transforming education into an efficient machine "based on high quality performance data" that can reveal "what constitutes best practice" (Blake et al., 2000, p. 8). This corporate vision that has grown strong in recent decades views educational problems as technical issues and questions of input-output, placing education within the paradigmatic of machine efficiency. It is quite plain that from this modernist perspective "high quality performance" translates into the teacher being an efficient communicator of the expert designed curriculum. Communication in this perspective is held to be the operation of a code, a pure medium, that is, a vehicle only, in which may be inscribed a body of practical thought to be directly transmitted with minimum or no interference from the act itself. Communication in and of itself is seemingly nothing, it is the communication *of* something, and therefore the sole focus is on that something—content or input. What occurs in-between the "input" and the "output" is apparently of no consequence. Therefore it is not surprising that the notion that good teaching practice can be codified and freely transmitted to bring about reform in schooling is the basis of a lot of research and writing in education.

However, given what we have seen above, there maybe a basic error lurking in such thinking. Commenting on Deleuze and Guattari's work, Massumi (1992) writes:

> Language may convey codes in the form of identity categories or general ideas... To the extent that it does, it can be said to function ideologically... The distinction between a code and a language is an important one that is not often made in semiotics. What is lost when it is not made is the whole political dimension of language. (p. 188)

This paper will emphatically draw the distinction between language and code and explore the political and performative dimension of the communicative act. I will attempt to do so, first, by bringing to the fore the reversibility between content and expression that shows the hierarchy between them to be a false one. This will challenge a key assumption in the instrumentalist view that the mode of expression is secondary or largely epiphenomenal to content. And second, I will show that there occur material exchanges between language and bodies by means of a certain confrontation of forces that dramatically politicizes the communicative act.

To put it differently, while "codification" of language and "free transmission of data" make the assumption of unproblematic communication, something that is possible only in a repeatable, context free world, I will attempt to show that in embroiled, embodied, lived life contexts, an act of communication is literally an embodied act. It is more than simply transmission of content but occurs through the warping of contingent totalities of semantic relationships that are at the same time the inauguration or transformation of physical micro-worlds. My project here is to show that beneath the sea of dominant significations lie flows and currents of transformations that are not simply signifiers but expressional crossovers into corporeality. The point is that if language and bodies are inextricably interrelated in this manner, expression becomes a key face of the political not as rhetoric but as an event in and of itself.

The argument proceeds thus: The pulsion or movement of a communicative act, in its very passage, changes the social body; and the body, in turn, reconstitutes the "message" over the socius. Inherent in this reciprocal movement are both an overt, conjunctive, dominant message, as well as a *disjunctive, uncontrollable transformation* and becoming. Grasping this subordinate and subversive movement we come to realize a communicative act as something more than a transmission of content. It is thus that we can propose a different way of thinking about exchange between bodies that constitutes the possibility of insurgent and corporeal murmurs that escape codification. In other words, even as messages appear codified at one level, a different and disjunctive activity may be going on simultaneously at another level that may have liberatory potential. The concurrent presence of both levels of activity ensures that the conditions of possibility for transgression of the dominant order of signification lie in the situation itself.

Recognizing expression as the real active face of language is a departure from the conventional order; it suggests performativity as primary. While codification often serves the normative and standardizing impulse and can be considered as a statist or corporatist activity, here I propose to show that even as we use language in normative modes it may unravel in significant ways to peveal an otherness that is freeing. For those od us who are closely attentive to the moments in a liberatory pedagogy, communication that bears on its own communicability is of the essence, for

> what human beings have to communicate to each other is above all a pure communicability (that is, language), politics then arises as the communicative emptiness in which the human...emerges as such (Agamben, 2000, p. 96).

Language or communicability itself is the wonder, and not merely what it says, for language must presuppose itself, without which no exchange is possible. This presupposition as a condition of possibility is an irrepressible opening ahead of every statement that makes language oscillate paradoxically as an apriori as well as a spokenness. It is the very possibility of language and the linguistic act that generates an opening within which also arise human potentiality, if potentiality can be thought of as collective will. The prospect of communication and politics therefore arise simultaneously. That is to say, the very attempt to communicate is political, for it sets in motion, besides dominant significations, a chasm that triggers disturbances within transversal layers and concentric webs of semantical relationships. It is the becoming of the human itself that is at stake in communicative acts and not the mere description of events.

A code, on the other hand, is an abstraction, a separation of the subject and utterance, and not the living exchange that is an unfolding of the being-in-language of the human in all its immense multiplicity. Therefore language as code and transmission is, in a sense, always already colonized, at the service of disciplinary bodies. Rather than invest in "best practices" that is the instrumentalist codification, I will show that the subversive movements hinted at above undermine the normative assumptions underpinning linguistic events, but even more, illustrate the surreptitious coming together of language and bodies by means of certain transformations that traverse both words and things. In order to examine this subversive process that underlies communicative acts I will begin by introducing a few useful conceptual tools below.

THE ORDER-WORD

Language, according to Deleuze and Guattari (1987), is not a literal conveyance of meaning but operates in a field of *implicit presuppositions* or collective assemblages from which the semantic content cannot be separated:

> It then becomes clear that the statement is individuated, and enunciation subjectified, only to the extent that an impersonal collective assemblage requires it and determines it to be so. (p. 80)

Collective assemblages are the dominant webs and networks of implicit pre-suppositions on the "surface" of which meaning or semantic content appears as a precipitate or an effect. Each utterance triggers a certain motion or pulsion in such networks giving rise to what is generally called meaning. To put it differently, recognition of enunciation is dependent on the action upon and within collective assemblages that are set in motion by a certain communicative act. The power of the assemblage, in large part, lies in its dispersal throughout the socius, its hiddenness equal in degree to its ubiquity. Meaning, therefore, is never in language alone, but in the manner in which collective assemblages traverse the network of social forces operating at a particular moment.

Further, this leads us to consider what Deleuze and Guattari (1987) call the order-word:

> We call *order-words*, not a particular category of explicit statements (for example, in the imperative), but the relation of every word or every statement to implicit presuppositions, in other words, to speech acts that are, and can only be, accomplished in the statement. Order-words do not concern commands only, but every act that is linked statements by a "social obligation." Every statement displays this link. The only possible definition of language is the set of all order-words, implicit presuppositions, or speech acts current in a given language at a given moment. (p. 79)

Borrowing the notion of the speech-act from J. L. Austin's *How To Do Things With Words,* Deleuze and Guattari modify it for their own purpose. Language, they say, is neither merely informational nor communicational, but is more a leaping from order-word to order-word, punctuated by action, as each statement *performs an act or an act is performed* in the statement. The order-word is thus a marshaling process that makes the utterance into an enunciation, and language remains no longer a mere carrier of information, but is a force or "pulsion".

Let us emphasize, that order-words do not refer merely to the imperatives in any language, but are constitutive of every statement. For, there can be no utterance without context or implicit presuppositions, and an action is performed in that very flash of connection to context, obligation, or presupposition. In other words, contrary to the Derridean conception of language as a free play of signifiers, "the expressed is not fundamentally a signified caught in the interplay of signifiers. Instead it is a function involving a real transformation" (Massumi, 1992, p. 18). A word is what a word does or prevents from doing.

To give an instance of this let us take the case of the ongoing "war" in Iraq. From the beginning, the debate on Iraq was borne by a set of terms that acquired "meaning" within an existing collective assemblage, a set of implicit presuppositions within the constructs of which meaning and response were sought. For instance, the use of the term "war," among other things, as a given descriptor of military action against Iraq inoculated the ground, so to speak, legitimizing aggression even before the debate had properly begun. Thereafter, the discourse quickly got bogged down in arguments about whether this was a just war. The question was never raised: "On whose terms is this a war?" In the case of the two countries involved — US and Iraq — the sheer disproportion and asymmetry in size and military strength made it a travesty to describe the situation as war. But if it was not war, then US military incursion had to be necessarily a criminal operation, the fact of which of course could not be admitted at any cost. So it was absolutely imperative to normalize the venture from the very beginning by calling it war, to codify it.

To put it differently, half the battle in legitimizing the venture lay in creating the semantic terrain on which such action could be projected as part of a society's normalized domain of defensive responses. The main work therefore was to cast what was essentially military adventurism in terms of a *collective assemblage* that would contain the debate in specific ways. In this case, in order to accept war, one had to first agree that it *is* war, not criminal adventurism, that was being posited, and once this work was done much had been accomplished. For "war" has the implicit presupposition of the existence of more or less balanced forces, and therefore a historical legitimation.

Let us next take a very different example that will attempt to further clarify the issue of collective assemblages. Let us look at the concept of healthcare that is everywhere these days, an unquestioned term in the public discourse as well as in private concerns. But when one stops to think about the notion, it is obvious that the massively entrenched discourse, the associated "health" industry, the colossal insurance network, and the related budgetary appropriations have little to do with health as such. They are, instead, concerned with disease and treatment, with drugs, doctors, hospitals, and the vast pharmaceutical industry. But although this fact is obvious, it is not admissible or "visible" within the operative collective assemblage. Everyone wants health, and therefore disease care, which is what it is about, is invisibilized, along with lifestyles and societal conditions that prevent health.

The "collective assemblage" underlying the notion of healthcare, which is the indirect discourse of implicit presuppositions, impels us into accepting the very opposite of health as the paradigm of healthcare. So when public officials talk about healthcare, or unions negotiate to expand its coverage, or when private individuals agonize about it, in each case the parameters of the enunciations are determined by the existing collective assemblage, and have little to do with the reality of caring for health as such. In other words, it is almost impossible to escape the discourse of implicit presuppositions and the collective assemblages that medicalize health. This medicalization of health makes sure that healthcare invokes myriad connections to drugs and medicine and to doctors and dentists as modern and efficient expressions of caring for health, and few other options are visible or available. The very meaning of health is created and managed within the set of existing presuppositions.

The above examples show that the real function of language is not communication of what is, nor is it simply mediated exchange, but rather "impulsions" that bring about or obscure certain thought-actions in a shifting field of pre-suppositions:

> What becomes of a meaning encounter is attributable to its unique and contingent "context," the nondiscursive network of forces within which particular speaking bodies are positioned and which ordains what those bodies say-do. (Massumi, 1992, p. 30).

From the examples discussed above this becomes abundantly clear. The logic of war quickly gains ground when the nondiscursive network of forces—hegemonic desires, appeasement of the electorate, control of resources, political gains—within the context of which it is invoked are already converging toward a set of objectives, even if the situation is misrepresented as war. In the second example, both management and unions tend to gain when they reach agreement on "healthcare" benefits, no matter that health as such is not involved in any way. The set of implicit presuppositions in each case is intersected by the nondiscursive forces to produce what we call "meaning" that is acceptable within a given context.

In the examples discussed above, war or health can be seen as order words. Going back to our example on the Iraq invasion, as the rhetoric leapt from WMD to war, the skies of Baghdad lit up with spectacular bombs that a "civilized" world watched with "awe" on television, shielded by the symbolic. "War" focuses on leaders and spectacular activity, discounting the reality of humans and the land. In the same way, when we listen to spiraling "healthcare" costs, the order word leaps quickly to questions about prescription drugs etc., ever impelling us into forms of thought-action within the contingent totality of the existing features of a collective assemblage. The order word "health" prevents deeper questions—about the social order, work conditions, ingrained habits, the social encouragement to passivity and other such possible factors in health—from emerging. In both cases, the enunciatory forces that are massed along certain fronts or lines do a specific kind of work of meaning management that makes the communicative act an intensely

political one. Having grasped this, the next step is to explore the nature of the actions that proceed from the order-word. For the order word does not merely organize social discourse but also affects bodies directly, intimately.

THE TWO TRANSFORMATIONS

Within the schemata presented here, there are at least two kinds of transformations or interchanges that occur between language and bodies: the incorporeal and the corporeal. Let us first look at Deleuze and Guattari's (1987) notion of *incorporeal transformations*:

> The incorporeal transformation is recognizable by its instantaneousness, its immediacy, by the simultaneity of the statement expressing the transformation and the effect the transformation produces...The order-words or assemblages of enunciation in a given society (in short, the illocutionary) designate this instantaneous relation between statements and the incorporeal transformations or noncorporeal attributes they express. (p. 81)

A declaration of war, although it may be expressed as a statement, changes everything instantaneously. The order word triggers a plethora of affect as it insinuates itself into daily modes of being. In an instant everything has changed. This is not the mere anticipation of an event but its very construction. Even before there is the general mobilization, the jingoistic fervor etc., the social atmosphere and the beings in it are variously transformed, re-experiencing primal instincts that are invested in the word itself. Consequently, we can say that *language itself turns out to be an event and not merely a description of events*. Further,

> the expressions or expresseds are inserted into or intervene in contents, not to represent them but to anticipate them or move them back, slow them down or speed them up, separate or combine them, delimit them in a different way. The warp of the instantaneous transformations is always inserted into the woof of the continuous modifications. (p. 86)

In other words, the order-word "intervenes" to alter the vectors in a field of relations, splice experience, recombine emotion, slow down or speed up affective transformations, draw limits around the event. Thus words do not merely represent things or states, they anticipate them, lie in wait for them, as it were. The incorporeal transformation is a convenient syntagma that captures a slice of the pragmatics.

Next I will consider the notion of corporeal transformation. An assemblage of enunciation does not speak merely *of* things; it speaks *on the same level as* states of things themselves. In other words, the enunciation is more than just a linguistic phenomenon; it is a body confronting other bodies. This confrontation and consequent interchange may be called *corporeal transformation*, bringing together the semiotics and pragmatics in a ceaseless interplay. A dramatic instance of this coming together of semiotic and material components is as follows:

> Sometimes the semiotic components are more deterritorialized than the material components, and sometimes the reverse. For example, a mathematical complex of signs may be more deterritorialized than a set of particles; conversely, the particles may have experimental effects that deterritorialize the semiotic system. (p. 87)

Here, "deterritorializing" may be approximately taken to mean fundamentally unsettling, or knocked into a different orbit or trajectory. A new mathematical relationship may radically alter the relations between particles, bringing about a transformation in the relevant micro-world; equally, fresh experimental evidence may upset older calculations, requiring a change in the symbolic. Thus, we see that there is no hierarchy of levels between content and expression, or language and bodies, and while it is a material confrontation, they ceaselessly pass into each other: "We constantly pass from order-words to the "silent order" of things (p. 87). It is in this moment of passage that we glimpse the subversive processes that underlie signification. It is in this moment of passage that we taste a certain freedom to create and be created from amidst the language that we use on a daily basis.

How do we conceive of the relationship between the two transformations? We can say that the corporeal and the incorporeal *reciprocally presuppose* one another. There is no incorporeal transformation without the movement between language and bodies, and so also the other way around. In the fresh becomings between language and bodies the two transformations constitute successive micro-openings that allow the possibility of micro-worlds of change and new formations.

Having seen what is involved in acts of communication, we have to seize the underlying tectonic movements and ride them toward a liberatory performativity, never letting out of sight the multiple ways in which language itself subverts dominant significations, deterritorializing or pushing outward so far as to be able to evade capture by the order word. In other words, through our very analysis of the order word, in parsing the forces that come into play, we create the possibility of escaping the order word. Like a storm cloud within which rages high velocity winds and streams of ions, language contains intense turbulences that are inseparably linked to performativity and that have liberatory potential. We will cap our analysis next by articulating a function that combines the transformations and allows us to see more clearly the effects of the performativity.

THE EXISTENTIALISING FUNCTION

It is on the note of reversibility between content and expression and incessant performativity that this discussion turns, a language phenomenon that we will call, after Guattari (1995), the "existentialising function." This function can be thought of as the movement between signs and substance (or language and bodies) that creates various kinds of part-subjects that are transitory, sometimes fleeting, not fully determined. A sound or sign melds with our physico-affective matrix producing a certain diffraction in our substantiation, just as our bodies emit "particles" that are part affect part sign, which in turn affect other bodies. Thus, part-subjects are intermediate subjects that are not fully words or things; something in-between that are in the process of becoming, of emergence. Eventually these fragments will be appropriated either by language or by bodies, depending on which side is more deterritorialized, that is, momentarily more knocked off its settled properties, as we have seen earlier. Like bone that melds with invasive matter bodies meld with signs producing new copulatives and articulations. Similarly, signs capture bodily matter to form new intensities. But their greatest utility for us lies in their state of flux. For it is in these sub-determined states expression can use part subjects as channels for its own movement, and reciprocally, bodies can use them for becoming through time, to engage in their own incessant becoming. From our perspective, this matter of performativity within language has four major consequences that I will outline below.

First, such activity makes it "impossible to conceive of language as a code, since a code is the condition of possibility for *all* explanation" (Deleuze & Guattari, 1987, p. 78). Performativity makes it clear that underneath the over-determination of the order-word, there are, at the heart of language, silent struggles that are suppressed for dominant meanings to emerge. Whereas a code is transparent, a set of all possibilities, language is emergent, murky, ambiguous, the result of action, conflict and ever becoming, and hence communicability itself cannot be codified, for it is prior to all codes.

Second, performativity and pragmatics within language also make it misleading to conceive of speech merely as the communication of information since information presupposes an objective, static content. This means that pedagogically humans must take the linguistic act more seriously, study the act of communication itself, the very gesture of language, and not just focus on content and its transmission. Such study brings into view a wholly different dynamic involving the linguistic event. It introduces a moment of hesitation, a murmur into language at the very moment of speech, revealing the turbulence and the surging of uncontrollables and the intuition of part subjects.

Third, performativity makes it impossible to define semantics and syntactics as independent of pragmatics since now we have the act enfolded in it. The implication of this is that resistance as ceaseless activity within language can be primary: in fact, the very gesture of languaging can be thought of as resistance even as it participates in producing dominant significations, since the passage between words and things is forever spilling out of and exceeding the normative.

And fourth, the meaning and syntax of language can no longer be defined independently of the speech acts they presuppose, and so the very notion of meaning is problematized with its obvious consequences for the conservation of intent. The ever-lurking gap between language and meaning is a communicative emptiness in which, as we saw in Agamben earlier, "the human emerges as such." The human here in no way indicates something essential, but new alignments of potentialities that drifts out of safe-harbors, riding minor swells of becoming-expression, opening up empty spaces in our bindings, at our limits.

Taken together, there is an ongoing activity that is ever-present as differential murmurs between the order of things and the order of words. A conception of language along these lines places the being of the human at the intersection of this reciprocal movement. It is important to raise this conception to the level of conscious activity as human praxis for the purpose of freeing communication from the order word. To put it differently, in decomposing the order word we come upon subterranean movements that may be liberating. The macro level phenomenon of communication can no longer conceal the subversive processes underneath. Knowledge of the reciprocal existentialising function is a corporeal knowledge that allows for the existing exploitative coherence of the world serving elite causes to be reconfigured locally. Such knowledge can produce a fresh collage, a sudden flash of insurgency in the false terror that binds our subjectivities.

As often heard in the esoteric discourse on creative activity that a writer/artist/thinker descends from or somehow circumvents her/his sociality to the sub-individual dungeons below where lie the subterranean flows that attend her work, so must each one of us reach for the incessant activity that bring forth part subjects, the involuntary murmurs beneath language that reciprocally reconstruct the collage and fragments of which we are put together. Thus the comprehension that words and bodies pass into one another, and in passage produce the communicability not of pure content but of communication itself, replaces settled realities by the perception of a generative function. From a transcendent position in which form and content as well as subject and message are distinct, we enter an immanence that is a zone of positive in-difference. The existentialising function is a direct challenge to the conception of communication as transmission of code. The stodgy instrumentality and end-gaining purposiveness represented by the latter conception gives way to an attitude that has the look of a serious kind of play. And at the same time we now have a new respect for language as a mode of our becoming in the real. This is not codification of content but a clash of forces and a mixing of the corporeal and the incorporeal that does not present ease of capture.

CONCLUSION

Does this mean language can never function as code? It certainly can. The trouble starts when we *equate* language and code. That is when we lose sight of the ongoing slippages and interchanges between the order of things and the order of words. This is certainly not to take the linguistic turn and claim there is nothing other than textuality. On the contrary, it is to say that language turns up in the transformation of the physical just as the physical fundamentally alters language. There is an intense and incessant reciprocal relationship. Together they produce transient part-subjects which eventually fall either on the side of language or on the side of things depending on which side is in greater flux at any given moment. Is this then a Hegelian dialectical movement between opposites? That is not the case either. There is no progressive movement here, no gradual unfolding of historical *telos*. The encounters are random and disjunctive rather than producing some kind of definite or higher synthesis.

Pedagogically, this confrontation and the disjunctive part-subjects are of critical importance for they allow us to partake in the social production of being. The existentialising function is a powerful concept that allows us to escape order words that encapsulate settled realities. The ancient opposition between words and things is seen to break down at certain junctures as words deterritorialize and insinuate themselves in the order of things, as well as the other way around, demonstrating that we have real means of constructing less alienating and more creative worlds. Of practical importance is the close attention paid to language not merely as carrier of information but as pro-voking the construction of micro-worlds. It means that we reinvent language as gesture, as becoming. Anthropologically we see hints of such processes among ancients such as certain Asiatic peoples, American Indians, and others, whose ritualized languages often were more than mere representation. The very use of language was inventing a mode of being and becoming, picking a particular way through reality, bringing into effect certain forms, transformations.

One last thing needs to be said. The body is often seen as the private, and language, on the other hand, as the most public sphere of shared meanings. In grasping the existentialising function and the formation, at the micro level, of part-subjects, the separation of the public and the private becomes a tenuous affair. As Judith Butler (2004) has often said, at critical existential moments we begin to become undone. In undertaking such an experiment as outlined here, we directly participate in public life but in an unusual manner; we engage in recrafting the body politic at the minoritarian level through the generation of a space where corporeal singularities and the linguistic sign lose their clear boundaries, transforming each other. War and health, that, from our examples, seemed like externalities governed by the order word, now seem much closer once we work through the implicit presuppositions or collective assemblages that give rise to their social form. Kept separate, the order of words and the order of things make reality appear very sewn up. But as we come to be undone from either end, the forces that shape macro phenomena seem not as remote and our ability to influence them not as improbable.

REFERENCES

Agamben, G. (2000). *Means without end: Notes on politics*. Minneapolis, MN: University of Minnesota Press.

Austin, J. L. (1962). *How to do things with words*. Cambridge, MA: Harvard Univepsity Press.

Blake, N., Smeyers, P., Smith, R., & Standish, P. (2000). *Education in an age of nihilism*. New York: Routledge-Falmer.

Butler, J. (2004). *Precarious life: The powers of mourning and violence*. New York: Verso.

Deleuze, G. (1994). *Difference and repetition*. New York: Columbia University Press.

Deleuze, G., & Guattari, F. (1987). *A thousand plateaus: Capitalism and schizophrenia*. Minneapolis, MN: University of Minnesota Press.

Derrida, J. (1982). *Margins of philosophy*. Chicago: University of Chicago Press.

Foucault, M. (1972). *The archaeology of knowledge*. New York: Pantheon.

Guattari, F. (1995). *Chaosmosis: An ethico-aesthetic paradigm*. Bloomington: Indiana University Press.

Habermas, J. (1984). *The theory of communicative action*. Boston: Beacon Press.
Massumi, B. (1992). *A user's guide to capitalism and schizophrenia: Deviations from Deleuze and Guattari*. Cambridge, MA: MIT Press.
Wittgenstein, L. (2001). *Philosophical investigations*. Malden, MA: Blackwell.

Kaustuv Roy
College of Education
Louisiana State University
USA

INNA SEMETSKY AND TERRY LOVAT

12. KNOWLEDGE IN ACTION: TOWARDS A DELEUZE-HABERMASIAN CRITIQUE IN/FOR EDUCATION

This chapter juxtaposes the thought processes of Gilles Deleuze and Jurgen Habermas as they relate to the idea of practical knowledge with the view of becoming able to re-conceptualise education in terms of multiple sets of socio-cultural practices. The idea of juxtaposing is based on Richard Bernstein's model of "the new constellation" (Bernstein, 1995) that, rather than comparing and/or contrasting two theories, aims to construct a common, shared plane between the two.

Bernstein (1971, 1983, 1995) addressed the intersections of continental and pragmatic philosophical thought both from substantive and methodological perspectives. He specifically acknowledged the importance and value, for both traditions, of the so-called experimental knowing that he considered to be essentially a practical art leading to results that are cumulative and not defined strictly by adherence to an *a priori* theoretical judgment. The common, *pragmatic*, denominator is evident in the philosophical and theoretical legacy of both Deleuze (cf. Semetsky, 2004, 2006) and Habermas (cf. Lovat, 2004, Biesta, 1994, Gibbs, 2000). The *constellation* metaphor helps us in addressing the seemingly "shared assumptions, commitments and insights" (Bernstein, 1983, p. 2) in their respective philosophies, notwithstanding the fact that Habermas' work is grounded in critical theory while that of Deleuze – in cultural and literary criticism.

The recent comprehensive volume "Theory for Education" (Dimitriadis & Kamberelis, 2006) devotes a chapter to Deleuze and Guattari, among names ranging from Bakhtin to Bourdieu to bell hooks to Lacan to Lev Vygotsky, while any reference to Habermas is conspicuously missing. A brief recourse to Habermas in this chapter will both complement and strengthen the case for Deleuze-Guattari's influential critique in educational theory and pedagogical practice. Several of Deleuze's philosophical works were written together with social psychologist and practicing psychoanalyst Felix Guattari, such a collaboration indeed bringing philosophy "proper" into closer contact with socio-cultural issues and practical concerns. Deleuze-Guattarian approach to knowledge as contextual and situated in a shared cultural milieu is akin to "the fascination of children with... Winnie the Pooh, and...Alice's adventures – also a favourite pastime of logicians, mathematicians, and physicists – [and] attests to their import to 'primitive' perceptual and conceptual modes, keenly picked up by ...Gilles Deleuze" (Merrell, 1996, p. 141). Deleuze's method does not rely on the absolutes but aims "to bring into being that which does not yet exist" (Deleuze, 1994, p. 147). In his move against the Cartesian method, Deleuze speaks of *paideia* stating that for Greeks

I. Semetsky (ed.), Nomadic Education: Variations on a Theme by Deleuze and Guattari, 171–182.

thought is not based on a premeditated decision to think. The true thought does not passively display propositional statements in the analytical manner; instead one must construct an active line of flight, a way to/of knowing. Thought thinks "by virtue of the forces that are exercised on it in order to constrain it to think. ... Thinking, like activity, is always a second power of thought, [and] not the natural exercise of a faculty. ... A power, *the force of thinking,* must throw it into a becoming-active" (Deleuze, 1983, p. 108). These *outside* forces belong to the socio-cultural, public, milieu and not to a private world of a Cartesian subject. The value of knowledge as the product of such thinking is in its practical import, that is, the way we will act, think, and feel – in short, assign meaning to our own experience in the world – as the pragmatic effect of the said knowledge.

Habermas (1972; 1974), distinguishing between knowledge as an epistemic unity and conceptions of it as being fragmented or divided, posited unity in knowledge that may be nonetheless impelled by three distinctive cognitive interests, which render three different ways of knowing. In other words, knowledge itself is a unity (even along traditional disciplinary divisions), but we come to know most fully in three different ways. First, a cognitive interest in technical control renders a way of knowing described as empirical-analytic, reducing the true thought to instrumental rationality. This is a way of knowing that serves our interest in capturing the "facts and figures" of scientific data. Data relevant to this kind of knowing would most reliably be contained in official documents, history books and websites, with methodologies around document analysis or statistical analysis being most likely to produce the optimal knowing. The Habermasian perspective would suggest that, even at the optimal level of empirical-analytic kind, knowing is far from complete because only one of the operative cognitive interests has been satisfied. A second cognitive interest lies in understanding the meanings that underlie the empirical-analytic data. These meanings are derived from intersubjective encounters and so the way of knowing that is impelled is described as historical-hermeneutic and always communicative. At the level of communicative action (contra rationalistic strategic action) knowledge comes about as a practical result of human encounters, negotiations, interactions and interpretations. The interest here is in ascertaining what the facts and figures mean, how we should understand and deal with them and, ultimately, find our most meaningful way of acting in the real world in light of them. Data relevant to this way of knowing is unlikely to be found in documents and history books but possibly in historical fiction and personal websites. It might also be found in some forms of media, more likely in the opinion pages than in the news sections of newspapers and more likely in independent radio and TV than in commercial broadcasts. Hence, the methodologies to produce such knowing would include ethnography, open-structured interviews and personal or biographical stories. Habermas, however, does not draw a line of great divide between empirical-analytic and historical-hermeneutic ways of knowing that would have resulted in their being in some form of competition; rather they act in a complementary manner. Second, and of greater import, he sees neither way of knowing, nor even the conjunction of both, as comprising the complete unity of knowledge.

On their own or together, these ways of knowing are inadequate as they can still leave us un-free, un-emancipated in our knowing and captive in the shadowy world of half-truths. It is in this acknowledgment and in a continuous search that yet another cognitive interest comes into play giving rise to an emancipating process equivalent to a third way of knowing. In other words, as much as it is human to want to know the facts and the deeper meanings behind those facts, it is just as important to critically evaluate them in a "self-reflective" way of knowing. In either or both of the first two ways of knowing, we are liable to delusion of one sort or another. Even the coalescence of two ways of knowing is inadequate because we may still be insulated from critiques that are outside our immediate frame of reference, personal perspective or point of view. The third way is derived from a necessary commitment to ongoing critical appraisal of the nature and function of the ways of knowing themselves, to the sources of our knowledge and the uncovering of partial, skewed or blatantly fallacious evidence, and, finally, to self-knowing.

This new quest, which is as much methodological as theoretical, is what Habermas describes as *praxis*, or action upon reflection, when a participative and transformative action is made possible. It is a practical way of knowing that engages both self and others at the level of the whole person that exceeds even an intersubjective experience. The third way of knowing can be summed up in that there is no knowing without knowing the knower. This coalescence of cognitive and holistic practical action is at the centre of Habermas' critical theory and it forces us to scrutinize and appraise the adequacy of both facts and our understanding of the facts as well as to re-valuate their meanings. Without critical thinking, the data derived from knowledge gathering can become a means of bondage, rather than emancipation, or a way of oppressing people and keeping their minds captive. Typically, methods most appropriate to this mode of knowing will include the most open forms of ethnography, unstructured interview, phenomenological engagement and in-group dynamics, friendly and unfriendly, and finally, intense forms of honest self-reflection that may include esoteric practices like meditation and prayer. For Habermas (1984; 1987; 1990), when the self-reflective knower comes to see her own life-world as just one that functions in a reciprocal manner among the myriad of life-worlds of others and so develops tolerance of other views and positions then the communicative capacity is achieved. Communicative action is impelled when the self-reflective knower takes a step beyond mere tolerance of other beliefs and values to accept a responsibility and take a stand for justice if one's integrity is at stake. All knowing has an ethical component in its relation to practical action. The self-reflective element in knowing is the means by which values implicit in the process of knowing become explicit to the knower. Herein, Habermas' theory of knowledge becomes *ipso facto* a moral philosophy.

In a different language, but with the same political and ethical vigour, Deleuze introduces his notion of *nomadic becoming* as an unorthodox process of thinking, knowing and practical self-formation. Nomadic inquiry supplements a narrow path of strict analytical reasoning (akin to Habermas' first cognitive way) with a broader format of diverse and spacious forms of mapping, employed in the methodologies of contemporary cultural studies. The nomadic methodology accords with the implied relation between practice and theory, in which the theory-practice nexus (indeed, central to pragmatism) is defined by everyday engagements with knowledge production. This method considers every value judgment analogous to making a conjecture, which is to be tested in practice in the context of changing problematic of circumstances, situations and social conditions. Theory and practice are interrelated in that theory performs a practical function of being used for the re-valuation of novel modes of existence through creating new and better-informed concepts and meanings in a self-reflective way. In a pragmatic sense, a number of possible consequences can never be fully exhausted. So the methods of inference are by necessity not syllogistic but *nomadic*.

Deleuze's *nomad* metaphor carries a topological nuance, "a fate of place" (Casey, 1997); indeed the whole philosophy of place is exemplified in Deleuze and Guattari's (1994) explicitly naming their approach *Geophilosophy*. This metaphor, by being used with regard to the question of sources of knowledge permits a shift of focus from the static body of knowledge to the dynamic process of knowing, with the latter's having far-reaching implications for education as a developing and generative practice. The alternative law that guides nomads in their travels is not *logos*, but *nomos*, a human construct. Nomadic place is always intense because the nomads' existence is inseparable from the region in space that they occupy. Their relation to the territory is being continuously, as Deleuze says, de-territorialized, implying the significance of a direction but simultaneously affirming the multiplicity of paths that nomadic tribes wander along in their movement in the "smooth space" (Deleuze & Guattari, 1987, p. 371) of the *steppe*.

The adjective *smooth* is contrasted with *striated,* both terms defining different musical forms: striated – as ordered by rigid schemata and point-to-point connections ensuring a linear and fixed structure, and smooth – as irregular, open and hetero-geneous, dynamical structure of fluid forces, "a field ...wedded to nonmetric, acentered, rhizomatic multiplicities" (Deleuze & Guattari, 1987, p. 381) and filled with the polyvocality of directions. Deleuze uses the word *polyvocality* stressing the very physicality of the way of knowing embodied in action. In order to find one's way, one's bearing or whereabouts in the smooth space of steppe or sea, one must feel as much as see or listen. Nomad is always in-between, always in the process of becoming, "the life of nomad is the intermezzo" (Deleuze & Guattari, 1987, p. 380), distributed at once between here and there, between now and then, "always the day before and the day after" (Deleuze, 1995, p. 77). Nomad's way is an immanent trajectory and not a transcendental end as some strategic goal, a deviant footpath and not the royal road. As a symbol for *becoming-other,* nomads always "transmute and reappear in the lines of flight of some social field" (Deleuze, 1995, p. 153). But for Deleuze, social and psychological dimensions interpenetrate, and from the epistemological perspective, nomadic ideas would be, in Deleuze's words, intensive multiplicities distributed in the smooth space.

The logic of the included middle and the phenomenology of nomads' lived experience preclude the nomadic ideas from meeting "the visual condition of being observable from a point in space external to them" (Deleuze & Guattari, 1987, p. 371) – quite in accord with Habermas' asserting the necessity of intersubjectivity and communicative action. Nomads must continuously adapt and readapt themselves to the open-ended world, in which even the line of horizon may be affected by the changing conditions of wind, shifting sands or storms so that no single rule or knowledge of the static facts would ever assist nomads in their navigations. They must be ready for sudden changes and critical appraisals and re-appraisals of real-life situations: "the local operations of relay must be oriented by the discovery (and often continual rediscovery) of direction" (Casey, 1997, p. 306).

Calling himself a pluralist, Deleuze has been employing metaphors and cartographies aiming at the mapping of the new directions for praxis. While Deleuze's theoretical explorations of education *per se* were not explicit, in his description of the experimental course he taught, he compared it with the investigative research conducted in a laboratory:

> Giving courses has been a major part of my life, in which I've been passionately involved. ... It's like a research laboratory: you give courses on what you are investigating, not on what you know. It takes a lot of preparatory work to get a few minutes of inspiration. ... [W]e rejected the principle of 'building up knowledge ' progressively: ... everyone took what they needed or wanted, what they could use (Deleuze, 1995, p. 139).

Recognizing the narrow view of education, Deleuze calls for education of the senses by means of exploring the faculties of perception not limited to the passive reception of the data of pure sense-impressions. His pluralism is a kind of constructivism because human interactions create a social network of "self-other" relations to be explored anew in the plurality of situations and contexts, the changing spatio-temporal dynamisms of which demand a novel understanding of collective experiences, that is, creating or inventing a set of new concepts and meanings as a means for re-valuation of experience, therefore constructing one's identity in practice.

One's identity, like Alice 's behind the looking glass, is always contested: the seemingly paradoxical element of changing one's identity leads to the self-identity itself losing its stable meaning. It reflects on the dynamics of becoming-other and discarding or transforming the values that were once established. Individuation depends on "the harshest exercise in depersonalization" (Deleuze, 1995, p. 6), and "experimentation on ourselves is our only identity, our single chance for all the combinations which inhabit us" (Deleuze, 1987, p. 11), expressed in the folding of forces. The sense of the self as singular is derived from the process of becoming not limited to just a cognising subject but holistically encompassing a particular event in a context described by Deleuze as "a draft, a wind, a day, a time of day, a stream, a place, a battle, an illness" (Deleuze, 1995, p. 141). It is an experiential situation distributed along the space-time continuum that leads to the creative individuation, to a practical constitution of a subject-in-action.

Such a singular self is not reduced to any a-social individualism; just the opposite, individuation and socialisation coalesce for Deleuze and Habermas alike. The self becomes capable of multiple "leaps from one soul to another, 'every now and then' crossing closed deserts. ... And from soul to soul it traces the design of an *open* society, a society of creators" (Deleuze, 1991, p. 111). The "now and then" are distinctive points, or events that represent the changing modes of existence. It is an experiential event that affects the shape, in almost mathematical terms, of one's life by virtue of itself being a variation on the curve that gives this or that shape to any figure. The liberation of the self and its entering society occur because of the process described as a mode of knowing and becoming in a form of "their circular play in order to break the circle" (Deleuze, 1991, p. 111). The interplay, or inter-subjectivity, of the self and the greater social world populated by others creates an interval between the pressures of society and the disputes of the individual. This gap is creative and productive by embodying the circle of a free play that "no longer has anything to do with an individual who contests ...nor with a society that constrains" (Deleuze, 1991, p. 111): such is Deleuze and Guattari's transformational pragmatics that both originates within and spills over into practical action thus making a difference, or what Habermas originally described as *praxis*.

The transformation occurs in the middle and muddle of life *per se*, and the quality of experience includes multiplicities of events, giving rise to meaning, producing plural truths – without a capital "T" – contingent on the context of local situations. The dynamics of knowing constitutes a long experiential affair, a process that would require, for Deleuze, practical wisdom in a Spinozian sense. The notion of truth in Deleuze's philosophy may be considered a nomadic concept *par excellence*. Truth, like any other concept, is not out there waiting to be discovered in its pre-existing domain of references to propositions. It "has to be created" (Deleuze, 1995, p. 126) and is bound to be affected by, and to affect in turn, a series of falsifications, so in the final analysis it is falsity that will have been producing truth by its own becoming-other. The false has its own power, and the latter can be realized not in *form*, but in trans-*form*-ation. The field of knowing is greater than truth which is to be generated at each given moment and, for Deleuze, "there is no other truth than the creation of the New: creativity, emergence " (Deleuze, 1989, pp. 146-147), or giving meaning to one's existence rather than discovering its eternal and invariant form.

Experience is rendered meaningful not by grounding empirical particulars in preconceived abstract universals but by experimentation, that is, by treating any concept in a manner quite similar to Habermas' critical theory, that is:

> as object of an encounter, as a here-and-now, ... from which emerge inexhaustibly ever new, differently distributed 'heres' and 'nows'. ... I make, remake and unmake my concepts along a moving horizon, from an always decentered center, from an always displaced periphery which repeats and differentiate them (Deleuze, 1994a, pp. xx-xxi).

Deleuze uses a powerful visual metaphor to describe the transformation and, by means of this image, accentuating also the significance allotted in his philosophy not to the point, but to the line: "One must multiply the sides, break every circle in favor of the polygons" (Deleuze, 1987, p. 19). For Deleuze,

> once one steps outside what's been thought before, once one ventures outside what's familiar and reassuring, once one has to invent new concepts for

unknown lands, then methods and moral systems break down and thinking becomes, as Foucault puts it, a "perilous act", a violence, whose first victim is oneself (Deleuze, 1995, p. 103).

The notion of critical freedom is implicit in Deleuze 's philosophy and is essentially different "from the standard liberal concepts of positive and negative freedom" (Patton, 2000, p. 83). Liberal thought, rather than taking into consideration the overall conditions of change as a *whole,* assigns to an individual self the center-stage of a volitional and constituting subject, thus conflating a whole with its single part. By contrast, Deleuze's poststructuralist "subject" continuously exercises the critical freedom of constituting herself which takes place through social fields, the very notion of the field implying the collective and distributed nature of the subjectivity-in-process as always already becoming-other.

For Deleuze and Guattari, liberation does not mean being free to manipulate a supposedly external reality (in the manner of technical control) by the subject that would have been located outside of that very arrangement she herself imposed on the world. Instead liberation consists in the free expression of forces so that the subject herself becomes constituted at the ontological level. Only if and when "thought is free, hence vital, nothing is compromised. When it ceases being so, all other oppressions are also possible, and already realized, so every action becomes culpable, every life threatened" (Deleuze, 1988, p. 4). In a democratic society, as Deleuze understands it, the power of thinking should be exempt from "the obligation to obey" (Deleuze, 1988, p. 4). The subject is never an isolated independent individual but is the most versatile component of the whole collective system. Two educational philosophers, Leach and Boler (1998), noticed that Deleuze situates the complex notion of freedom

> within and as part of the development of nature, rather than its conquest and mastery ... Deleuze 's philosophical urgencies have resulted in elaborations of alternative accounts of the processes constitutive of subjectivity (Leach & Boler, 1998, p. 155).

The Deleuzian nomadic subject is able to avoid being forever stuck in the infamous vicious circle because it is free to break things open: it lives by its philosophy – and philosophy in virtue of the practical creation of concepts is, for Deleuze (as for Habermas), an ethical way of life – both putting theory into practice and forming new meanings contingent on the dynamics of experience. Martin Joughin, in his introduction to Deleuze's book on Spinoza (1992), notices that for Deleuze,

> the development of a "philosophy " is traced from some version of an initial situation where some term in our experience diverges from its apparent relations with some other terms, breaking out of that "space " of relations and provoking a reflection in which we consider reorientations or reinscriptions of this and other terms within a "virtual " matrix of possible unfoldings of these terms and their relations in time .... Such a "philosophy" comes full-circle when the "subject" ... "orients" its own practical activity of inter-pretation, evaluation or orientation of the terms of experience within this universal matrix it has itself unfolded (Joughin in Deleuze, 1992, p. 9).

Two important educational implications follow: first, a moral subject can never be reduced to an individual agent but is always intersubjective in that it depends on relational dynamics and communicative practices within social milieus; second, such an agency defined as a relational self (that is, always already becoming-other) must embody a creative thinker because she must continuously evaluate new experiences and create new meanings in the process of 'making sense' out of problematic, conflicting and baffling situations or moral dilemmas that abound in contemporary life and that crucially depend on our improved social relations with others. The autonomy of the subject is never "given" but should be "taken" and is contingent on the act of shared communication embedded within the experiential situation. Deleuze 's conceptualisation of becoming asserts a self-*becoming*-autonomous, as if tending to its own ideal limit, as a continuous function of experience capable of making a difference. Difference has to be perceived – felt, seen, heard, touched – in order of itself making a difference, that is, creating "a local integration moving from part to part and constituting smooth space in an infinite succession of linkages and changes in direction" (Deleuze & Guattari, 1987, p. 494). The integration into (self-)reflective thinking is possible only in the physical world of action. This mode of philosophical thinking utilises "the points of transition, the conceptual shifts, the subtleties, and extra-textual uses" (Peters, 2004, p. 217) at the practical, cultural level.

The ontological priority of relations, for Deleuze, "is not a principle, it is a vital protest against principles" (Deleuze, 1987, p. 55). Relations may change, but it does not mean that the terms necessarily change too; what would change is a set of circumstances, the context. Deleuze is adamant that if relations are irreducible to their terms, then the whole dualistic split between the sensible and the intelligible, between thought and experience, between ideas and sensations becomes invalid and what is in operation is the dynamical, experimental and experiential logic of becoming which is not "subordinate to the verb to be" (Deleuze, 1987, p. 57), or to static being. It is a set of relations that are capable of constructing the unpredictable experiential world, which unfolds in a seemingly strange manner, resembling:

> a Harlequin's jacket or patchwork, made up of solid parts and voids, blocs and ruptures, attractions and divisions, nuances and bluntnesses, conjunctions and separations, alternations and interweavings, additions which never reach a total and subtractions whose remainder is never fixed. ... This geography of relations is particularly important ... one must make the encounter with relations penetrate and corrupt everything, undermine being ... (Deleuze, 1987, pp. 55-57).

This philosophy would not conform to the schematics of the progressive and uninterrupted building-up of knowledge toward some higher ideal end. Progress of the latter kind, for Deleuze and Guattari, would represent "the submission of the line to the point" (Deleuze & Guattari, 1987, p. 293), that is a return to representational thinking and the idea of the correspondence theory of truth, a regress indeed. For Deleuze, the very spirit of experimentation rejects the binary opposition between universals and particulars and combines in itself mysticism with the mathematicism of concepts: for example, Leibniz 's infinitesimal calculus becomes compatible with philosophy as a virtual form of thinking. In this respect, the mathematical form cannot be taken away from natural laws; the latter are models and not just straightforward expressions of preexisting linguistic truths (cf. DeLanda, 2002). Deleuze stresses an impersonal and collective nature of the language-system by referring to the concept of the fourth person singular as the specific language expressing the singularity of the event. Subjective voice has to be more than personal by virtue of it being embedded in the free indirect discourse. The subject who (as if) speaks in the fourth person singular is not the *a priori* given intentional and speaking subject. As becoming, developing, and learning by means of multiple interactions embedded in experiential events, it is a collective subject capable of overcoming the Cartesian dualism. An event *per se* is as yet subject-less because it is always of the nature of relationships, in which the distinction between first, second or third person is not at all clear. The subject "speaking" in the fourth person singular belongs to the multiplicity functioning

in the form of undetermined infinitive. ... It is poetry itself. As it expresses in language all events in one, the infinitive expresses the event of language – language being a unique event which merges now with that which renders it possible (Deleuze, 1995, p. 185).

Event is always an element of becoming, and the becoming is unlimited. That's why Deleuze describes events by means of infinitive verbs or (present continuous) gerunds: they are as yet subject-less. Thinking as a process replaces the Cartesian point of departure in the form of "I think" thereby closing off the dualistic split between (supposedly private) language and (public) world.

Analytic philosophy presents language as a system of representations *a priori* distinguished from signs (cf. Tiles & Tiles, 1993). The representational system presupposes a class of things represented, which are not representations themselves, that is, objects in the world are posited as existing outside language. A linguistic sign (and other regimes of signs would be ignored in the empirical-analytic mode of knowing) represents transparently or literally. On this account, poetic language, which "represents" symbolically, that is, it does not represent in a strict sense, cannot be "objective". Not so for Deleuze or Habermas. In fact, Habermas, commenting on Cassiser's philosophy of symbolic forms in his book *The Liberating Power of Symbols: Philosophical Essays,* says that the function of any symbol is to establish the necessary connection in the greater social context: "Mind only makes contact with its environment in a mediated way" (Habermas, 2001, p. 24).

Foucault in *The Order of Things,* regarding language as a system of representations vs. a system of signs, rightly noticed that the language and the world form a single semiotic fabric, that is, things in the world also function as signs. We may say that things are *like* signs, that is, the relationship is analogical and not strictly logical or identical as in the system of representations. That's why Deleuze, in his characteristical manner, expresses the difference by contrasting the habitual logical copula "is" with the radical conjunction "and", the latter indeed would have been exemplifying the Habermasian *unity* of knowledge.

The interpenetration of thought and life, the ontological unity of subjects and objects, lead to Deleuze 's defining his discipline, philosophy, as an enterprise both *critical* and *clinical* (Deleuze, 1997). We have already been discussing the critical aspect in detail, both from Deleuzian and Habermasian perspectives. As for the meaning of *clinical,* as used by Deleuze, it is not derived from some discourse on pathology; instead its focus is the model of vitality, life and health. Deleuze (1995) refers to Nietzsche who tells us that artists and philosophers are the physicians of civilization. Philosophers, writers, and artists are first and foremost symptom-atologists; they read, interpret and create signs that "imply ways of living, possibilities of existence, [signs are] the symptoms of life gushing forth or draining away. ... There is a profound link between signs, events, life and vitalism" (Deleuze, 1995, p. 143). For Deleuze, critical and clinical aspects resonate and are bound to educate each other, and the ways of knowing are not limited to scientific facts, or understanding a concept, or interpreting a meaning of a novel, or even "reading" a painting. It is the ethical task as a re-valuation of experience which is "clinical" by virtue of its both implying a diagnosis of a particular mode of existence by means of assessing its symptoms, that is reading them as the signs of the here-and-now in the present, and because of making a decision, a value-judgement, in virtue of becoming emancipated and free to choose the next "nomadic" direction, thereby creating a new map and even a new territory. Yet, Deleuze is careful to point out the ambivalence of his concept of the line of flight. It is becoming-other that is created by the movement along this line, hence the significance of the clinical aspect of nomadic inquiry:

> What is it which tells us that, on a line of flight, we will not rediscover everything we were fleeing? ... How can one avoid the lines of flight becoming identical with a pure and simple movement of self-destruction; Fitzgerald's alcoholism, Lawrence's disillusion, Virginia Woolf 's suicide, Kerouac's sad end? ... [L]iterature is thoroughly imbued with a somber picture of demolition, which carry off the writer. ... How to get past the wall while avoiding bouncing back on it, behind, or being crushed? ... How to shatter even our love in order to become finally capable of loving? (Deleuze, 1987, pp. 38-46)

The answer is unequivocal, though. Because becoming is always in the present, although the present *per se* is elusive, making becoming all the more difficult and challenging, one does not have to remember and does not have to predict. One will become capable of loving again if there is no remembrance of the painful past. Because one never knows in advance, there are only explorations and experimentations. Only then the flight along the lines of becomings is towards life, towards the real.

How can education in the form of nomadic inquiry be implemented in practice? How can knowledge be enacted? Nel Noddings begins her latest book "Critical lessons: What our schools should teach?" (2006) by noticing that when the United States invaded Iraq in 2003, many public school teachers were forbidden to discuss the war in their classrooms thus missing on an opportunity of exercising critical thinking even as such a restriction on free discussion appears to be simply outrageous in a liberal democracy. Assuming that such a discussion indeed is taking place, we may imagine the aforementioned three modes of knowing in this context. First, this real-life event (in a Deleuzian sense) entails the knowledge of the facts and figures, getting information on as much details as possible, when and where the event took place, how long it persisted, which countries were involved, how much it cost, how many lives were lost from which nationalities, and an almost endless array of data that would constitute a Habermasian empirical-analytic way of knowing. Second, knowing about the War in Iraq would require intellectual depth and much listening, especially with those most involved and affected, that is, those who have experienced war in their actual practice and have this event embedded into their personal (hi)story. Third, critical evaluation demands self-reflection on all our past and present (and even a possible anticipated future) knowledge, when engaging with those views that might seem most unfamiliar and uncomfortable to us. We will be enacting interpersonal relations at the community level even with those people whose views might seem to be most repugnant to us, putting all our unreflective assumptions, biases and prejudices through the sifter that critically appraises the possible sources of our erstwhile knowing. These sources will include those documents and history books that provided us with our empirical-analytic knowing, all those interpersonal encounters and interpretations that constitute our historical-hermeneutic knowing, and even those very personal sources that have formed the perceived basis of our self-reflectivity. These latter sources will encompass our families, religious beliefs and cultural values, and our sense of personal identity. The self-reflective knower must take responsibility for her own actions and reactions, for the consciousness and the "will that the event creates in us" (Deleuze, 1990, p. 148), as well as for understanding the perspective of the other because "there is something to be learned from each person involved" (Gibbs, 2000, p. 160) in the process of genuine communicative action. Finally, we will be confronting ourselves, including our own comfort zones of knowing, those familial, cultural, religious and dispositional preferences that, having provided a feeling of inner security, have become part of our identity thereby engaging in the practice of becoming-other in the same time as becoming real authentic selves.

REFERENCES

Bernstein, R. J. (1971). *Praxis and action*. Philadelphia: University of Pennsylvania Press.

Bernstein, R. J. (1983). *Beyond objectivity and relativism: Science, hermeneutics and praxis.* Philadelphia: University of Pennsylvania Press.

Bernstein, R. J. (1995). *The new constellation: The ethical-political horizons of modernity/ postmodernity.* Cambridge: MIT Press.

Biesta, G. J. J. (1994). Education as practical intersubjectivity. Towards a critical-pragmatic understanding of education. *Educational Theory, 44*(3), 299–317.

Casey, E. S. (1997). *The fate of place: A philosophical history.* Berkeley: University of California Press.

DeLanda, M. (2002). *Intensive science and virtual philosophy.* London, New York: Continuum.

Deleuze, G. (1987). *Dialogues* (with Claire Parnet) (H. Tomlinson & G. Burchell, Trans.). New York: Columbia University Press.

Deleuze, G. (1988). *Spinoza: Practical philosophy* (R. Hurley, Trans.). San Francisco: City Lights Books.

Deleuze, G. (1989). *Cinema 2: The time-image* (H. Tomlinson & R. Galeta, Trans.). Minneapolis, MN: University of Minnesota Press.
Deleuze, G. (1990). *The logic of sense* (M. Lester, Trans.). New York: Columbia University Press.
Deleuze, G. (1991). *Bergsonism* (H. Tomlinson, Trans.). New York: Zone Books.
Deleuze, G. (1992). *Expressionism in philosophy: Spinoza* (M. Joughin, Trans.). New York: Zone Books.
Deleuze, G. (1994). *Difference and repetition* (P. Patton, Trans.). New York: Columbia University Press.
Deleuze, G. (1995). *Negotiations 1972–1990* (M. Joughin, Trans.). New York: Columbia University Press.
Deleuze, G. (1997). *Essays critical and clinical* (D. W. Smith & M. Greco, Trans.). Minneapolis, MN: University of Minnesota Press.
Deleuze, G., & Guattari, F. (1987). *A thousand plateaus: Capitalism and schizophrenia* (B. Massumi, Trans.). Minneapolis, MN: University of Minnesota Press.
Deleuze, G., & Guattari. F. (1994). *What is philosophy ?* (H. Tomlinson & G. Burchell, Trans.). New York: Columbia University Press.
Dimitriadis, G., & Kamberelis, G. (2006). *Theory for education.* New York, London: Routledge.
Gibbs, R. (2000). *Why ethics? Signs of responsibilities.* Princeton, NJ: Princeton University Press.
Habermas, J. (1972). *Knowledge and human interests* (J. Shapiro, Trans.). London: Heinemann.
Habermas, J. (1974). *Theory and practice* (J. Viertal, Trans.). London: Heinmann.
Habermas, J. (1984). *The theory of communicative action* (Vol. I, T. McCarthy, Trans.). Boston: Beacon Press.
Habermas, J. (1987). *The theory of communicative action* (Vol. II, T. McCarthy, Trans.). Boston: Beacon Press.
Habermas, J. (1990). *Moral consciousness and communicative action* (C. Lenhardt & S. W. Nicholsen, Trans.). Cambridge, MA: MIT Press.
Habermas, J. (2001). *The liberating power of symbols: Philosophical essays* (Studies in Contemporary German Social Thought) (P. Dews, Trans.). The MIT Press.
Leach, M., & Boler, M. (1998). Gilles Deleuze: Practicing education through flight and gossip. In M. Peters (Ed.), *Naming the multiple: Poststructuralism and education.* Westport, Connecticut & London: Bergin & Carvey.
Lovat, T. (2004). Aristotelian ethics and habermasian critical theory: A conjoined force for proportionism in ethical discourse and Roman Catholic moral theology. *Australian E-Journal of Theology, 3.* http://dlibrary.acu.edu.au/research/theology/ejournal/aejt_3/Lovat.htm
Merrell, F. (1996). *Signs grow: Semiosis and life processes.* Toronto: University of Toronto Press.
Noddings, N. (2006). *Critical lessons: What our schools should teach.* Cambridge University Press.
Patton, P. (2000). *Deleuze and the political.* London & New York: Routledge.
Peters, M. A. (2004). Editorial: Geophilosophy, education and the pedagogy of the concept. In I. Semetsky (Ed.), *Educational philosophy and theory,* special issue *Deleuze and education 36*(3), 217–226.
Semetsky, I. (2004). The role of intuition in thinking and learning: Deleuze and the pragmatic legacy. *Educational philosophy and theory* (Vol. 36, No. 4, pp. 433–454). UK: Blackwell Publishers.
Semetsky, I. (2006). *Deleuze, education and becoming.* Rotterdam, The Netherlands: Sense Publishers.
Tiles, M., & Tiles, J. (1993). *An introduction to historical epistemology: The authority of knowledge.* Cambridge, MA: Blackwell Publishers.

Terry Lovat
The University of Newcastle
Australia

Inna Semetsky
The University of Newcastle
Australia

ELIZABETH A. ST.PIERRE

13. DELEUZIAN CONCEPTS FOR EDUCATION: THE SUBJECT UNDONE

Deleuze and Guattari (1991/1994) write that "the greatness of philosophy is measured by the nature of the events to which its concepts summon us or that it enables us to release in concepts" (p. 34). I find this one of those provocative Deleuzian statements that seems straightforward but is best considered askew. If you go after it head on, it will unravel even as your understanding increases. This is fine with me; in fact, I have become quite fond of this way of reading, which Deleuze (1990/1995) explains quite beautifully in the following long quote that will set up the rest of this essay quite nicely:

There are, you see, two ways of reading a book; you either see it as a box with something inside and start looking for what it signifies, and then if you're even more perverse or depraved you set off after signifiers. And you treat the next book like a box contained in the first or containing it. And you annotate and interpret and question, and write a book about the book, and so on and on. Or there's the other way: you see the book as a little non-signifying machine, and the only question is 'Does it work, and how does it work?' How does it work for you? If it doesn't work, if nothing comes through, you try another book. This second way of reading's intensive: something comes through or it doesn't. There's nothing to explain, nothing to understand, nothing to interpret. It's like plugging in to an electric circuit. I know people who've read nothing who immediately saw what bodies without organs were, given their own 'habits,' their own way of being one. This second way of reading's quite different from the first, because it relates a book directly to what's Outside. A book is a little cog in much more complicated external machinery... This intensive way of reading, in contact with what's outside the book, as a flow meeting other flows, one machine among others, as a series of experiments for each reader in the midst of events that have nothing to do with books, as tearing the book into pieces, getting it to interact with other things, absolutely anything...is reading with love. That's exactly how you read the book. (pp. 7-9)

I was happy to come upon this description of reading and be granted permission to give up the pretense of signifying and "making meaning" in the old way because this is exactly how I had read Deleuze (in fact, this is the way I've always read everything). I had plugged into his circuits and, without thinking too much about it, found myself plugging his concepts into everything in my life so that it has become different than it was before. I expect the pleasure of reading great philosophy is the thrill that even a non-philosopher can find in events (a life) that were once impossible.

I. Semetsky (ed.), Nomadic Education: Variations on a Theme by Deleuze and Guattari, 183–196.
© 2008 Sense Publishers. All rights reserved.

In my teaching, I have found that my students often respond as I do to Deleuze and Guattari's (1991/1994) philosophy, whose object, the philosophers say, is "to create concepts that are always new" (p. 5) even if others may not know "the problems to which those concepts are a response" (Deleuze, 1990/1995, p. 136). Indeed, readers seem to happily take up and use concepts such as *multiplicity*, *bodies-without-organs*, *faciality*, and *insomnia* in response to their own problems, perhaps because, as Ronald Bogue (1996) points out, there is an "impersonality" in Deleuze's style such that he "eliminates in his writing the personal—the anecdotal, memory-laden, intentional subject" (p. 252). I will return to this notion of the impersonal subject later, but I expect it is this very impersonality that allows one to "lift a dynamism out of the book entirely, and incarnate it in a foreign medium" (Massumi, 1987, p. xv) without feeling particularly anxious about whether one has been true to Deleuze and "gotten it right." This is not to say that we should not read Deleuze, and Deleuze and Guattari, long and hard, but, as Brian Massumi (1987) explains, Deleuze and Guattari "steal from other disciplines with glee, but they are more than happy to return the favor" (p. xv). What is exciting for those who plug a Deleuzian machine into another machine is that different assemblages become possible that could make available the "nonthought within thought" (Deleuze & Guattari, 1991/1994, p. 59) that some of us long for.

John Rajchman (2001a) explains how Deleuzian concepts travel as follows:

We might then imagine Deleuze's philosophy as built up in a way such as this: there are different conceptual "bits," each initially introduced in relation to a particular problem, then reintroduced into new contexts, seen from new perspectives. The coherence among the various bits shifts from one work to the next as new concepts are added, fresh problems addressed; it is not given by "logical consistency" among propositions, but rather by the "series" or "plateaus" into which the conceptual pieces enter or settle along the web of their interrelations.... The bits thus don't work together like parts in a well-formed organism or a purposeful mechanism or a well-formed narrative—the whole is not given, and things are always starting up again in the middle, falling together in another looser way. As one thus passes from one zone or "plateau" to another and back again, one thus has nothing of the sense of a well-planned itinerary; on the contrary, one is taken on a sort of conceptual trip for which there preexists no map—a voyage for which one must leave one's usual discourse behind and never be quite sure where one will land. (pp. 21-22)

So you will never get to the bottom of a concept like *multiplicity*, you will never be able to figure out what it *really means*, nor, if you become the least bit Deleuzian, will you want to. Rather than asking what a concept means, you will find yourself asking, "Does it work? what new thoughts does it make possible to think? what new emotions does it make possible to feel? what new sensations and perceptions does it open in the body?" (Massumi, 1992, p. 8). You soon give up worrying about what Deleuze might have *intended* and use him in your own work "to free life from where it's trapped, to trace lines of flight" (Deleuze, 1990/1995, p. 141) into a different way of being in the world.

For how can one read a philosopher like Deleuze and not be transformed in some way? Once you have used the *nomad, rhizome, haeceity, middle, line of flight* to think the world, you live differently. At least, that's what I believe. Todd May (1996) explains that Deleuze's ontology is "built upon the not-so-controversial idea that how we conceive the world is relevant to how we live in it." This belief leads us "toward the idea that we ought to conceive understandings that at least permit and perhaps encourage better—and alternative—ways of living in the world we conceive" (p. 295).

Of course, many of us in education believe we need new concepts in order to think and live education differently. Deleuze (1990/1995), like many educators, worries that we are "turning education into a business" (p. 182) as we introduce policies such as "continual training" (p. 175) (being condemned to lifelong learning), forms of continuous assessment,...the related move away from any research in universities, 'business' being brought into education at every level." (p. 182). These trends, he writes, convey "what it means to talk of institutions breaking down: the widespread progressive introduction of a new system of domination" (p. 182).

Recently, the U.S. Department of Education's new Institute of Educational Sciences (IES), the governmental body responsible for setting the standard for and funding educational research, has indeed introduced a new system of domination that privileges randomized experimental trials as the gold standard for scientific-based research (SBR) or evidence-based research (EBR) in education (see St.Pierre, 2002; St.Pierre, in press; the November 2002 special issue of *Educational Researcher*). This particular form of domination is described by IES as a methodological issue, but it is, of course, also epistemological, since the federal government has determined that a certain research method produces the truest, most rational knowledge. The IES is rapidly putting into place a structure that attempts, in every respect, to discipline and control the field of educational research and, by extension, the broader field of education. This domination begins with the training of researchers and extends to the dissemination of research findings—in the databases of the new *What Works Clearinghouse*—to those whom Grover J. (Russ) Whitehurst, the new Director of IES, refers to as our "customers"—practitioners, school superintendents, and legislators.

At a Presidential Invited Session (session # 29.011) at the 2003 annual meeting of the American Educational Research Association (AERA), Whitehurst chided several hundred researchers who attended the session about the misfit between research presented at the meeting and research that would help school superintendents decide "what works." He instructed researchers to do applied rather than basic research that is "overly theoretical" and to focus on getting the "right answer," on designing "practical delivery systems," and on offering "product support." He read titles of conference sessions (not actual session titles, but titles constructed from actual session titles) that he said "would not help school superintendents" decide "what works best for whom in what circumstances." The titles he chose to reject used concepts specific to queer theories, feminist theories, post-colonial theories, and postmodern theories, among others. Praising sessions on "teacher quality" and "alternative teacher certification," he specifically stated that "our customers do not need postmodern methods." In effect, Whitehurst directed educational researchers to use that what John Willinsky (2001) calls the "top-down linear R&D models of the 1950s and 1960s" (p. 7), erasing at least the last 50 years of social science and educational theory and research that has attempted "to produce different knowledge and produce knowledge differently" (St.Pierre, 1997a, p. 175). Deleuze's 1990 statement identifying the desire of some to turn education into a business has become federal policy in the United States.

We are in desperate need of new concepts, Deleuzian or otherwise, in this new educational environment that privileges a single positivist research model with its transcendent rationality and objectivity and accompanying concepts such as randomization, replicability, generalizability, bias, and so forth—one that has marginalized subjugated knowledges and done material harm at all levels of education, and one that many educators have resisted with some success for the last 50 years. We seem to be in a time warp, when the overcoding machine of "State science" (Deleuze & Guattari, 1980/1987), p. 362), or what Sandra Harding (1991) calls "science-as-usual" (p. 1), once again attempts to control education. Deleuze & Guattari (1991/1994) write that "philosophy thus lives in a permanent crisis" (p. 82); and we are indeed in crisis at the beginning of the 21st century as the educational philosophy privileged by the federal government imposes on all who care deeply about education "flimsy concepts" that are "too regular, petrified, and reduced to a framework...the most universal concepts, those presented as eternal forms or values [that] are the most skeletal and least interesting" (Deleuze & Guattari, 1991/1994, p. 83). In the last decades, these stale concepts have been used to the limit and used up in many instances, but it should not be surprising,that "transcendence is inevitably reintroduced" (Deleuze & Guattari, 1991/1994, p. 51) when "functionaries who, enjoying a ready-made thought, are not even conscious of the problem and are unaware even of the efforts of those they claim to take as their models" (Deleuze & Guattari, 1991/1994, p. 51). If the functionaries in the IES were aware of such efforts in the history of positivism, their model, they might hesitate to reintroduce as the gold standard guiding educational research a philosophy whose limits and dangers have been so well tested and documented. I am reminded here of Gayatri Spivak's (1993) comment that she does not understand why "people who do not have the time to learn should organize the construction of the rest of the world" (p. 187).

But where do we go from here? Hal Foster (1996) writes that a "regime of power also prepares its resistance, calls it into being, in ways that cannot always be recouped" (p. 212), and Foucault (1984/1987) writes that when relations of power are fixed in an asymmetrical way "the problem is in fact to find out where resistance is going to organize" (p. 12). There are many in education who have been resisting the federal government's current vision of science, an old vision newly deployed, for quite some time. Unfortunately, as Deleuze (1990/1995) writes, "stupidity's never blind or mute" (p. 129), and those who disagree with the

State science of the IES must organize their resistance and take care that their critique is seen and heard at this critical time.

Deleuze (1965/2001b) says "we know full well that some values are born old and from their birth exhibit their conformity, their conformism, their inability to upset any established order" (p. 81). One form of resistance to the scientism produced by the old values of government functionaries involves accomplishing scholarship that critiques those values and introduces concepts that upset the established order. This essay participates in that resistance, illustrating how Deleuzian concepts keep the field of play open, becoming, rhizomatic, with science springing up everywhere, unrecognizable according to the old rules, coming and going in the middle, "where things pick up speed" (Deleuze & Guattari, 1980/1987, p. 25). We might remember in this time of stifling conservatism Deleuze's (1990/1995) description of the work of philosophy: "Philosophy's like a novel: you have to ask 'What's going to happen?,' 'What's happened?' Except the characters are concepts, and the setting, the scenes, are space-times. One's always trying to bring something to life, to free life from where it's trapped, to trace lines of flight" (p. 140-141). We may, indeed, feel trapped, but we have the pleasure of plugging the Deleuzian machine into other machines we are thinking/being/doing to produces assemblages that take us elsewhere.

Writing about students who took his courses, Deleuze (1990/1995) explains, "nobody took in everything, but everyone took what they needed or wanted, what they could use" (p. 139). I have greedily taken concepts I could use from Deleuze and traced lines of flight, not away from, but into the turbulence of this life I live as an educator, searching for smooth spaces in which something different might happen. "Of course, smooth spaces are not in themselves liberatory. But the struggle is changed or displaced in them, and life reconstitutes its stakes, confronts new obstacles, invents new paces, switches adversaries. Never believe that a smooth space will suffice to save us" (Deleuze & Guattari, 1980/1987. p. 500). Heeding this caution about the romance of liberation, I nevertheless find a stubborn pleasure in Deleuzian affirmation, which John Rajchman (2001a) says "requires a belief or trust in the world and what may yet transpire in it, beyond what we are warranted to assert" (p. 76), an affirmation that is about a "belief of the future, in the future" (Deleuze, quoted in Rajchman, 2001a, p. 76). This reminds me of what Tony Kushner (quoted in Lather, 1995) calls a" non-stupid optimism" (p. 3) and Cornell West (1995), an "audacious sense of hope." Reading Nietzsche, Deleuze (1962/1983) writes that "*to affirm is not to take responsibility for, to take on the burden of what is, but to release, to set free what lives.* To affirm is to unburden: not to load life with the weight of higher values, but *to create* new values which are those of life, which make life light and active" (p. 185).

And this becomes practical work, this making life light and active, and I will now return to my earlier comments following this essay's first long quote in which Deleuze describes the different ways one might read a book. When I first read Deleuze, I was in the middle of an event, a life-long qualitative research project that uses Foucault's ethical analysis, care of the self (Foucault, 1984/1985), to investigate the arts of existence, or practices of the self 36 older white southern women who live in my hometown have used during their long lives in the construction of their subjectivities. I at once put Deleuze to work in that study—a "flow meeting other flows" –even though I'm sure I didn't understand his work— "there's nothing to explain, nothing to understand, nothing to interpret" (Deleuze, 1990/1995, p. 9). Concepts like the fold, the nomad, and the rhizome were immediately useful and helped me try to think outside both the overcoded qualitative research process and the notions of the subject I had studied.

I desperately needed what many educational researchers need when we're intensely living "fieldwork, textwork, and headwork" (Van Maanen, 1995, p. 4)—I needed new language, new concepts to help me describe, for example, the field when I could no longer locate the place in which I worked, to describe space/time when I no longer lived a linear time, to describe myself when I was no longer the subject I had been given in advance of living with these women *in medias res.* Deleuze (1969/1990) asks us to think differently so as "not be unworthy of what happens to us" (p. 149), and the ethical imperatives of this study have demanded that I become a different subject than the present, knowing, coherent individual defined, in large part, by the Enlightenment. As Foucault (1982) writes, "Maybe the target nowadays is not to discover what we are but to refuse what we are . . . we have to promote new forms of subjectivity through the refusal of this kind of individuality" (p. 216).

In the following section, I will try to describe how I think with Deleuzian concepts in this study of subjectivity that is characterized by "folding, unfolding, refolding" (Deleuze, 1988/1993, p. 137) and how they help me try to "free the art of seeing from its subordination to prior concept or discourse" (Rajchman, 2001a, p. 129). I believe this is science in its most provocative form, this business of "extending the original plane by giving it new curves, until a doubt arises" (Deleuze & Guattari, 1991/1994, p. 57), a doubt that undoes the old plane "blow by blow" (Deleuze & Guattari, 1991/1994, p. 76) and carries us "across our thresholds, toward a destination which is unknown, not foreseeable, not preexistent" (Deleuze & Parnet, 1977/1987, p. 125). This science undoes State science at every turn and requires we rethink the subject, for me, the most difficult task of my life.

THE SUBJECT UNDONE

All my work focuses on the problem of the *subject*, and I have become particularly intrigued by poststructural descriptions of subjectivity, specifically, those of Foucault. In the course of his work, Foucault moved through various conceptions of the subject: a subject dispersed in discourse (e.g. Foucault, 1979) a subject constituted in discourse (e.g., Foucault, 1961/1965, 1975/1979), and a subject constituted in practice (e.g., 1984/1983, 1984/1985, 1984/1987, 1984/1988, 1985/1986, 1988, 1997). In my study with the older women of Milton, I used the latter conception, in which Foucault describes how the ancient Greeks developed an ethos called "care of the self" that enabled one to produce oneself as the "ethical subject of one's actions " (Foucault, 1984/1985, p. 26). This theory of the subject worked well in that research project. It suited the data I collected from the women, and it pushed me into new ways of thinking about both subjectivity and ethics in a postmodern world (see St.Pierre, 2003).

About the same time, I began to read Deleuze and Guattari and came upon the following sentences that astounded me: "You are longitude and latitude, a set of speeds and slownesses between unformed particles, a set of nonsubjectified affects. You have the individuality of a day, a season, a year, a *life*... or at least you can have it, you can reach it...It should not be thought that a haecceity consists simply of a décor or a backdrop that situates subjects... It is the entire assemblage in its individuated aggregate that is a haecceity" (Deleuze & Guattari, 1980/1987, p. 262). Here, *haecceity*—a concept used by Duns Scotus (c. 1266-1308) to indicate how one thing/person is distinct from another because of some individuating essence—represents "an hour of a day, a river, a climate, a strange moment during a concert can be like this—not one of a kind, but the individuation of something that belongs to no kind, but which, though perfectly individuated, yet retains an indefiniteness, as though pointing to something 'ineffable'" (Rajchman, 2001a, p. 85). Deleuze and Guattari (1980/1987) provide an example from literature, as they so often do, "The thin dog is running in the road, this dog is the road,' cries Virginia Woolf. That is how we need to feel...A haecceity has neither beginning nor end, origin nor destination; it is always in the middle. It is not made of points, only of lines. It is a rhizome" (p. 263).

I had no difficulty thinking that the dog is the road; I readily recognized that composition, that complication, that assemblage, of the dog and the road and everything else in that event. Because the human/nonhuman binary had always troubled me, I had no difficulty thinking of myself—the human—as an assemblage with the earth, space/time, speeds, intensities, durations, lines, interstices, hydraulics, turbulances, folds (Deleuze 1993/1988)—the nonhuman. According to Goodchild (1996), this kind of thinking "is not a question of anti-humanism, but a question of whether subjectivity is produced solely by internal faculties of the soul, interpersonal relations, and intra-familial complexes, or whether non-human machines such as social, cultural, environmental, or technological assemblages enter into the very production of subjectivity itself (p. 151). This Deleuzian assemblage made sense to me. *I got it*, or, rather, I plugged it (however one makes sense of *it)* into my own musings about subjectivity and it worked.

Having found inadequate the descriptions of the subject I had studied, as they all must be, I believed the concept haecceity, as described by Deleuze and Guattari, gestured toward a kind of individuation I believed I had always lived. As is my wont, I began to write my way toward this new concept in conference papers and journal articles since I at last had language to describe a problem I had lived but not labeled, so to speak. I surely didn't "understand" it, but as Deleuze and Guattari (1980/1987) write, "we will never ask what a book means, as signified or signifier; we will not look for anything to understand in it. We will ask what it functions with, in connection with what other things it does or does not transmit intensities, in what other multiplicities its own are inserted and metamorphosed" (p. 4). The concept, haecceity, and other related Deleuzian concepts, had been inserted in my life, and I was not the same.

In order to have some sense of this very different notion of individuation, I will provide a brief and cursory discussion of some writing by Deleuze, Deleuze and Guattari, and others that describe it in more detail. For example, in the following quote, Deleuze (1990/1995) points out its impersonal nature:

> When I said Félix and I were rather like two streams, what I meant was that individuation doesn't have to be personal. We're not at all sure we're persons: a draft, a wind, a day, a time of day, a stream, a place, a battle, an illness all have a nonpersonal individuality. They have proper names. We call them "hecceities." [sic] They combine like two streams, two rivers, They express themselves in language, carving differences in it, but language gives each its own individual life and gets things passing between them. If you speak like most people on the level of opinions, you say, "me, I'm a person," just as you say "the sun's rising." But we're not convinced that's definitely the right concept. Félix and I, and many others like us, don't feel we're persons exactly. Our individuality is rather that of events, which isn't making any grand claim, given that hecceities can be modest and microscopic. I've tried in all my books to discover the nature of events; it's a philosophical concept, the only one capable of ousting the verb "to be" and attributes (p, 141).

More specifically, he says, "What we're interested in, you see, are modes of individuation beyond those of things, persons, or subjects: the individuation, say, of a time of day, of a region, a climate, a river or a wind, of an event. And maybe it's a mistake to believe in the existence of things, persons, or subjects" (Deleuze, 1990/1995, p. 26).

Now what is one to make of this last sentence? How can we not believe in the existence of things, persons, or subjects? Aren't they real? Aren't they true? Haven't we believed in them all our lives and lived accordingly? Weren't we born into language that describes the world and ourselves in a certain way such that I am able to think of myself as "I" and believe I am a unique, autonomous, knowing, rational, conscious individual "endowed with a will, a freedom, an intentionality which is then subsequently 'expressed' in language, in action, in the public domain" (Butler, 1995, p. 136)? Surely I exist ahead of language and apart from everything else in the world. Who/what am I if I am not that "I"? How does one think/live outside "I"? Why should one want to? As mentioned earlier, Deleuze might respond to that last question by saying that we might live differently if we conceive the world differently.

In this regard, I believe Rajchman (2001a) is right when he cautions that if we do rethink subjectivity "the question then becomes how to conceive of our ethos— our 'modes of being'—in a manner no longer based in identity" (p. 92). What would it mean for ethics if we could no longer install or restore subjectivity as the foundation of responsibility? What would it mean for relations if they did not involve pre-existent, self-contained individuals identifying and interacting with each other within the structure of some a priori space/time but, instead, were an individuation that was always starting up again in the middle of a different temporality, in new assemblages, never fully constituted, fluid, a flow meeting other flows? The following provides some sense of how Deleuze (1969/1990) thinks of ethics: "To the extent that events are actualized in us, they wait for us and invite us in... 'Everything was in order with the events of my life before I made them mine; to live them is to find myself tempted to become their equal, as if they had to get from me only that which they have that is best and most perfect.' Either ethics makes no sense at all, or this is what it means and has nothing else to say: not to be unworthy of what happens to us" (pp. 148-149). That last phrase has shifted the way I think about ethics and my life (a life).

As to how Deleuze came to question "I,"— "traps of consciousness...what John Locke called 'the self,' (p. 8)—Rajchman (2001b) explains that Hume helped Deleuze connect empiricism and subjectivity differently so that the "self"—"the phenomenological anchoring of a subject in a landscape" (p. 10)— becomes an artifice, a philosophical fiction. Deleuze then conceives life as an empiricist concept with "quite different features than those Locke associated with the self—consciousness, memory, and personal identity. It unfolds according to another logic: a logic of impersonal individuation rather than personal individualization, of singularities rather than particularities. It can never be completely specified" (Rajchman, 2001b, p. 8). Foucault (1983/1988) situates Deleuze's work on Hume (1953/1991) and Nietzsche (1962/1983)—work that indicates "a dissatisfaction with the phenomenological theory of the subject" (p. 24)—within more general concerns about this theory in French philosophy in the1960's.

Needless to say, Deleuze demands we interrogate our ordinary habits of saying "I." In Deleuzian terms, "'I' is not an expressive subject, only a linguistic marker indicating what body is addressed by the whispered imperative immanent to that particular position within that particular state of things" (Massumi, 1992, p. 33). Foucault (1971/1972), in a similar vein, writes that "the subject of the statement should not be regarded as identical with the author of the formulation—either in substance, or in function. He is not in fact the cause, origin, or starting-point of the phenomenon of the written or spoken articulation of a sentence" (p. 95). Butler (1995) says much the same thing, "That an 'I' is founded through reciting the anonymous linguistic site of the 'I' (Benveniste) implies that citation is not performed by a subject, but is rather the invocation by which a subject comes into linguistic being" (p. 135). If we think of Descartes' (1637/1993) statement, "I think, therefore I am" (p. 19), we can see that, for a very long time, we have used the grammatical "I" as a linguistic index to produce ourselves as a certain kind of subject. Goodchild (1996) explains it this way:

> The process of subjectificaton takes place when a subject of enunciaton, the speaker, recoils into the subject of the statement. Its dominant reality is given by the range of statements which are possible for it. One learns the range of possible options that one is allowed to think, believe, want, or love from those given within society: a subject of enunciation forms it consciousness of itself out of the statements which it is able to make as a subject of a

statement. Descartes' *cogito*, often considered the founding of modern subjectivity, is exemplary in this respect: 'It think [subject of the statement, independent of its object] therefore [movement of recoiling] I am [the subject of the statement now designates the subject of enunciation].' The speaker then knows himself as a thinking substance. (p. 148)

Now, even though I have produced myself within this "grammar of the subject" (Butler, 1992, p. 9), and been hailed as such (Althusser, 1979/1971) all my life, I do not doubt that the "personalizing identification" (Rajchman, 2001a, p. 90) of the humanist, phenomenological subject is a fiction (as are all theories of the subject), albeit a maximally powerful rhetorical fiction. Michel Foucault, Judith Butler, Donna Haraway, Gayatri Spivak, Jacques Derrida, and others had warned me of that incorrigible illusion before I came to Deleuze. Their work confirmed the fragility of a subject whose legitimacy had become increasingly suspect in my life's everydayness. Deleuze (1986/1988) writes, "we continue to produce ourselves as a subject on the basis of old modes which do not correspond to our problems" (p. 107).

My problems, as I did "science" in Milton, asked something different of subjectivity, and I was drawn to the "impersonal individuations" (Rajchman, 2001b, p. 8) of Deleuze and Guattari because these concepts "have a necessity, as well as an unfamiliarity, and they have both to the extent they're a response to real problems," (Deleuze, 1990/1995, p. 136), problems I encountered in fieldwork related to time, space, and so forth (see St.Pierre, 2003), which may or may not be similar to the problems Deleuze encountered.

As I mentioned earlier, Deleuze and Guattari do not believe that smooth spaces will save us, nor can we entirely escape subjectivity. "You have to keep enough of the organism for it to reform each dawn; and you have to keep small supplies of significance and subjectification, if only to turn them against their own systems when the circumstances demand it, when things, persons, even situations, force you to; and you have to keep small rations of subjectivity in sufficient quantity to enable you to respond to the dominant reality." (Deleuze & Guattari, 1980/1987, p. 160). Does this response, as Foucault suggests, involve refusing the reality of what we are and, as a consequence, the life such a subject compels? Perhaps. At this point in my thinking, I usually return to Butler's (1995) question, "how is it that we become available to a transformation of who we are, a contestation which compels us to rethink ourselves, a reconfiguration of our 'place' and our 'ground'" (p. 132)? What must happen for us to rethink the "I" we were born into? Foucault (1981/2000), explaining the impetus for his various projects, offers the following rationale: "every time I have tried to do a piece of theoretical work, it has been on the basis of elements of my own experience: always in connection with processes I saw unfolding around me. It was always because I thought I identified cracks, silent tremors, and dysfunctions in things I saw, institutions I was dealing with, or my relations with others, that I set out to do a piece of work, and each time was partly a fragment of autobiography" (p. 458). Theory seldom springs forth from nothing but is most often produced in response to problems of everyday living.

Now you might ask what this discussion of subjectivity in Deleuze has to do with education and science, and I would respond—everything, everything. All of education and science is grounded in certain theories of the subject; and if the subject changes, everything else must as well. Fortunately, Deleuze gathers an audience in unexpected Nietzschean fashion, shooting out concepts like arrows that are picked up by chance and used in strange new ways. I have certainly seen my own students in all areas of education produce simply thrilling lines of flight in response to concepts like the rhizome, nomad, bodies-without-organs, and so forth. In regard to science, specifically, every single category of the structure of conventional, interpretive qualitative inquiry came loose from its moorings in the phenomenological subject when I engaged Deleuzian concepts in my study with the women of Milton (see, for example, St.Pierre, 1997a, 1997b). Deleuze (1994) pushes language and thought to the limit so that one stammers or stutters, becoming "a foreigner in his own language" (p. 25). As Bogue (1996) explains, "If there is stuttering in Deleuze, it is a conceptual stuttering, a stuttering of thought itself" (p. 262). Deleuzian concepts can indeed crack open the "grid of intelligibility" (Foucault, 1976/1978, p. 93) that structures the subject, education, and science so tightly.

In a time when many educators are terribly concerned about the fate of education, we might do well to remember Foucault's (1980/2000) advice about how to resist oppressive relations of power:

> I'm very careful to get a grip on the actual mechanisms of the exercise of power; I do this because those who are enmeshed, involved, in these power relations can, in their actions, their resistance, their rebellion, escape them, transform them, in a word, cease being submissive. And if I don't say what needs to be done, it isn't because I believe there is nothing to be done. On the contrary, I think there are a thousand things that can be done, invented, contrived by those who, recognizing the relations of power in which they are involved, have decided to resist them or escape them. From that viewpoint, all my research rests on a postulate of absolute optimism. I don't construct my analyses in order to say, "This is the way things are, you are trapped." I say these things only insofar as I believe it enables us to transform them. Everything I do is done with the conviction that it may be of use (pp. 294-295).

Resistance in the educational community to government mandates has already begun and will continue as we analyze the mechanisms of power that the Department of Education has put into place. We live in a time out of joint, a time of conservatism that threatens to overwhelm us at every turn, yet Deleuze helps us imagine a time to come in which the struggle may change.

At the end, I return to the beginning of my adventure with Deleuze, which commenced with a problem of subjectivity, caused to a great extent by a problem of space/time. Sometimes in Milton when I was folding in Foucault's care of the self, *le travail de soi sur soi*, and, at the same time, unfolding in a Deleuzian (1965/2001a) "qualitative duration of consciousness without a self" (p. 25), I felt so smooth that I found myself living "memor[ies] of the future" (Deleuze, 1986/1988,

p. 107), a future in which the conditions of thought are such that neither the subject, nor education, nor science, as they are presently configured, are possible. In such a future, education might be more worthy of and might not betray those who come to it with hopes and dreams of splendid transformation.

REFERENCES

Althusser, L. (1971). Ideology and ideological state apparatuses (Notes towards an investigation). In L. Althusser (Ed.), *Lenin and philosophy and other essays* (B. Brewster, Trans., pp. 127–186). New York: Monthly Review Press. (Reprinted from *La Pensée*, 1970)

Bogue, R. (1996). Deleuze's style. *Man and World, 29*, 251–268.

Butler, J. (1995). For a careful reading. In S. Benhabib, J. Butler, D. Cornell, & N. Fraser (Eds.), *Feminist contentions: A philosophical exchange* (pp. 127–143). New York: Routledge.

Deleuze, G. (1983). *Nietzsche and philosophy* (H. Tomlinson, Trans.). New York: Columbia University Press. (Original work published 1962)

Deleuze, G. (1988). *Foucault* (S. Hand, Trans.). Minneapolis, MN: University of Minnesota Press. (Original work published 1986)

Deleuze, G. (1990). *The logic of sense* (C. V. Boundas, Ed., M. Lester, Trans.). New York: Columbia University Press.

Deleuze, G. (1991). *Empiricism and subjectivity: An essay on Hume's theory of human nature* (C. V. Boundas, Trans.). New York: Columbia University Press. (Original work published 1953)

Deleuze, G. (1993). *The fold: Leibniz and the baroque* (T. Conley, Trans.). Minneapolis: University of Minnesota Press. (Original work published 1988)

Deleuze, G. (1994). He stuttered. In C. V. Boundas & D. Oklowski (Eds.), *Gilles Deleuze and the theater of philosophy* (pp. 23–29). New York: Routledge.

Deleuze, G. (1995). *Negotiations: 1972–1990* (M. Joughin, Trans.). New York: Columbia University Press. (Original work published 1990)

Deleuze, G. (2001a). Immanence: A life. In *Pure immanence: Essays on a life* (A. Boyman, Trans., pp. 53–102). New York: Zone Books. (Original work published 1965)

Deleuze, G. (2001b). Nietzsche. In *Pure immanence: Essays on a life* (A. Boyman, Trans., pp. 53–102). New York: Zone Books. (Original work published 1965)

Deleuze, G., & Guattari, F. (1987). *A thousand plateaus: Capitalism and schizophrenia* (B. Massumi, Trans.). Minneapolis: University of Minnesota Press. (Original work published 1980)

Deleuze, G., & Guattari, F. (1994). *What is philosophy?* (H. Tomlinson & G. Burchell, Trans.). New York: Columbia University Press. (Original work published 1991)

Deleuze, G., & Parnet, C. (1987). *Dialogues* (H. Tomlinson & B. Habberjam, Trans.). New York: Columbia University Press. (Original work published 1977)

Descartes, R. (1993). *Discourse on method* [original date of publication 1637] *and meditations on first philosophy* [original date of publication 1641] (D. A. Cress, Trans.). Indianapolis: Hackett Publishing Company.

Foster, H. (1996). *The return of the real: The avant-garde at the end of the century*. Cambridge, MA: MIT Press.

Foucault, M. (1965). *Madness and civilization: A history of sanity in the age of reason* (R. Howard, Trans.). New York: Vintage Books. (Original work published 1961)

Foucault, M. (1972). *The archaeology of knowledge and the discourse on language* (A. M. S. Smith, Trans.). New York: Pantheon Books. (Original work published 1971)

Foucault, M. (1978). *The history of sexuality: An introduction* (Vol. 1, R. Hurley, Trans.). New York: Vintage Books. (Original work published 1976)

Foucault, M. (1979). What is an author? In J. V. Harari (Ed.), *Textual strategies: Perspectives in post-structuralist criticism* (pp. 141–160). Ithaca: Cornell University Press. [no translator given]

Foucault, M. (1979). *Discipline and punish: The birth of the prison* (A. Sheridan, Trans.). New York: Vintage Books. (Original work published 1975)

Foucault, M. (1982). The subject and power. In H. L. Dreyfus & P. Rabinow (Eds.), *Michel Foucault: Beyond structuralism and hermeneutics* (pp. 208–226). Chicago: University of Chicago Press.

Foucault, M. (1988). Critical theory/intellectual history. In *Politics, philosophy, culture: Interviews and other writings, 1977–1984* (J. Harding, Trans., pp. 17–46). New York: Routledge. (Original work published 1983)

Foucault, M. (1984). On the genealogy of ethics: An overview of work in progress. In P. Rabinow (Ed.), *The Foucault reader* (pp. 340–372). New York: Pantheon Books. (Interview conducted 1983)

Foucault, M. (1985). *The history of sexuality. The use of pleasure* (Vol. 2, R. Hurley, Trans.). New York: Vintage Books. (Original work published 1984)

Foucault, M. (1986). *History of sexuality. The care of the self* (Vol. 3, R. Hurley, Trans.). New York: Vintage Books. (Original work published 1985)

Foucault, M. (1987). The ethic of care for the self as a practice of freedom. In J. Bernauer & D. Rasmussen (Eds.), *The final Foucault* (R. Fornet-Betancourt, H. Becker, A. Gomez-Müller, Interviewers; J. D. Gauthier, Trans., pp. 1–20). Cambridge, MA: The MIT Press. (Interview conducted 1984)

Foucault, M. (1988). Technologies of the self. In L. H. Martin, H. Gutman, & P. H. Hutton (Eds.), *Technologies of the self: A seminar with Michel Foucault* (pp. 16–49). Amherst, MA: University of Massachusetts Press.

Foucault, M. (1988). An aesthetics of existence. In L. D. Kritzman (Ed.), *Politics, philosophy, culture: Interviews and other writings, 1977–1984* (A. Fontana, Interviewer; A. Sheridan, Trans., pp. 47–53). New York: Routledge. (Reprinted from *Panorama*, April 25, 1984)

Foucault, M. (1997). *Ethics: Subjectivity and truth* (P. Rabinow, Ed., R. Hurley et al., Trans.). New York: The New Press.

Foucault, M. (2000). Interview with Michel Foucault. In J. D. Faubion (Ed.), *Power* (D. Trombadori, Interviewer; pp. 239–297). New York: The New Press. (Original work published 1980)

Foucault, M. (2000). So is it important to think? In J. D. Faubion (Ed.), *Power* (pp. 454–458). New York: The New Press. (Original work published 1981)

Goodchild, P. (1996). *Deleuze and Guattari: An introduction to the politics of desire*. London: Sage.

Harding, S. (1991). *Whose science? Whose knowledge? Thinking from women's lives*. Ithaca, NY: Cornell University Press.

Lather, P. (1995). *Naked methodology: Researching the lives of women with HIV/AIDS*. Paper presented at the Revisioning Women, Health and Healing: Feminist, Cultural and Technoscience Studies Perspectives conference, San Francisco, CA.

Massumi, B. (1987). Translator's foreward: Pleasure of philosophy. In G. Deleuze & F. Guattari (Eds.), *A thousand plateaus: Capitalism and schizophrenia* (B. Massumi, Trans., pp. ix–xv). Minneapolis, MN: University of Minnesota Press.

Massumi, B. (1992). *A user's guide to capitalism and schizophrenia: Deviations from Deleuze and Guattari*. Cambridge, MA: The MIT Press.

May, T. (1996). Gilles Deleuze and the politics of time. *Man and World, 29*, 293–302.

Rajchman, J. (2001a). *The Deleuze connections*. Cambridge, MA: The MIT Press.

Rajchman, J. (2001b). Introduction. In G. Deleuze (Ed.), *Pure immanence: Essays on a life* (A. Boyman, Trans.). New York: Zone Books.

Spivak, G. C. (1993). *Outside in the teaching machine*. New York: Routledge.

St. Pierre, E. A. (1997a). Methodology in the fold and the irruption of transgressive data. *International Journal of Qualitative Studies in Education, 10*(2), 175–189.

St. Pierre, E. A. (1997b). Nomadic inquiry in the smooth spaces of the field: A preface. *International Journal of Qualitative Studies in Education, 10*(3), 363–383.

St. Pierre, E. A. (2002). "Science" rejects postmodernism. *Educational Researcher, 31*(8), 25–27.

St. Pierre, E. A. (in press). Refusing alternatives: A postmodern ethics of inquiry. *Qualitative Inquiry.*

St. Pierre, E. A. (2003). Care of the self: The subject and freedom. In B. Baker & K. E. Heyning (Eds.), *Dangerous coagulations?: The uses of Foucault in the study of education*. New York: Peter Lang.

Van Maanen, J. (Ed.). (1995). *Representation in ethnography*. Thousand Oaks, CA: Sage Publications.

West, C. (1995, February 24). Lecture, "Race matters," given at the Ohio State University.

Willinsky, J. (2001). The strategic education research program and the public value of research. *Educational Researcher, 30*(1), 5–14.

Elizabeth A. St.Pierre
The University of Georgia
USA

CONTRIBUTORS

Ronald Bogue is Distinguished Research Professor of Comparative Literature at the University of Georgia. Among his many books are *Deleuze and Guattari* (1989), *Deleuze on Literature* (2003), *Deleuze on Cinema* (2003), *Deleuze on Music, Painting, and the Arts* (2003), and *Deleuze's Wake: Tributes and Tributaries* (2004). Email: rbogue@uga.edu

Brett Buchanan is Assistant Professor of Philosophy at Laurentian University, Canada. He has recently published in *Proteus* and *Abécédaire de Martin Heidegger*, and has just completed a manuscript entitled *Onto-Ethologies*. Email: bbuchanan@laurentian.ca

David R. Cole is Senior Lecturer in English and Pedagogy, University of Technology, Sydney, Australia, Lindfield Campus. He published in the literary e-zine at http://www.sageofcon.org/ez7/nf/dc.htm and also wrote a novel about Colombia called *A Mushroom of Glass*. Email: David.Cole@uts.edu.au

Claire Colebrook is Professor of Modern Literary Theory at the University of Edinburgh, UK. She has published several books on gender, literary theory, Deleuze and irony. She is currently completing a book on happiness. Email: ccolebro@staffmail.ed.ac.uk

Jacques Daignault's (University of Quebec, Canada) last book *(H)opéra pour Geneviève* (2002) witnessed his political, existential and theological research interests which took form of a philosophical, pedagogical, novel-like and autobiographical story. Email: jacques@levinux.org

Gary Genosko is Canada Research Chair in Technoculture at Lakehead University in Thunder Bay, Ontario, Canada. Currently he is preparing a manuscript titled *Félix Guattari: A Political Chaodyssey*. He is editor of *The Guattari Reader* (1996), and author of *Félix Guattari: An Aberrant Introduction* (2002), and *The Party Without Bosses: Lessons on Anti-Capitalism from Lula da Silva and Félix Guattari* (2003). Email: genosko@lakeheadu.ca

Noel Gough is Foundation Professor of Outdoor and Environmental Education at La Trobe University, Australia. His publications focus on research methodology and curriculum studies, with particular reference to environmental education, science education, internationalisation and globalisation. He is editor of *Transnational Curriculum Inquiry*, the journal of the International Association for the Advancement of Curriculum Studies. Email: N.Gough@latrobe.edu.au

Zelia Gregoriou is Assistant Professor in Philosophy and Theory of Education at the University of Cyprus. She is a member and Policy Expert of The Mediterranean

Institute of Gender Studies. Her research and publications focus on poststructuralist philosophers of ethics and subjectivity with regard to multiculturalism, identity, recognition, cultural narratives, memory and otherness, trauma and mourning. She writes poetry. Email: gregoriou@ucy.ac.cy

Eileen Honan is Senior Lecturer in English and Literacy Education at The University of Queensland, Australia. Her research includes developing methodological applications in educational research of Deleuze and Guattari's philosophical work, and working with teachers in the area of theoretical issues related to literacy teaching practices. Email: e.honan@uq.edu.au

David Lines is Associate Head of Music (Research) at the University of Auckland, New Zealand. His research interests include contemporary/artistic perspectives of educational philosophy, music education and interdisciplinary performance projects in music. Email: d.lines@auckland.ac.nz

Terence Lovat is Professor of Education and Pro Vice-Chancellor (Education and Arts) at The University of Newcastle, NSW, Australia. He was a foundation member of the Board of the Carrick Institute for Learning and Teaching in Higher Education. He has authored, co-authored or edited five major academic texts and numerous journal articles and book chapters. He is a member of the International Values Education Research Consortium at the University of Minnesota, USA. Email: Terry.Lovat@newcastle.edu.au

Todd May is Kathryn and Calhoun Lemon Professor of Philosophy at Clemson University, USA. He has published seven books in Continental philosophy, focusing on the work of Michel Foucault and Gilles Deleuze. His book on Ranciere is forthcoming with Edinburgh University Press and Penn State Press. He has also been focusing on the rights of Palestinians. Email: mayt@clemson.edu

Kaustuv Roy teaches political and social theory in the College of Education at Louisiana State University. His book *Neighborhoods: War, Politics, and Education* is published by Sense Publishers. Email: kroy@lsu.edu

Marg Sellers is Programme Leader, Teaching and Educational Studies Centre of Learning, Whitireia Community Polytechnic, Porirua, Aotearoa, New Zealand. She is currently a PhD candidate at The University of Queensland, Australia, researching young children's understandings of curriculum alongside Deleuze's philosophical concepts. Email: m.sellers@paradise.net.nz

Inna Semetsky is a Research Academic at the Institute of Advanced Study for Humanity (IASH), The University of Newcastle, NSW, Australia. Her 2006 book *Deleuze, Education and Becoming* is published by Sense Publishers. In 2007 she guest-edited a special issue "Semiotics and Education" of Studies in Philosophy and Education (Springer). Email: Inna.Semetsky@newcastle.edu.au

Elizabeth Addams St.Pierre is Professor of Language & Literacy Education and Affiliated Professor of both the Qualitative Research Program and the Women's Studies Institute at the University of Georgia, USA. Her research is grounded in poststructural theories of language and subjectivity and focuses on a critique of both scientifically based research and conventional qualitative research methodology. Email: stpierre@arches.uga.edu

Lightning Source UK Ltd.
Milton Keynes UK
07 September 2010

159531UK00001B/60/P